Rhetoric In Shakespeare's Time

Literary Theory
of Renaissance Europe

by

SISTER MIRIAM JOSEPH, C.S.C.

A Harbinger Book

HARCOURT, BRACE & WORLD, INC.
NEW YORK AND BURLINGAME

To SISTER M. MADELEVA, c.s.c.

Poet and Educator

CONTENTS

Part Two

Part Two of the work on which this edition is based, *Shakespeare's Use of the Theory*, has been omitted except for its Conclusion which appears, slightly expanded, in its original place. Original page numbers have been retained for convenience in reference. Thus page 285 here follows immediately after page 42.

*Part Three: The General Theory of Composition and Reading
As Defined and Illustrated by Tudor Logicians and Rhetoricians*

As C. S. Lewis in his illuminating work *The Allegory of Love* (1936) helped modern readers to recapture the art of reading allegory, a form of composition very familiar to medieval and Renaissance readers, so this book aims to help modern readers respond to effective devices of rhetoric and logic so familiar to every Renaissance schoolboy in England, Germany, France, Spain, and Italy that not only the novelists and poets but even the dramatists could and did count on the spontaneous response of an ordinary mixed popular audience of their day. That this is true is evident from numerous passages in many plays, for example, in Jonson's *The Alchemist* 4.2.21-28, 63-66; *Cynthia's Revels* 4.3.160-201; Shakespeare's *Taming of the Shrew* 1.1.32; *The Merry Wives of Windsor* 4.1.16-80; *Love's Labor's Lost* 1.2.1-129; 5.1.18, 67; 5.2.106-408; *As You Like It* 5.1.52; *Hamlet* 5.2.110-187 (notice line 137); *Twelfth Night* 1.5.55, 64-78. Why and how this is true becomes clear from the account of the schoolboy's training, all in Latin and Greek textbooks (summarized on pages 8-13), and from the adult's continuing interest in the corresponding English works. The popularity and vitality of these latter (which are the basis of my book—see pages 13-16) were demonstrated by their wide circulation.

My major contribution to the theory is the insight into the intimate relationship which Renaissance men habitually perceived between rhetoric and logic and my systematic reorganization presented on page 36 whereby I clarify this relationship and make intelligible to modern readers valuable devices and distinctions long obscured both by obsolete terms and by the traditional classification presented on page 35. Descended as it is from Isocrates, Aristotle, Cicero, Quintilian, Bede, and others, much of this theory also helps us understand classical and medieval literature. Yet, as explained on pages 38-39, I cannot be accused of imposing a twentieth century view on the sixteenth century writers, readers, and theorists, for my organization is based on Aristotle's work whose pattern they knew well. Furthermore, Peacham and Melanchthon show both implicit and explicit awareness of the relation. Melanchthon, in fact, made a substantial but relatively small beginning, although he did not go on to make the complete reclassification which I offer.

This book is an abridgment of my *Shakespeare's Use of the Arts of Language* published by Columbia University Press in December 1947, with a second printing in 1949. The present edition omits Part II, *Shakespeare's Use of the Theory*, except the Conclusion. This Conclusion points up specifically the marvelous results Shakespeare achieved through this technique, which were shown in detail in the omitted pages.

I think that the advantages of retaining the original paging outweigh the unusual but not too disconcerting gap. Retaining unchanged also the bibliography, footnotes, and the whole index preserves the recognition and awareness of the cooperation which is as necessary in literary research as in scientific achievement. The complete index, with its references to T. W. Baldwin's work in all three parts of my unabridged book, fortifies my summary on pages 8-13 of outstanding points in his monumental (1525 pages), remarkably authenticated, but expensive work and makes its immense values better known. Furthermore, the alphabetical listing on pages 413-15 of figures of speech and vices of language under Figures (see headnote to Index) shows both the amazing extensiveness of the Renaissance concept and the parallel relation between Parts II and III of my original book.

This abridgment presents the complete general theory of composition and reading as it was stated in the works of the three Tudor groups, and as in fact it was universal in European countries during the Renaissance. It does not deal with the structure of specific literary forms like epic, drama, lyric, or prose romance, but with that other part of literary theory which today we call texture as contrasted with structure. It makes accessible to the modern student in the very words of the Tudor theorists, their amazing analysis of thought and expression now available only in the rare book rooms of a very few libraries. Probably without knowing the name epistrophe Abraham Lincoln spoke at Gettysburg those memorable words of hope that "government of the people, by the people, for the people shall not perish from the earth." We all cherish and admire this skillful repetition, which is only one of the many that continually reoccur in Lyly's *Euphues* and Sidney's *Arcadia*. Both these Renaissance works seem to the modern reader a peculiar and highly embroidered prose, but how many recognize precisely the differences in their patterns of embroidery? Sidney heartily disliked some patterns that Lyly especially favored. Any device can be overused or delightfully used. To know intelligently and systematically, to recognize and to name the devices that enriched the great works of the Renaissance can be a valuable and a rewarding experience. And that is the fundamental purpose of this book.

PREFACE

THE RHETORICAL and logical theory current during the Renaissance and its influence on the literature of the time have engaged the attention of many scholars interested in the period, among whom the following may relevantly be mentioned here. William Lowes Rushton, in *Shakespeare and 'The Arte of English Poesie'* (Liverpool, 1909), pointed out parallels between passages in Shakespeare and definitions and illustrations in the *Arte*. Gladys Doidge Willcock and Alice Walker edited a reprint of Puttenham's *Arte of English Poesie* (Cambridge, 1936) with an illuminating introduction and notes. Miss Willcock has also written essays on Shakespeare's use of rhetoric. Veré L. Rubel selected certain figures of speech from Puttenham's *Arte* and in her *Poetic Diction in the English Renaissance* (New York, 1941) illustrated their use in the work of the poets from Skelton through Spenser, after some preliminary notice of their use by Chaucer. Frank P. Wilson, in "Shakespeare and the Diction of Common Life," *Proceedings of the British Academy*, Vol. XXVI (1941), examined Shakespeare's use of three figures: paronomasia (a form of pun), the image, and the proverb. William G. Crane, in *Wit and Rhetoric in the Renaissance* (New York, 1937), particularly noted the relation of the rhetorical figures of thought to the logical topics of invention and emphasized the importance of both logic and rhetoric in developing the "wit" deemed necessary for the composition of all forms of Renaissance literature. Rosemond Tuve, in "Imagery and Logic: Ramus and Metaphysical Poetics," *The Journal of the History of Ideas*, III (October, 1942), 365–400, showed the intimate connection of logic and rhetoric with poetic composition in the work of Elizabethan writers and cited examples from Spenser, Sidney, Marlowe, and Donne. Hardin Craig, in "Shakespeare and Formal Logic" (*Studies in English Philology; a Miscellany in Honor of Frederick Klaeber* (Minneapolis, 1929, pp. 380–96), demonstrated Shakespeare's knowledge and use of the terms and processes of formal logic, and Allan H. Gilbert, in "Logic in the Elizabethan Drama," *Studies in Philology*, XXXII (October, 1935), 527–45, illustrated the use of logic by other Elizabethan dramatists from Lyly to Shirley. T. W. Baldwin, in *William Shakspere's Small Latine and Lesse Greeke* (Urbana, 1944), adduced evidence to prove not only that Shakespeare had a thorough and systematic knowledge of rhetoric and logic but also that he gained this knowledge from the Latin textbooks regularly studied in the Tudor grammar schools and that he employed in the composition of his plays and poems both techniques and materials derived from these Latin texts. Baldwin illustrates Shakespeare's use of particular forms of composition, as for example various forms of the oration described in the *Rhetorica ad C. Herennium* and in Quintilian's *Institutio oratoria.*

The contribution of the present work is to present in organized detail essentially complete the general theory of composition current during the Renaissance (as contrasted with special theories for particular forms of composition) and the illustration of Shakespeare's use of it. A few examples from the work of other Elizabethan writers are included for the sake of comparison. There are in Shakespeare's works many comments on the arts of language, that is, on grammar, rhetoric, and logic. Most of them are assembled at the beginning of Chapter II, a few at the opening of other chapters and sections of chapters. Remarks which are virtually definitions of figures of speech or obvious references to them are placed where the given figure is treated. The Renaissance classification of puns among highly esteemed figures may be mentioned as one instance in which the sixteenth-century theory sheds light on Shakespeare's work, for he uses puns in the most serious contexts, a fact which surprises and even offends many modern readers. The expository intention of the present study precludes the omission of any part of the general theory of composition, however unimportant, although it permits emphasis of the more significant parts. It also precludes continuous treatment of any one play and necessitates the use of scattered quotations from all of them. There is, however, a somewhat sustained treatment of particular plays at the close of sections in Chapters III, IV, and V.

Quotations from Renaissance works, except Shakespeare's, reproduce the spelling and punctuation of the time, but mere typographical peculiarities, such as the interchange of *u* and *v* and the use of *i* for *j,* have been modernized. The quotations from Shakespeare follow the text of George Lyman Kittredge's edition of *Shakespeare's Complete Works* (Ginn and Company, 1936).

My indebtedness to scholars to whose work mine is related at many points is acknowledged specifically in the footnotes and generally in the bibliography. For facilities necessary to carry on this study, particularly the use of rare books, and for their unfailing courtesy I desire to thank staff members of the libraries of Columbia University (including the main library, the law library, special collections, the Plimpton Library, and the library of Teachers College), the New York Public Library, the Library of Congress, the libraries of the University of Chicago, and the Newberry Library. I thank the authorities of the Huntington Library for permission to quote from Fenner's *The Artes of Logike and Rhetorike*, and the following publishers for permission to incorporate copyrighted material: Oxford University Press and the Clarendon Press for passages from Hardin Craig, *The Enchanted Glass*, George Stuart Gordon, S.P.E. Tract 29, C. S. Lewis, *The Allegory of Love*, Frank P. Wilson, "Shakespeare and the Diction of Common Life," from *The Works of Aristotle Translated into English*, and from the Oxford editions of Spenser, Lyly, Jonson, Thomas Wilson, *The Arte of Rhetorique*, Mulcaster, *Elementarie*, *The Pilgrimage to Parnassus*, and *Elizabethan Critical Essays*; the Cambridge University Press, for passages from E. E. Kellett, *Suggestions*, and from Cambridge editions of Puttenham's *The Arte of English Poesie* and the works of Sidney; Yale University Press for passages from Hoskyns, "Direccions for Speech and Style"; and the University of Illinois Press for passages from T. W. Baldwin, *William Shakspere's Small Latine and Lesse Greeke*.

I wish to express my sincere gratitude to Professor Harry Morgan Ayres, Professor Oscar James Campbell, and Professor Donald Lemen Clark, of Columbia University, for their direction of this work and for their helpful criticism.

I am deeply grateful to Mother M. Rose Elizabeth, superior general of the Congregation of the Sisters of the Holy Cross, to Mother M. Una, provincial, to Mother M. Vincentia, former superior general, to Mother M. Verda, former provincial (now deceased), and to Sister M. Madeleva, president of Saint Mary's College, Notre Dame, for the opportunity to pursue the studies which led to the writing of this book. To my colleague Sister Maria Teresa I owe thanks for typing the manuscript and for friendly criticism.

S. M. J.

Saint Mary's College, Notre Dame
Holy Cross, Indiana
Sept. 15, 1947

KEY TO REFERENCES

THEORETICAL WORKS

Blundeville	Thomas Blundeville, *The Arte of Logick* [1599], London, 1617.
Day	Angel Day, *The English Secretorie, with a Declaration of Tropes, Figures and Schemes* [1592], London, 1635.
Fenner	Dudley Fenner, *The Artes of Logike and Rhetorike*, Middelburg, 1584.
Fraunce, *AR*	Abraham Fraunce, *The Arcadian Rhetorike*, London, 1588.
Fraunce, *LL*	Abraham Fraunce, *The Lawiers Logike*, London, 1588.
Hoskyns	John Hoskyns, *Direccions for Speech and Style* [wr. *ca.* 1599], printed from MS Harley 4604 in *The Life, Letters, and Writings of John Hoskyns*, pp. 114–166, by Louise Brown Osborn, New Haven, 1937.
Lever	Raphe Lever, *The Arte of Reason, Rightly Termed, Witcraft*, London, 1573.
Peacham, 1577	Henry Peacham, *The Garden of Eloquence*, London, 1577.
Peacham	Henry Peacham, *The Garden of Eloquence*, London, 1593.
Puttenham	George Puttenham, *The Arte of English Poesie* [1589]; ed. by Gladys Doidge Willcock and Alice Walker, Cambridge, 1936.
Sherry	Richard Sherry, *A Treatise of Schemes & Tropes*, London, 1550.
Sherry, 1555	Richard Sherry, *A Treatise of the Figures of Grammer and Rhetorike*, London, 1555.
Wilson, *AR*	Thomas Wilson, *The Arte of Rhetorique* [1553]; ed. by G. H. Mair, Oxford, 1909.
Wilson, *RR*	Thomas Wilson, *The Rule of Reason, Conteining the Art of Logike* [1551], London, 1567.

SHAKESPEARE'S PLAYS

A & C	The Tragedy of Antony and Cleopatra
AW	All's Well That Ends Well

AYLI	As You Like It
CE	The Comedy of Errors
Cor.	The Tragedy of Coriolanus
Cym.	Cymbeline
Ham.	The Tragedy of Hamlet, Prince of Denmark
1H4	The First Part of King Henry the Fourth
2H4	The Second Part of King Henry the Fourth
H5	The Life of King Henry the Fifth
1H6	The First Part of King Henry the Sixth
2H6	The Second Part of King Henry the Sixth
3H6	The Third Part of King Henry the Sixth
H8	The Famous History of the Life of King Henry the Eighth
JC	The Tragedy of Julius Caesar
KJ	The Life and Death of King John
Lear	The Tragedy of King Lear
LLL	Love's Labour's Lost
MA	Much Ado about Nothing
Mac.	The Tragedy of Macbeth
MM	Measure for Measure
MND	A Midsummer Night's Dream
MV	The Merchant of Venice
MWW	The Merry Wives of Windsor
Oth.	The Tragedy of Othello, the Moor of Venice
Per.	Pericles, Prince of Tyre
R2	The Tragedy of King Richard the Second
R3	The Tragedy of King Richard the Third
R & J	The Tragedy of Romeo and Juliet
RL	The Rape of Lucrece
Son.	Sonnets
T & C	The Tragedy of Troilus and Cressida
Tem.	The Tempest
TGV	The Two Gentlemen of Verona
Tim.	The Life of Timon of Athens
Tit.	The Tragedy of Titus Andronicus
TN	Twelfth Night; or, What You Will
TNK	The Two Noble Kinsmen
TS	The Taming of the Shrew
V & A	Venus and Adonis
WT	The Winter's Tale

PART ONE

INTRODUCTION

CHAPTER I

THE GENERAL THEORY OF COMPOSITION AND
OF READING IN SHAKESPEARE'S ENGLAND

SCHOLARS have endeavored, especially in recent years, to show by historical studies how Shakespeare's plays were influenced in form and content by such matters as stage conventions and conditions of production,[1] by current doctrines of science, philosophy, and physiology,[2] or even by something apparently as remote as the bishops' order of June 1, 1599, prohibiting the printing of satires and epigrams.[3] If such historical studies illuminate for the modern reader certain plays of Shakespeare, as many agree they do, then the recovery of the current theory of composition, which enters into the very form and texture of all Shakespeare's plays and was the common idiom of his time, should likewise be of value.

The extraordinary power, vitality, and richness of Shakespeare's language are due in part to his genius, in part to the fact that the unsettled linguistic forms of his age promoted to an unusual degree the spirit of free creativeness, and in part to the theory of composition then prevailing. It is this last which accounts for those characteristics of Shakespeare's language which differentiate it most from the language of today, not so much in the words themselves as in their collocation. The difference in habits of thought and in methods of developing a thought results in a corresponding difference in expression principally because the Renaissance theory of composition, derived from an ancient tradition, was permeated with formal logic and rhetoric, while ours is not.

The purpose of this study is to present to the modern reader the general theory of composition current in Shakespeare's England. A general theory of composition, and correlatively of reading, is to be understood as one which underlies all special forms, such as the oration, the epic,

[1] As in the work of E. E. Stoll and E. K. Chambers.
[2] See Spencer, *Shakespeare and the Nature of Man*; Curry, *Shakespeare's Philosophical Patterns*; L. B. Campbell, *Shakespeare's Tragic Heroes, Slaves of Passion*.
[3] See O. J. Campbell, *Comicall Satyre and Shakespeare's 'Troilus and Cressida'*; also, his *Satire in Shakespeare*.

the drama, whether in prose or in verse. The Elizabethan critical essays unequivocally witness to the fact that the art of composition was then conceived as a body of precepts laid down in works on the three arts of language: grammar, rhetoric, and logic. Since grammar in its aesthetic aspects is treated in the works on rhetoric, the general theory of composition is to be sought in the works on rhetoric and logic which circulated in Tudor England. These include the *Rhetorica ad C. Herennium*, treatises by Cicero, Quintilian, and Aristotle, and Renaissance works directly or indirectly derived from them and often designed to lead into them. The Renaissance rhetoricians may be considered for the moment in two classes: those who in addition to a work on rhetoric, treating comparatively few figures of speech, wrote a companion work on logic; and those who deal only with the figures of speech, distinguishing from about ninety to one hundred and eighty figures, and who may therefore be called the figurists. A concordance of the Tudor figures approximates two hundred.

This study undertakes to establish four points: first, that the general theory of composition and of reading current in Shakespeare's England is to be found in one form in the contemporary works on logic and rhetoric combined; second, that it is to be found in another form in the work of the figurists which, surprisingly, treats of approximately the same matter as do the logic and rhetoric texts combined; third, that these two forms, though outwardly different, are fundamentally alike; fourth, that the theory in its entire scope, whether in the one form or in the other, is, with two or three negligible exceptions, illustrated in Shakespeare's plays and poems, where it contributes to the power and richness of his language and even of his thought, while it accounts for certain peculiar differences between the characteristic mode of expression of his time and of ours. Included also in this study are the vices of language, treated by the figurists in connection with the figures of grammar, and the fallacies and captious arguments, treated by the logicians in connection with correct forms of reasoning. Shakespeare makes capital use of them to create humor and to depict villainy and low life.

In the light of this theory it becomes evident, first, that Shakespeare's development of his subject matter and his mode of expression in his plays and poems are characteristic of his time; secondly, that he utilized every resource of thought and language known to his time; thirdly, that his genius, outrunning precept even while conforming to it, transcends that of his contemporaries and belongs to all time.

1. The Concept of Art in Renaissance England

In the late sixteenth century the Renaissance in England, no longer occupied primarily in making the acquaintance of ancient classics or in translating them or in composing imitations in Latin, was well advanced in its third phase: the later Elizabethan writers were eagerly and patriotically bent on creating literature in the vernacular inspired not only by the ancient classics but also by the new vernacular literatures of Italy and France. Spenser's simultaneous devotion to Aristotle, Plato, Theocritus, Bion, Vergil, Ariosto, Tasso, Mantuan, Marot, the French Pléiade, and Chaucer, and above all his desire to enrich English poetry by art comparable to that of other nations, exemplified the spirit of the time. The Elizabethan literary critics and poets, no less than the rhetoricians and logicians, insisted on the importance of precepts and theory in the creation of literature. Richard Mulcaster, Spenser's teacher at the Merchant Taylors school in London, with a robust faith in the artistic capacities of English, confidently asserted that "our natural tung" is "as readie to anie rule of Art, as anie other is." [4] George Puttenham conceived of art as "a certaine order of rules prescribed by reason, and gathered by experience." [5] Undertaking to write an *Arte of English Poesie* (1589) he reasoned:

Then as there was no art in the world till by experience found out: so if Poesie be now an Art, & of al antiquitie hath bene among the Greeks and Latines, & yet were none, untill by studious persons fashioned and reduced into a method of rules & precepts, then no doubt may there be the like with us. (p. 5)

Artificial was accordingly, as Puttenham pointed out, a word of praise.

Man also in all his actions that be not altogether naturall, but are gotten by study & discipline or exercise, as to daunce by measures, to sing by note, to play on the lute, and such like, it is a praise to be said an artificiall dauncer, singer, & player on instruments, because they be not exactly knowne or done, but by rules & precepts or teaching of schoolemasters. (p. 305)

In the Renaissance "to imitate the excellentest artificiality of the most renowned worke-masters that antiquity affourdeth" [6] was the ideal which

---

[4] Mulcaster, *Elementarie* (1582), ed. by E. T. Campagnac, p. 59.
[5] Puttenham, *The Arte of English Poesie*, ed. by Gladys Doidge Willcock and Alice Walker, p. 5.
[6] Gabriel Harvey, from *Pierce's Supererogation*, 1593, in *Elizabethan Critical Essays*, ed. with an introduction by G. Gregory Smith (hereafter cited as Smith), II, 277.

many of the greatest writers, such as Tasso and Spenser, sought to achieve. A lack of art was regarded as intolerable by Thomas Nashe: "Nothing is more odious to the Auditor then the artlesse tongue of a tedious dolt." [7] Nashe was quick to note, however, the even greater importance of experience:

Endevour to adde unto Arte Experience: experience is more profitable voide of arte then arte which hath not experience. Of it selfe arte is unprofitable without experience, and experience rashe withoute arte. [8]

Art, as Richard Rainolde explained, supplements and perfects the gifts of nature.

Nature hath indued every man, with a certain eloquence, and also subtilitee to reason and discusse, of any question or proposicion propounded, as *Aristotle* the Philosopher, in his Booke of *Rhetorike* dooeth shewe. . . . therefore Nature itself beyng well framed, and afterward by arte and order of science, instructed and adorned, must be singularlie furthered, helped, and aided to all excellencie, to exquisite invencion, and profound knowledge, bothe in *Logike* and *Rhetorike.* In the one, as a Oratour to pleate with all facilitee, and copious-lie to dilate any matter or sentence: in the other to grounde profunde and sub-till argument, to fortifie & make stronge our assercion or sentence, to prove and defende, by the force and power of arte, thinges passyng the compasse & reach of our capacitee and witte. [9]

In his "Apologie for Poetrie" Sir Philip Sidney expressed the current con-viction that the arts are derived from nature and have nature for their object.

There is no Arte delivered to mankinde that hath not the workes of Nature for his principall object, without which they could not consist, and on which they so depend, as they become Actors and Players, as it were, of what Nature will have set foorth. So doth the Astronomer looke upon the starres, and, by that he seeth, setteth downe what order Nature hath taken therein. . . . The Grammarian speaketh onely of the rules of speech; and the Rethorician and Logitian, considering what in Nature will soonest prove and perswade, thereon give artificiall rules. (Smith, I, 155)

The three arts of language, observed Puttenham, while derived from nature, bring it to perfection only through exercise.

[7] Nash, from "The Anatomie of Absurditee," 1589, Smith, I, 335.
[8] *Loc. cit.*
[9] Rainolde, *A Booke Called the Foundacion of Rhetorike,* fol. iͬ.

But what else is language and utterance, and discourse & persuasion, and argument in man, then the vertues of a well constitute body and minde, little lesse naturall then his very sensuall actions, saving that the one is perfited by nature at once, the other not without exercise & iteration? . . . And yet I am not ignorant that there be artes and methodes both to speake and to perswade and also to dispute, and by which the naturall is in some sorte . . . relieved in his imperfection . . . in which respect I call those artes of Grammer, *Logicke*, and *Rhetorick* . . . by long and studious observation rather a repetition or reminiscens naturall, reduced into perfection, and made prompt by use and exercise. . . . Also in that which the Poet speakes or reports of another mans tale or doings, as *Homer* of *Priamus* or *Ulisses* . . . in that he speakes figuratively, or argues subtillie, or perswades copiously and vehemently, he doth as the cunning gardiner that using nature as a coadjutor, furders her conclusions & many times makes her effectes more absolute and straunge. (pp.305 ff.)

Art, then, according to Tudor critics and poets, is assumed to rest on a body of precepts derived from nature, and both composition and reading are to be guided by the three ancient interrelated arts of language. Raphe Lever noted what every humanist considered a truism, that

artes are knit together in such a bande of knowledge, that no man can be cunning in anye one but he must have some knowledge in manye.[10]

Montaigne, well known in England, especially in Florio's translation, explained more specifically the interrelatedness of the liberal arts.

The Logitian referreth himselfe to the Grammarian for the signification of words: the Rethoritian borroweth the places of arguments from the Logitian: The Poet his measures from the Musitian. The Geometrician his proportion from the Arithmetician.[11]

Ben Jonson conceived the ideal poet as one in whom the gifts of nature are perfected by the knowledge and exercise particularly of the three arts of language, in addition to ethics.

I would leade you to the knowledge of our *Poet*, by a perfect Information, what he is, or should bee by nature, by exercise, by imitation, by Studie; and so bring him downe through the disciplines of Grammar, Logicke, Rhetoricke, and the Ethicks, adding somewhat, out of all, peculiar to himselfe, and worthy of your Admittance, or reception.[12]

[10] Raphe Lever, *The Arte of Reason, Rightly Termed Witcraft*, p. 90.
[11] "An Apologie of *Raymond Sebond*," in Montaigne, *Essayes*, tr. by John Florio, ed. by Thomas Seccombe, II, 307.
[12] Jonson, *Discoveries*, ed. by Maurice Castelain, p. 122.

It is clear that the men of Shakespeare's time, no less than those of classical antiquity and the Middle Ages, held the basic theory of composition and of reading to lie in the arts of grammar, logic, and rhetoric, which guide and govern all discourse. They believed that the poet, the orator, and the prose narrator, each having distinct and peculiar problems of his own, inevitably draw upon these wider arts of language for the general theory which must underlie all special forms of composition.

2. *Training in the Arts in Renaissance England*

A thorough training in the arts of language was the fundamental aim of the grammar schools of Tudor England.[13] These schools were patterned on Saint Paul's, London, re-founded in 1510 by Dean Colet, whose friend Erasmus, then in England, planned the curriculum and wrote or helped to write many of the textbooks, which continued to be used throughout the century. These textbooks, imbued with the literary spirit of Erasmus, exemplified the ideals and methods of studying the classics which he set forth systematically in his *De ratione studii,* composed at the end of the fifteenth century and published in 1512. It is no mere coincidence that the early leaders of the Renaissance in various countries were schoolmasters and authors of school texts which were used internationally: Erasmus, Agricola, Vives, Melanchthon, Sturm. They cultivated the ground from which flowered the great vernacular literatures. Ariosto, Ronsard, and Shakespeare learned through training in Latin to write superbly in their own tongues.

There is no external proof that Shakespeare attended grammar school. It may be presumed, however, that he did. Very likely after learning his ABC's and catechism in English in petty school he entered Stratford grammar school, about 1571, and followed the curriculum and texts which had become practically uniform by mid-century.

The aim of the grammar-school curriculum was to enable the student to read, write, and speak Latin, to acquaint him with the leading Latin classics and a few of the Greek, and to infuse into him sound moral and religious principles. The method prescribed unremitting exercise in grammar, rhetoric, and logic. Grammar dominated the lower forms, logic and rhetoric the upper. In all forms the order was first to learn precepts, then to employ them as a tool of analysis in reading, and finally to use them as a guide in composition. Much of the reading, especially in the lower

---

[13] See T. W. Baldwin, *William Shakspere's Small Latine and Lesse Greeke.*

forms, was selected with a view to furnishing moral and religious instruction.

The boy learning the rules of accidence bit by bit in Lily's Latin grammar would apply them first in construing *Sententiae pueriles, Catonis disticha moralia,* and a Latin version of Aesop's fables, and then in translating English into Latin. The making of Latins might begin with mottoes from the *Satellitium* of Vives or *Sententiae Ciceronis* dictated in English by the teacher; the boy's Latin rendering could then be compared with the original. The English Bible would furnish longer passages for translation into Latin, the favorites being the Psalms and the books of moral wisdom, Proverbs, Ecclesiasticus, Wisdom, and Ecclesiastes. To these might be added Job, Isaiah, and Genesis. Meanwhile colloquial Latin would not have been neglected. The *Linguae Latinae exercitatio* of Vives, with its typical conversations related to the various phases of school life, would prepare the boy to obey the rule requiring that all conversation, even at play, be carried on in Latin. The *Dialogi sacri* of Castalio and the colloquies of Erasmus would lead into Terence, the perfection of colloquial Latinity. Plautus and a Latin translation of Lucian might also be used. It was customary, in some schools at least, for the boys to take part in a Latin play at Christmas and just before Lent. The play might be by Terence or by Plautus or it might be composed by the schoolmaster himself. The study of poetry would begin with the Italian Renaissance poets Mantuan and Palingenius, who wrote in Latin.

In the upper forms a closely interrelated group of texts embodied the precepts of logic-rhetoric which were to guide the study of literature and composition. The boy must first be grounded in the topics of logic through Cicero's *Topica* before he could properly understand the one hundred and thirty-two figures of speech defined and illustrated in Susenbrotus' *Epitome troporum ac schematum et grammaticorum et rhetoricorum.* A mastery of the topics and figures was presupposed in *De duplici copia verborum ac rerum,* by Erasmus, which explained the two modes of varying in order to secure copiousness: first of diction, chiefly by means of the figures and a wide vocabulary, second of matter, by employing the topics of logic. In *Modus conscribendi epistolas* Erasmus applied these principles to letter writing. The boy would next observe these precepts exemplified in the classical authors and finally apply them to the composition of Latin epistles, first in prose and then in verse. Cicero's epistles furnished models for prose, those of Horace and the

Heroidum epistolae of Ovid for verse. The *Ars poetica* of Horace was both an epistle and a treatise on poetry supplementing the prosody, which constituted the fourth division of grammar. The epistle thus provided an easy transition from prose to verse, both in reading and in composition.

The poetry read would include Ovid's *Metamorphoses, Fasti, Tristia, Amores,* Vergil's *Eclogues, Georgics, Aeneid,* Lucan's *Pharsalia,* Horace's odes, and satires of Horace, Juvenal, and Persius. Pupil-teaching was a common device which impressed a lesson doubly upon the mind of the student. The boys would memorize Ovid's *Metamorphoses* at the rate of twelve lines a week, five hundred lines a year, for two or more years. A form would recite to the one next above it, which in turn would recite to the one higher. Thus were poetic rhythms, as distinguished from mere meter, fixed in the ears of the students as an aid in writing verse. Elizabethan poetry illustrates the results of this method. A customary exercise was to compose Latin prose and then turn it into one or more prescribed metrical forms. Accordingly Jonson, who said that he composed in prose and then turned the prose into verse, merely continued to do in English what he had learned to do in Latin grammar school. The method of studying poetry involved daily exercises in grammar, rhetoric, and logic. In a work like Melanchthon's *Erotemata dialectices* the boy learned the forms of propositions and the rules of the syllogism. In reading a poem he would construe, parse, scan, describe the metrical form, point out the topics and forms of logic and the figures of rhetoric, and then write verses of his own in imitation. The figures were particularly valued as an aid in the reading and writing of poetry.

Precepts for fourteen minor forms of prose themes preliminary to the oration were studied in Aphthonius' *Progymnasmata.* Sentential and moral matter valuable for writing such themes was furnished in the collections of Erasmus, *Adagia, Apophthegmata,* and *Parabolae* and in Pliny's *De historia naturali.* The histories of Livy, Sallust, Caesar, Justin, Valerius Maximus, and Lucius Florus provided further matter. From the *Rhetorica ad C. Herennium* and Quintilian's *Institutio oratoria* the student received instruction in reading and writing orations and thereby reached the summit of achievement in grammar school. Cicero's orations, his *Tusculanae disputationes, De officiis, Paradoxes, Somnium Scipionis, De amicitia,* and *De senectute* would be studied with attention to grammatical constructions, logical arguments, and rhetorical figures and forms. The three arts would then be applied to writing, in imitation, orations of the three recognized kinds—judicial, deliberative, and demonstrative—in which much of the moral matter from the reading was introduced.

Meanwhile the study of Greek grammar presented in Latin would also have begun, with accompanying construing and parsing in Latin of Greek sentences and the translation of Latin sentences into Greek. Next would follow the reading and writing of longer passages in prose and verse, with attention to constructions, topics, figures, and the changing of verse to prose and prose to verse. The Greek New Testament, Isocrates, and Homer were most often required for reading, but the curriculum might include Aesop, Lucian, Demosthenes, Hesiod, Pindar, Euripides, Xenophon, Dionysius of Halicarnassus, Plutarch, Theocritus, Heliodorus, Saint Basil's epistles.

This program of studies necessitated a strenuous routine. The order of the day in the Tudor grammar schools prescribed rising at five; class from six to nine; breakfast; class from nine-fifteen to eleven; dinner; class from one to five; supper. After supper, from six to seven, the pupils recited to their fellows what they had learned during the day. The lessons drilled on in the morning were regularly recited in the afternoon, and all the work of the week was reviewed in recitation on Fridays and Saturdays. A week devoted to repetitions tested the accomplishments of the thirty-six weeks of the school year. A sixteenth-century schoolmaster estimated that one hour of instruction would require at least six hours of exercise to apply the principles to writing and speaking.

T. W. Baldwin, upon whose recent work the preceding summary is based, has shown that an Elizabethan would understand Ben Jonson's ascription to Shakespeare of "small Latine and lesse Greeke" as meaning that Shakespeare had the regular grammar school education of the time. In the university the same authors were studied on a higher level, and others, including Aristotle, were added. Using sixteenth-century editions of annotated grammar-school texts along with such contemporary school aids as the Latin-English dictionaries of Withals, Baret, and Cooper and collections of quotations such as *Polyanthea* and Octavianus Mirandula's *Illustrium poetarum flores,* Baldwin finds internal evidence, some of it certain, some of it probable, that Shakepeare was acquainted in the original Latin with all of the books mentioned above except Cicero's orations, *De amicitia* and *De senectute,* the histories of Sallust, Caesar, Justin, and Valerius Maximus, Horace's satires, and Lucan's *Pharsalia.* Of the Greek readings, he finds some probability only for the New Testament. It is not unlikely, however, that Shakespeare knew at least some of the books which he did not use as sources of material or of techniques in his writing. Baldwin concludes:

William Shakspere was trained in the heroic age of grammar school rhetoric in England, and he shows knowledge of the complete system, in its most heroic proportions. He shows a grasp of the theory as presented by the various texts through Quintilian. He shows a corresponding grasp upon all the different compositional forms of prose for which the theory prepared. And this is true whether or not Shakspere ever went to school a day. Manifestly, the sensible thing to do is to permit him to complete Stratford grammar school, as there is every reason to believe that he did.[14]

Particularly interesting is Baldwin's demonstration that Shakespeare's famous lines on the seven ages of man, beginning "All the world's a stage," were derived primarily from Palingenius' *Zodiacus vitae* (which borrowed from Vives, Ovid, and Saint Chrysostom) and secondarily from Susenbrotus, Proclus, Horace, and Lambinus' notes on Horace. Palingenius was also a source, along with Saint Chrysostom, Job, and Isaiah, of a beautiful passage in *The Tempest* (4.1.152–58).[15] In *Love's Labour's Lost,* when Holofernes quotes the opening lines of the eclogues of Mantuan, his words would have awakened reminiscences of school days in Shakespeare's contemporaries.

> Fauste, precor, gelida, quando pecus omne sub umbra
> Ruminat, and so forth. Ah, good old Mantuan! (4.2.95)

Baldwin's study [16] throws light particularly on three characters: Holofernes, the schoolmaster, Sir Nathaniel, the text-parading curate, and Hamlet, the Wittenberg scholar. According to Baldwin an Elizabethan audience would easily have recognized the satirical rogue referred to by Hamlet (2.2.198) as Juvenal,[17] and the book Hamlet was reading (in the first version of the play) just before he began to dispute with himself, "To be or not to be—that is the question" (3.1.56), as Cicero's *Quaestiones Tusculanae,* "the first and fundamental text for a scholar's consolation in doubts of death."[18]

---

[14] *Ibid.,* II, 378.   [15] *Ibid.,* I, 652–77.

[16] In reviewing Baldwin's work, Tucker Brooke comments on its importance to students of Shakespeare: "Many passages in the plays and poems are either explained or given a fuller meaning by Baldwin's analysis of the techniques and textbooks through which Elizabethan schoolboys were trained; and this exegesis will hereafter be ignored by teachers at their peril." *Modern Language Notes,* LX (February, 1945), 126.

[17] T. W. Baldwin, *op. cit.,* II, 526.   [18] *Ibid.,* II, 607; 601–8.

After demonstrating that the Latin textbooks used in grammar school are not only the source of many passages in Shakespeare's works but also the basis of his conscious use of technicalities and of his "mastery of the system as a whole, not merely of a few chance definitions," [19] Baldwin observes: "It would be possible to show how he has used without pointing to the fact this great body of rhetorical knowledge, but that is beyond our present scope." [20] To show how Shakespeare used the whole body of logical-rhetorical knowledge of his time is essentially the undertaking of the present study. Although Baldwin justly maintains that "in these Latin texts is the main stream; the English rhetorics are only the eddies," [21] yet, because the English works on logic and rhetoric were translations and adaptations of the Latin textbooks used in the grammar schools of Tudor England, they can furnish an authentic contemporary account of Renaissance theory in language which, though slightly antiquated, has obviously an advantage in an investigation that aims, not at the discovery of specific sources, as Baldwin's does, but at the reconstruction of the general theory of the time. Furthermore, the English works had a wide circulation in Elizabethan England, and there is evidence that some of them were known to Shakespeare.

3. The English Works on Logic and Rhetoric

The following are the extant sixteenth-century works in English on logic and rhetoric, arranged in three groups. At the beginning of each group is at least one Renaissance Latin work to which the English works are closely related, usually through adaptation or translation.[22]

GROUP 1: THE TRADITIONALISTS

Aphthonius, *Progymnasmata;* tr. by Agricola and Cataneus, ed. by Lorichius; 1542.

Philippus Melanchthon, *Institutiones rhetoricae*, Haganoa, 1521.

—— *Elementa rhetorices*, Wittenberg, 1531.

—— *Erotemata dialectices*, Basel, 1521.

Leonard Cox, *The Arte or Crafte of Rhethoryke*, London, *ca.* 1530.

Thomas Wilson, *The Rule of Reason, Conteining the Art of Logike*, London, 1551.

—— *The Arte of Rhetorique*, London, 1553.

Richard Rainolde, *A Booke Called the Foundacion of Rhetorike*, London, 1563.

---

[19] *Ibid.*, II, 237.   [20] *Ibid.*, II, 238.   [21] *Ibid.*, II, 175.

[22] The dates are those of the first editions. The editions or reprints used in this study are listed in the bibliography. For key to abbreviations used for references see p. xiii.

Raphe Lever, *The Arte of Reason, Rightly Termed Witcraft*, London, 1573.
Thomas Blundeville, *The Arte of Logick*, London, 1599.

GROUP 2: THE RAMISTS

Petrus Ramus, *Dialecticae institutiones*, Paris, 1543.
Audomarus Talaeus, *Rhetorica*, 1544?
Dudley Fenner, *The Artes of Logike and Rhetorike*, Middelburg, 1584.
Abraham Fraunce, *The Lawiers Logike*, London, 1588.
—— *The Arcadian Rhetorike*, London, 1588.
Charles Butler, *Rhetoricae libri duo*, London, 1598.
—— *Oratoriae libri duo*, Oxford, 1629.
John Hoskyns, *Direccions for Speech and Style*, Harley MS 4604, written
    ca. 1600.

GROUP 3: THE FIGURISTS

Joannes Susenbrotus, *Epitome troporum ac schematum et grammaticorum et
    rhetoricorum*, Zurich, 1540.
Richard Sherry, *A Treatise of Schemes and Tropes*, London, 1550.
—— *A Treatise of the Figures of Grammer and Rhetorike*, London, 1555.
Henry Peacham, *The Garden of Eloquence*, London, 1577.
—— *The Garden of Eloquence*; corrected and augmented by the first author;
    London, 1593.
George Puttenham, *The Arte of English Poesie*, London, 1589.
Angel Day, *The English Secretorie* [1586]: with a declaration of tropes,
    figures, and schemes [this later part is added in the second edition]; London,
    1592.

These English works had in Tudor times a popularity, a vitality, and
an importance astonishing to us today, due in part to the use of illustrations
from matter of intense interest to the readers for whom the books were
designed. The Latin works were school texts, but the English books
circulated among adults, especially among those of the court and of the
upper and middle classes. From 1551 to 1595 there were at least seven
editions of Wilson's *Rule of Reason* and eight of his *Arte of Rhetorique*
which was written, so the title page informs us, "for the use of all such
as are studious of Eloquence"—as who in intellectual circles in Tudor
England was not? Puttenham explicitly stated that he wrote his *Arte*
for courtiers, and particularly for ladies, to assist them in composing and
in appreciating polite verse. He drew his illustrations chiefly from the
best English poets of his time, such as Wyatt, Surrey, Sidney, and Dyer.
Fraunce, too, capitalized on the lively interest in the new literature of
the vernaculars by illustrating the topics of logic and the various forms

of the syllogism from Spenser's *Shepheardes Calender;* the figures of rhetoric from Sidney's *Arcadia* and his songs and sonnets, from Tasso's *Gerusalemme liberata, Aminta,* and *Torrismondo,* from Du Bartas' *Judith* and *La Semaine,* from the sonnets and eclogues of Boscan and Garcilasso. Fraunce's illustrations from these leading English, Italian, French, and Spanish writers, along with examples from Homer's *Iliad* and *Odyssey* and from Vergil's *Eclogues, Georgics,* and *Aeneid* emphasized the likeness of Renaissance literature to the classics which inspired it, a likeness dear to the literary hearts of the time. Angel Day's work, which went through eight editions before 1626, appealed especially to the middle class by adapting the figures of rhetoric to the practical needs of letter writing. In an age ardently devoted to the reading of the Bible, Peacham, like his countryman the Venerable Bede eight centuries earlier,[23] assured his readers that a knowledge of the figures of rhetoric "helpeth much for the better understanding of the holy Scriptures," [24] from which he drew most of his examples. Fenner, in the three editions of his work, took all of the illustrations for both his logic and his rhetoric from the Bible. Blundeville, like Rabanus Maurus seven centuries earlier, valued logic as a means to find the truth in Scripture and to perceive and confute the subtle deceits of heretics. On his title page he asserted that logic is very necessary to all students in any profession in order to know "how to defend any Argument against all subtill Sophisters, and cavelling Schismatikes, and how to confute their false Syllogismes, and captious arguments." The religious controversies of the sixteenth century are reflected in many of the illustrations in Wilson's *Rule of Reason.*

Thus the Tudor rhetoricians and logicians enhanced the universally recognized merit of the arts they treated by illustrating their application to matters of vital interest among men of their own time: to the understanding of the ancient classics and of the new vernacular literatures, to composition, to the reading of the Scriptures, and to religious controversy. It is quite natural, therefore, that Elizabethan literature should reflect the current zestful interest in rhetoric and logic. As Hardin Craig has observed:

Elizabethan literature is alive with debate. . . . It is no wonder that drama flourished, which is itself an art of contest, dialogue and debate, agreement and disagreement. The reason for this preoccupation with controversial utterance . . . arises from the conception of logic (or rather dialectic) as an in-

[23] The Venerable Bede illustrated his *Liber de schematibus et tropis* wholly from the Bible.
[24] Peacham, *The Garden of Eloquence,* 1577, title page.

strument for the discovery of truth. . . . The syllogism, supplemented by an acute knowledge of the fallacies, was the chosen and obvious instrument for the discovery of truth—by deduction and induction. . . . every question has two sides, and . . . the acutest minds would habitually see both sides. Now, drama itself, as just said, is debate, and the issues it loves to treat are debatable issues. Shakespeare, the acutest of Renaissance thinkers, has . . . an ability to see both sides of a question, and a sympathy with all sorts and conditions of men. . . . No one can tell whether Bolingbroke or Richard II is in the right. Is it not fair, then, to regard Shakespeare as an exemplification of controversial broadmindedness in an age of advocacy? [25]

It is only in their choice of illustrations, and often not even in that, that the works of the Tudor rhetoricians and logicians can claim any originality or independence; their sources were principally Latin works of the Renaissance scholars, Erasmus, Agricola, Melanchthon, Ramus, Talaeus, Mosellanus, Susenbrotus, used singly or in combination and derived in their turn from earlier works reaching back through Quintilian, Cicero, and the *Ad Herennium* ultimately to Aristotle and Gorgias.

There are among the English authors of the Renaissance, as among the Latin, obvious differences that dispose them into the three groups which in the present study are called the traditionalists, the Ramists, and the figurists.

Thomas Wilson is eminently the traditionalist. His *Arte of Rhetorique* presents the whole of the classical tradition of rhetoric with its five parts: invention, disposition, elocution, memory, and delivery. The opinion, however, that it is the only English work of Tudor times which does so, requires qualification. Wilson is also a traditionalist in his work on logic. In treating of invention, he depends directly on Agricola,[26] whose work is in the main Aristotelian tradition. Lever and Blundeville follow Aristotle even more closely, but, like Wilson, admit accretions and modifications contributed in the intervening ages. Leonard Cox's rhetoric, the earliest one in English, is mostly a translation of that part of Melanchthon's which treats of invention, and is admittedly incomplete. Cox belonged to the circle of Erasmus and Sir Thomas More. Rainolde's book is a school text which explains how the topics of invention are to be applied in the composition of fourteen kinds of "Oracions" and illustrates each by example. Except for the illustrations, some of which are probably

---

[25] Craig, *The Enchanted Glass*, pp. 156 f.
[26] See Crane, *Wit and Rhetoric in the Renaissance*, p. 54.

original, it is derived from Aphthonius, whose *Progymnasmata* in Latin was a standard text in the sixteenth-century schools of England and of the continent and had been used in schools for centuries.[27]

The Ramists—as Ramus and his collaborator Talaeus and their English adapters, Fenner, Fraunce, Butler, and, to some degree, Hoskyns, may be called—depart from the Aristotelian tradition not so much in content as in pedagogical method and to a slight degree in terminology. Ramus and Talaeus insist that they follow Aristotle but do not hesitate to improve upon him and more especially upon the Aristotelians, whose sterile method of teaching they sought to vitalize by relating logic to literature and to the discourse of life and to clarify by making a clean-cut division between the functions of logic and rhetoric. To logic the Ramists assign invention, disposition, and memory inasmuch as it is aided most by method, a subdivision of disposition; to rhetoric they assign elocution and delivery. Thus the five parts of the classical tradition are embodied in their logic and rhetoric texts when taken together, as the Ramists explicitly asserted they must be, since the two supplement each other. To logic belong the two essential processes of composition, namely, the investigation of the desired subject by means of the topics of invention, and the organization of the material thus derived into appropriate logical forms by means of a suitable method. This they call genesis. The same principles employed to apprehend the meaning of what one reads or hears is analysis. For the Ramists the functions of rhetoric are but two: to beautify composition and make it emotionally effective by means of a comparatively few figures of speech and to contribute the graces of good voice and gesture in the delivery of a speech.

The figurists, as Susenbrotus, Sherry, Peacham, Puttenham, and Day may be named, appear on superficial examination to treat only of elocution and to omit the four other traditional parts of classical rhetoric. A closer examination of their work, however, shows that their concept of figures is so inclusive as to omit little of what has ever been included in a theory of composition, for the approximately two hundred figures of speech

[27] See Johnson, "Two Renaissance Textbooks of Rhetoric: Aphthonius' *Progymnasmata* and Rainolde's *A Booke Called the Foundacion of Rhetorike*," *The Huntington Library Quarterly*, VI (August, 1943), 427–44. Hermogenes, a second century Greek rhetorician, devised rules for twelve orations or elementary exercises in composition. Aphthonius, a fourth-century Greek rhetorician, increased the exercises to fourteen and added an illustrative example of each. In the sixteenth century Lorich's Latin edition of Aphthonius became the most widely used textbook of Latin composition; even Priscian's Latin translation, (*ca.* 500 A.D.) of Hermogenes yielded to it. Rainolde's book is adapted from Lorich. See also Crane, *op. cit.*, pp. 62–69.

which they distinguish represent an analysis of practically every aspect of grammar, logic, and rhetoric.

One of the conclusions to which the present study leads is that in the works of all three of these groups of Renaissance writers there is a fundamental likeness despite obvious differences, for in all of them are discernible, to a degree not hitherto adequately recognized, the dominant features of Aristotle's rhetoric.[28] The present study stresses the likenesses of the Tudor works to one another, not their differences, and the important features in which they are at one with the classical tradition, whether they drew their theory of composition directly from the ancient treatises, which were eagerly studied, or indirectly through contemporary works ultimately derived from them.

4. The Tradition

Gabriel Harvey, writing to Spenser, speaks of "the best Philosophers, and namely Aristotle, that poynt us . . . to the very fountaines and head springes of Artes and Artificiall preceptes" (Smith, I, 103). From Aristotle came the most important and influential treatises on the intimately related arts of logic, rhetoric, and poetic. Logic and rhetoric are concerned with the communication of ideas directly from mind to mind through words; poetic, with the communication of experience indirectly by the creation of illusion, into which the reader may enter imaginatively to share the experience vicariously. Aristotle defines poetic as imitation, the kind of composition whereby the writer speaks to the reader not directly but mediately through the interposed creations of his imagination, such imitation as we describe today as creative or imaginative writing. Poetic employs, but subordinates, the arts of logic and rhetoric and of course presupposes grammar as necessary to the intelligibility of any kind of verbal communication. In the *Poetics* Aristotle distinguishes six elements of tragedy: plot, characters, dianoia, diction, music, and spectacle. Where dianoia, or thought, rather than action determines the course of events, logic, rhetoric, and poetic are fused, functioning simultaneously, as in Plato's dialogues, which Aristotle regarded as poems.

In his works on logic Aristotle distinguishes three divisions: scientific demonstration, treated in his *Analytics,* its matter necessary premises true and primary, its instrument the demonstrative syllogism, its result knowledge through formal causes, that is, true and universal knowledge; dialectic, treated in the *Topics,* its matter probable premises discussed

[28] This is shown in detail in Part Three.

in the spirit of inquiry, its instrument the dialectical syllogism and induction, its result opinion probable, but not certain or strictly demonstrable; and sophistic, treated in *De sophisticis elenchis*, its matter premises that seem to be generally accepted or appropriate, but really are not, discussed by "those who argue as competitors and rivals to the death" [29] seeking by whatever means to refute the opponent, its instrument the sophistic syllogism, apparent reasoning either fallacious or inappropriate, its result apparent refutation of the opponent, refutation not absolute but only relative, in order thereby at all costs to gain the victory and to appear wise. Rhetoric, Aristotle says, is the counterpart of dialectic: like dialectic, it has for its matter the probable, for its aim persuasion. But as instruments of persuasion it employs the enthymeme as the counterpart of the dialectical syllogism, and the example as the counterpart of induction. Precisely because their proper subject matter is opinion, that is, the probable, rhetoric and dialectic have the capacity to generate arguments on both sides of a question. Hence rhetoric is sometimes, and dialectic always, a form of disputation. But in the oration, its most characteristic form, and in the debate, which is a series of orations on opposite sides, rhetoric advances by continued discourse, whereas dialectic, as illustrated in Plato's dialogues, advances by interrupted discourse, the give and take of question and answer, of objection and counter-objection. Rhetoric, as Aristotle defines it, is the faculty of observing in any given case the available means of persuasion, and since the orator addresses a popular audience including untrained thinkers, his appeal is threefold: to their reason (*logos*), to their feelings (*pathos*), and to their confidence in his character, that is, in his virtue, competence, courtesy, good sense, good will (*ethos*). It thus appears, says Aristotle, that rhetoric is an offshoot of dialectic (*logos*) and also of ethical studies (*ethos* and *pathos*).[30]

By the wholeness and balance of this well-constructed system, Aristotle corrected the one-sidedness and superficiality of Gorgias and Protagoras, which Plato had exposed, particularly in his *Gorgias*.

The tradition was transmitted to later ages principally through Cicero,[31] who modified and developed it in both theory and practice, drawing eclectically on Aristotle, on Isocrates, and to a relatively slight degree on his own teacher Hermagoras. Cicero subordinated logic to

[29] Aristotle *De sophisticis elenchis* 3.165^b 13, in *Works*, Vol. I, translated into English under the editorship of W. D. Ross. All citations from Aristotle are from this edition.

[30] Aristotle *Rhetoric* 1.2.1356^a 25. He treats of the emotions and passions in his *Ethics* and his *Rhetoric*; today these are regarded as primarily within the province of psychology.

[31] Cicero's work takes no account of the *Analytics* or the *Poetics* of Aristotle.

rhetoric and incorporated a great part of it in his rhetorical treatises. Every careful method of arguing, according to Cicero, has two parts: invention and judgment.[32] Aristotle, he says, seems to have been the chief discoverer of each; the Stoics diligently pursued the latter but disregarded the former. Cicero followed Isocrates rather than Aristotle in emphasizing the graces of style and the value of figures, and in his orations he employed the three styles—the lofty, the intermediate, and the plain. In his rhetorical treatises he gave rules for memory and for delivery. Therefore, in Cicero's work and through it, the division of rhetoric into five parts—invention, disposition, elocution, memory, and pronunciation—a division which he attributed to numerous writers before him,[33] became firmly established in the tradition.[34] It was primarily through his youthful *De inventione* and his orations that Cicero affected the rhetoric of the Middle Ages; and through these and his more mature works on rhetoric, especially the *De oratore,* which later became available, he continued to be a dominant influence in the Renaissance. The *Rhetorica ad C. Herennium,* probably by Cornificius, but wrongly attributed throughout the Middle Ages to his younger contemporary Cicero and owing its great influence in part to Cicero's name, was the first Latin work which treated the rhetorical figures stressed by Gorgias and his pupil Isocrates and became the principal link in transmitting them to its own and later ages. Quintilian's *Institutio oratoria,* based mainly on Cicero and recovered by scholars in the fifteenth century, strengthened the classical tradition. Aristotle, the *Ad Herennium,* Cicero, and Quintilian were studied directly in the schools during the Renaissance and were the chief ultimate sources of the works on rhetoric and logic, whether in Latin or in the vernaculars.

The sixteenth-century texts on rhetoric and logic make frequent explicit reference to Tully and Quintilian and also to Aristotle, though often these references, especially to the last, represent intermediary rather than direct acquaintance. Unquestionably there had been in the course of centuries shifts of emphasis and other distortions of the tradition, as

[32] Cicero *Topica* ch. 2. This division became standard in treatises on logic. Abraham Fraunce, in *The Lawiers Logike,* fol. 5ᵛ, notes that Aristotle himself commends this division in 8 *Topics* [ch. 1] and 3 *Rhet.* [ch. 1].

[33] Cicero *De inventione* 1.7.

[34] Richard McKeon, in "Rhetoric in the Middle Ages," *Speculum,* XVII (January, 1942), 1–32, p. 4, comments: "Whatever the estimate critics and historians are disposed to make of Cicero's achievement, originality, and consistency, his choices and emphases fixed the influence and oriented the interpretation of ancient thought, Greek as well as Latin, at the beginning of the Middle Ages and again in the Renaissance."

scholars have pointed out.[35] Yet the tradition persisted, and its features are discernible in all the works which circulated in Shakespeare's England. Despite obvious differences, the Renaissance works are essentially alike and at one with the classical tradition. They recognize as important the traditional five parts of rhetoric—invention, disposition, elocution, memory, and utterance—even when they do not explicitly treat all of them.

Two of these parts, memory and utterance, because they relate only to the oral delivery of a speech, may be passed over here with a brief notice. In his *Arte of Rhetorique* Wilson, the traditionalist, gives the lengthiest treatment of memory in the Tudor works. The Ramists held that memory is assisted most by method, the proper disposition or ordering of ideas in accordance with logical principles, and that it is therefore a part of logic. Wilson and the Ramists, following Cicero and the *Ad Herennium* in their treatment of delivery, which they called utterance, pronunciation, or action, divided it into two parts, voice and gesture.[36] The figurists did not deal with memory, but they took into account voice and gesture. By the figure mimesis, explained Peacham,

we counterfeit not only what one sayd, but also utteraunce and gesture, immitating everything as it was . . . cutting it shorte, or drawing it out a long, with stammering, with loude or loe voyce, lisping, nodding the head, wincking, frowning, smiling . . . (1577 ed., sig. O iiii ʳ)

A pittifull pronunciation is of great force: and moveth affections wonderfully, in expressing a wofull case, for the apte bending of the voyce to the quallity of the cause, is a Godly ornament in an Oratour. (*Ibid.*, sig. P iii ᵛ) . . . likewyse, that which the Oratoure hath uttered in whole and vehemente speech, he may repeate agayne with cold and quyet words. (*Ibid.*, sig. Q i ʳ)

In their attitude toward invention, disposition, and elocution, the traditionalists, Ramists, and figurists apparently differ, but the differences

[35] Among them are the following: C. S. Baldwin, *Ancient Rhetoric and Poetic; Medieval Rhetoric and Poetic; Renaissance Literary Theory and Practice;* Clark, *Rhetoric and Poetry in the Renaissance;* Crane, *Wit and Rhetoric in the Renaissance;* Hultzen, "Aristotle's 'Rhetoric' in England before 1600," an unpublished dissertation presented to Cornell University, 1932; Herrick, *The Poetics of Aristotle in England;* Spingarn, *A History of Literary Criticism in the Renaissance;* Abelson, *The Seven Liberal Arts; a Study in Medieval Culture;* McKeon, "Rhetoric in the Middle Ages," *Speculum,* XVII (January, 1942), 1–32; Faral, "Les Arts poetiques du XIIᵉ et du XIIIᵉ siècle," in *Bibliothèque de l'École des Hautes Etudes;* Haskins, *The Renaissance of the Twelfth Century;* Paetow, *The Arts Course at Medieval Universities; with Special Reference to Grammar and Rhetoric.*
[36] Shakespeare takes account of voice and gesture in Hamlet's advice to the players (2.1.1–39).

on closer examination are seen to be superficial rather than fundamental. Consequently these three parts need to be examined in more detail.

5. Invention and Disposition

Aristotle treated invention in the first seven of his eight books of *Topics,* or dialectic, and also in his *Rhetoric,* especially in Book II, Chapter 23, where he enumerates twenty-eight topics [37] from which a speaker or writer may draw matter for whatever discourse he wishes to develop. Cicero wrote his *Topica* in response to the request of his friend the lawyer Trebatius, who said he could not understand Aristotle's *Topics* and wished for a clearer and simpler statement of its substance. Cicero presented his list of the topics of invention with great clarity as complete and exhaustive.

Every rule necessary for the finding of arguments is now concluded; so that when you have proceeded from definition, from division, from the name, from conjugates, from genus, from species, from similarity, from difference, from contraries, from adjuncts, from consequents, from antecedents, from things incompatible with one another, from causes, from effects, from a comparison with things greater or less or equal—there is no topic of argument whatever remaining to be discovered.[38]

To these sixteen topics internal to the subject of inquiry he added a seventeenth, testimony, which does not depend on the art of the investigator, but requires recourse to external aids such as laws, contracts, witnesses, tortures, oaths, prophecies, divinations, and oracles. Testimony evokes belief if it proceeds from authority such as that derived from a man's character, knowledge, experience, age, or position.

Cicero's *Topica,* probably the clearest and most concise treatment of invention, was the standard text for beginning this study in the grammar schools of Tudor England. Regarded sometimes as a work on rhetoric, more often as one on logic, it became basic to all later studies of the kind. Whether the topics or places of invention belong to rhetoric, to logic,

[37] In the *Rhetoric,* Bk. III, ch. 15, Aristotle further enumerates sixteen lines of argument designed to allay prejudice. Their purpose is to promote *ethos* and *pathos;* their method, disputation: excuse, counterattack, admission of facts while denying alleged evil motives, etc. In Book II, ch. 24, Aristotle enumerates ten lines of spurious argument employed by the sophists.

[38] Perfecta est omnis argumentorum inveniendorum praeceptio, ut, cum profectus sis a definitione, a partitione, a notatione, a coniugatis, a genere, a formis, a similitudine, a differentia, a contrariis, ab adiunctis, a consequentibus, ab antecedentibus, a repugnantibus, a causis, ab effectis, a comparatione maiorum minorum parium, nulla praeterea sedes argumenti quaerenda sit. (*Topica,* 18.71)

or to both was a moot question. Aristotle had not clearly defined the relation between dialectical and rhetorical investigation; many of the topics in his *Rhetoric* were the same as those treated also in his *Topics*, or dialectic. According to Cicero, Hermagoras made the important distinction between thesis, the general or theoretical question, and hypothesis, the particularized or practical question, but then wrongly assigned both to the orator, whereas, remarks Cicero, the first belongs properly to the philosopher.[39] Accepting Cicero's view, Boethius in his *De differentiis topicis* came nearest to stating a clear distinction between dialectical and rhetorical investigation, but he admitted that the two tend to overlap; for, if the dialectician takes up a dispute as of persons or deeds, he will bring it under a general or philosophical question, which is his proper concern; likewise, if the rhetorician takes up a general question, he will treat it with reference to certain persons, times, deeds, circumstances, for such particularized questions are his proper concern.[40] The allocation of the topics of invention was the primary question dividing the traditionalists and the Ramists.

a. The Traditionalists.—The traditionalists held that the topics of invention belong to both logic and rhetoric. Thomas Wilson, in his *Arte of Rhetorique,* agreed with Boethius that while both the logical and rhetorical forms of investigation have their proper subject matter, they tend to overlap.

Thinges generally spoken without all circumstaunces, are more proper unto the *Logician,* who talketh of thinges universally, without respect of person, time, or place. And yet notwithstanding, *Tullie* doth say, that whosoever will talke of particular matter must remember, that within the same also is comprehended a general. (p. 2)

Cox, following Melanchthon, who had taken the position of Hermagoras, added to the generally recognized three kinds of orations—the deliberative, the judicial, and the demonstrative—a fourth kind, the logical, which deals with a general question, either simple, as what justice is, or compound, as whether justice be a virtue. It must be developed, says Cox, according to the precepts of logic, and set forth with the graces of rhetoric.

<hr>

[39] Cicero *De inventione,* 1.6. *Cf. De partitione oratoriae,* ch. 18. Also compare Aristotle, *Topics,* Bk. III, ch. 6, where he treats of the definite and indefinite thesis.
[40] Boethius (480?–524?) *De differentiis topicis,* in Migne *Patrologia Latina,* LXIV, 1177, 1205–6, 1216.

Nothinge can be perfectly and propryely knowen but by rules of Logike, whiche
is nothynge but an observacyon or a diligent markynge of nature . . . so then
the sure Judgement of argumentes or reasons muste be lernyd of the Logicyan
but the crafte to set them out with plesaunte fygures and to delate the matter
longith to the Rhetorycian.[41]

In *The Arte of Rhetorique* Wilson lists as places or topics of rhetorical
inquiry such practical and particularized questions as what was done, who
did it, where, with whose help, how, when. In a deliberative oration the
investigation would turn on whether the proposed action would be honest,
profitable, possible, necessary, difficult, easy, pleasant, safe, just, prudent,
honorable, according to custom. Most suited to a demonstrative oration
eulogizing a man, especially one dead, says Wilson, are the places of
persons, that is, gifts of mind, body, and fortune. He lists ten: ancestrie,
the Realme, the Shire, or Towne, the sexe or kinde, education, inclination
of nature, attempts worthie, wise counsaile given, time of departing this
worlde, his Tombe and all such honours as are used in Funeralles (*AR*,
p. 120). A judicial oration in particular would employ various forms of
testimony, such as laws, contracts, witnesses.

Wilson points out, however, the superiority even in rhetoric of the
more general topics of logic because they are more searching, more
fundamental.

I wish that every man should desire, & seeke to have his *Logique* perfit, before
he looke to profite in *Rhetorique,* considering the ground and confirmation
of causes, is for the most part gathered out of *Logique.* (*AR*, p. 113)

Places to confirme things are fower: Things honest, Profitable, Easie to be
done, Hard to be done. Many learned will have recourse to the places of
Logicke in steede of these fower places, when they take in hand to commend
any such matter. . . .

The places of *Logicke* are these. Definition, Causes, Parts, Effects, Things
adjoyning, Contraries. . . . I thinke these of *Logicke* must first bee minded,
ere the other can well be had. For what is he, that can cal a thing honest, and
by reason prove it, except he first know what the thing is: the which he cannot better doe, then by defining the nature of the thing. Againe, how shall I
know whether mine attempt be easie or hard if I knowe not the efficient cause,
or be assured how it may be done. In affirming it to bee possible, I shall not
better knowe it then by searching the ende, and learning by *Logicke,* what is
the finall cause of every thing. (p. 23)

[41] Cox, *The Arte or Crafte of Rhethoryke,* ed. by F. I. Carpenter, pp. 45–48.

The traditionalists Wilson, Cox, and Rainolde do not attempt in their works on rhetoric a general or systematic treatment of invention in one place. Instead, following their sources, they list for each kind of oration the topics best suited to it, sometimes combining the general topics of logic with the more particularized topics of rhetoric related to persons and circumstances. The pattern which Rainolde prescribes for composing a "Confirmacion" is limited to rhetorical topics.

1. It shall behove you first, for the entring of the oracion, to induce a reprehension againste those, whiche have confuted as a truthe, that which you will confirme.
2. In the seconde parte, place the exposicion and meanyng of the aucthours sentence.
3. Shewe the matter to be manifest.
4. Credible.
5. Possible.
6. Agreying to the truthe.
7. Shewe the facte comelie.
8. Profitable.[42]

For gnome, or sentence, "an oracion in fewe wordes, shewyng a godlie precept of life, exhorting, or diswayding," [43] he combines rhetorical and logical topics. The latter are marked with asterisks, supplied by the present writer.

1. The praise of the aucthour.
2. The Exposicion of the sentence.
* 3. A Confirmacion in the strength of the cause.
* 4. A conference, of the contrarie.
* 5. A similitude.
6. The example.
* 7. The testimonie of aucthours, shewing the like.
8. Then adde the conclusion.[44]

---

[42] Rainolde, *A Booke Called the Foundacion of Rhetorike*, fol. xxviii[v]. [43] *Ibid.*, fol. xx[r].
[44] That Shakespeare used these forms as presented by Aphthonius, whose work Rainolde adapted, is noted by T. W. Baldwin. When Malvolio, wearing yellow stockings cross-gartered, comes before Olivia, he confirms his hopes by checking with four of the rules of confirmation her reactions and the letter which he thinks she wrote to him: the matter is manifest (he has "limed" Olivia); it is credible and possible (he finds "no incredulous or unsafe circumstance"); it agrees with the truth ("concurs directly with the letter . . . everything adheres together.") (*TN*, 3.4.71–92.) King Henry IV concludes his apostrophe to sleep with the gnome, or sentence, "Uneasy lies the head that wears a crown" (*2H4*, 3.1.4–31). The matter of this speech is adapted from the annotations of the sixteenth-

Notwithstanding the clarity of Cicero's *Topica* and the wide use of his book as a school text and despite his claim that the seventeen topics of invention he treats are complete and exhaustive, a desire for more minute distinctions resulted in some diagreement among the traditionalists as to their number. Thomas Wilson, in *The Rule of Reason*, lists twenty-four places of logic; these are his translation into English of Agricola's re-working of the seventeen topics of Cicero and the twenty-four of Themistius, which Boethius had set side by side in his *De differentiis topicis*. Raphe Lever, while remaining within the traditional boundaries, attempted an avowedly original treatment by appointing the ten categories of Aristotle as places and adding and interlacing others which could not conveniently be referred to them, making in all twenty-four places, which he later subdivided to make forty-four. Furthermore, some of the logicians among the traditionalists entered territory usually assigned to rhetoric and grammar. Thus, Thomas Blundeville, in his table, lists seventeen places of persons as well as thirty-five places of things; [45] the latter include figurative speech and grammatical comparison of the positive, comparative, and superlative degrees.

Disposition, or arrangement of a speech, was explicitly discussed by only one of the Tudor rhetoricians. In *The Arte of Rhetorique* Wilson defined disposition as the ordering of the parts of an oration. He distinguished two kinds. The first is merely the traditional sequence: exordium, narration, confirmation, confutation, peroration. The second admits a variation from that order to gain certain desired effects, principally through the weighing of reasons and the placing of the strongest reasons at the beginning and at the end, the weakest in the middle. In his *Rule of Reason*, Wilson, like the other logicians of the traditionalist group, treated disposition or judgment in terms of definition, division, method, propositions, and the syllogism.

b. The Ramists.—The Ramists differed from the traditionalists in ignoring the rhetorical topics—such as the credible, the profitable, the difficult—and in considering only the logical topics. In opposition to the traditionalists they flatly denied that invention and disposition are common to both logic and rhetoric. They insisted that they belong only to

century editors of Aphthonius, and the framework is that of an illustration from Priscian which they added. *Op. cit.*, II, 322–27.

[45] Melanchthon, in his "Erotemata dialectices," also treats *loci personarum* (11) in addition to *loci rerum* (28). See *Opera, Corpus reformatorum*, ed. by Bretschneider and Bindseil, XIII, 659–63.

logic.[46] Abraham Fraunce states this position forcefully in *The Lawiers Logike.*

> What precepts soever the common Rhetoricians put downe for ordering of
> *Exordiums* and framing and disposing of the whole course of their speeche
> fitly and according to cause, auditors, time, place, and such like circumstances;
> all these I say, are altogether Logicall, not in any respect perteining to Rheto-
> ricke, but as a Rhetor may bee directed by Logicall precepts of judgement and
> disposition. (fol. 115 ʳ)

The Ramists asserted that neither the distinction between necessary
propositions and those merely contingent or probable nor that between
true propositions and false demands such separate treatment according
to subject matter as Aristotle had given in his *Analytics,* his *Topics* and
Rhetoric, and his *De sophisticis elenchis.* Fraunce reasons thus:

> Because of these two kinds of conceipts, *Aristotle* woulde needes make two
> Logikes, the one for Science, the other for Opinion: wherein (if so it may be
> sayde of so great a Philosopher) it seemeth hee was but an *Opinator.* For al-
> though among thinges conceaved and knowne, some bee necessary and unfal-
> lible, some doubtfull and contingent, yet the Arte of Knowing and Reasoning
> of the same (I meane Logike) is only one and the same, as the sight of the eye
> in perceyving all colours, bee they chaungeable or not chaungeable. And as
> well might a man say there must bee two arts of Grammer (if Grammer bee
> a distinct Art, one for courtly speeche, an other for country talke: or two
> distinct arts of making of cups, one for golden cuppes, an other for cuppes of
> silver, as two Logikes, one for unfallible Argumentes, and another for Con-
> tingent. Therefore one Logike suffiseth to dispute of all thinges, necessary or
> contingent whatsoever. Yet this one Logike her selfe in respect of her preceptes
> is always necessary and never contingent, for otherwise it were no Art, but
> the application of it may bee in contingent causes as well as necessary. (5 ᵛ)
> . . . as for the third kinde of Logike, which they call *Elenchticall,* seeing it is
> no Logike at all, but rather the abuse and perversion of Logike, I see no cause
> why it should be taught in Logike: yet if any man thinke that the true preceptes
> of Logike once knowne, will not be sufficient to descry the falsenesse of sophis-
> ticall argumentations, he may for his contentation seeke for a full discourse

---

[46] Thus Gabriel Harvey, in true Ramist fashion, divided the twelve books of Quintilian's
Institutio oratoria: "The first two bookes, preparative. The five next, Logique for Invention, and disposition. The fower following, Rhetorique for Elocution, & pronunciation:
Logique for memory: an accessary, and shaddow of disposition. The last, A supplement,
and discourse of such appurtenaunces, as may otherwyse concerne an Orator to knowe and
practise." Moore-Smith, *Gabriel Harvey's Marginalia,* p. 110. For a clear outline of the
Ramist theory on this point see p. 380, below.

thereof out of some commentarie, and not overcharge the Art it selfe with
unnecessary institutions. (6 ᵣ) . . . Artificiall Logike then is the polyshing
of natural wit, as discovering the validitie of everie reason, bee it necessary,
whereof cometh science: or contingent, whence proceedeth opinion. (5 ᵣ)

If, then, as the Ramists held, there is only one art of reasoning which
includes both the necessarily true and the probable, it follows that there
is only one art concerned with the invention and disposition of arguments,
the art of logic. On these premises the Ramists allocated to rhetoric only
style and delivery. Yet while insisting on this strict division, they, even
more than the traditionalists, emphasized the close relationship of logic
and rhetoric and the necessity of using both together as tools of analysis
or reading and of genesis or composition. For this reason the Ramist texts
are in pairs.[47] William Kempe and John Brinsley, schoolmasters who
wrote on education during Shakespeare's lifetime, were Ramists. In *The
Education of Children* (1588) Kempe describes the vital integration of
the three arts of language in grammar school practice.

First the scholler shal learne the precepts concerning the divers sorts of arguments in the first part of Logike, (for without them Rhetorike cannot be well
understood) then shall followe the tropes and figures in the first part of Rhetorike, wherein he shall employ the sixth part of his studie, and all the rest in
learning and handling good authors: as are *Tullies Offices,* his Orations,
Caesars Commentaries, Virgils Aeneis, Ovids Metamorphosis, and *Horace.*
In whom for his first exercise of unfolding the Arte, he shall observe the examples of the hardest poynts in Grammar, of the arguments in Logike, of the
tropes and figures in Rhetorike, referring every example to his proper rule, as
before. Then he shall learne the two latter parts also both of Logike and
Rhetorike. . . . And by this time he must observe in authors all the use of the
Artes, as not only the words and phrases, not only the examples of the arguments; but also the axiome, wherein every argument is disposed; the syllogisme, whereby it is concluded; the method of the whole treatise, and the
passages, whereby the parts are joyned together. Agayne he shall observe not
only every trope, every figure, aswell of words as of sentences; but also the
Rhetoricall pronunciation and gesture fit for every word, sentence, and affection.

And so let him take in hand the exercise of all these three Artes at once in
making somewhat of his owne, first by imitation . . . then let him have a

⁴⁷ Hultzen, in his "Aristotle's 'Rhetoric' in England before 1600," finds Fraunce's *Lawiers
Logike* and *Arcadian Rhetorike,* taken together, the nearest approach, and that not very
close, to Aristotle's *Rhetoric.* Butler in his *Oratoriae libri duo,* treats invention as the other
Ramists do in their logic texts. And under disposition, he treats the proposition and syllogism; but he subordinates logic to oratory in the manner of Cicero and Quintilian.

like theame to prosecute with the same artificiall instruments, that he findeth in his author.[48]

Brinsley explains in greater detail just how the precepts of logic and rhetoric were applied in composition.

For the manner of writing downe the Theames by schollers of judgement, it may not be amisse where leisure will serve, to cause the schollers to write them thus: In the first Margent towards the left hand, together with the severall parts of the Theame (as *Exord. Narratio, Confirmatio, Confutatio, Conclusio,* being set in great letters over against each part) to set also the heads of the severall arguments; chiefly against the Confirmation: as *Causa, Effectum:* like as *Apthonius* doth set his places, à *Causa,* à *Contrario.* And in the latter side of the page, towards the right hand, to set the severall tropes or figures, but in two or three letters. As for *Metonymia Efficientis,* no more but *Met. Effic.* or the like . . .[49]

In *The Scholemaster* Roger Ascham tells of the happy effects achieved by his royal pupil in applying the precepts of logic and rhetoric to her reading of the classics.

And a better, and nerer example herein, may be, our most noble Queene *Elizabeth* . . . the mynde by dailie marking, first, the cause and matter: than, the wordes and phrases: next, the order and compos[it]ion: after the reason and argumentes: than the formes and figures of both the tonges [Greek and Latin]: lastelie, the measure and compas of everie sentence, must nedes, by litle and litle drawe unto it the like shape of eloquence, as the author doth use, which is red.[50]

As to the number of topics, Brinsley had his pupils distinguish ten.

The following of those tenne first and chiefe heads of reasoning; to wit, from Causes, Effects, Subjects, Adjuncts, Disagreeable things, Comparisons, Notations, Distributions, Definitions, Testimonies, (to one of which each of *Apthonius* or *Tullies* places do belong) is farre the easiest, surest, and plainest way. (p. 183)

In addition to these ten, Ramus himself had listed conjugates. Merely by further subdivision, Butler showed twenty topics on his table, and Fraunce treated nineteen; both of these writers rejected notation and conjugates. All of the Ramists omitted antecedents and consequents.

---

[48] Kempe, *The Education of Children,* sig. G2ᵛ.
[49] Brinsley, *Ludus literarius; or, The Grammar Schoole,* ed. by E. T. Campagnac, p. 185.
[50] Ascham, *The Scholemaster,* fol., 35ʳ. Upton edition, p. 105.

With these exceptions their list of topics is, as Brinsley remarked, the same as Cicero's.

Nothwithstanding the variety of opinion as to the number of topics or places, there was complete unanimity among all Renaissance groups as to their nature, use, and importance. The traditionalist Wilson expresses the common judgment of the time in *The Rule of Reason* when he asserts:

A place is, the resting corner of an argument (fol. 37 ʳ) . . . [the orator] may have arguments at will, if he search the places which are none other thing, but the store house of reason and the fountaine of all wisedome. (fol. 61 ᵛ)

Thus we see how large the use is of these places, for not only shall any one bee able to speake right aptly, and very well to the purpose, whensoever he shal seeke out the trueth of any cause by diligent search, and raunging in these corners, but also hee shall largely set out his matter, with much delite, and orderly tel his tale, with singular profite, and passing gaine. And therefore I would wish that Logike were alwaies the square to rule our talke, and made the very touch stone to trie our reasons, such as in weightie matters, full ofte are alledged, and then I would not doubt, but that folly should the sooner bee espied, and wise mens sayinges the better estemed. (fol. 61 ʳ)

The practical use of logic [51] and rhetoric in the affairs of life is insisted on by Fraunce even more ardently than by Wilson.

Logike is an art of teaching . . . whose vertue is seene not onely in teaching others, but also in learning thy selfe, in discoursing, thinking, meditating, and framing of thine owne, as also in discussing, perusing, searching and examining what others have either delivered by speach, or put downe in writing; this is called *Analysis*, that *Genesis*, and in them both consisteth the whole use of Logike.

As farre then as mans reason can reach, so farre extendeth it selfe the use and vertue of this art of reasoning, . . . Men reason in schooles as Philosophers, in Westminster as Lawyers, in Court as Lords, in Countrey as worldly

[51] The most accessible Ramist work on logic is Milton's expansion of Ramus's *Dialectica*, entitled *Artis logicae plenior institutio, ad Petri Rami methodum concinnata*, ed. and tr. by Allan H. Gilbert, in *The Works of John Milton*, Vol. XI. In *The Pilgrimage to Parnassus* (*ca.* 1597) is a contemporary comment on the clarity of the Ramist method. Even Stupido can learn logic as Ramus presented it: "I have (I pray God prosper my labours!) analised a peece of an hommelie according to Ramus, and surelie in my minde and simple opinion Mr. Peter maketh all things verie plaine and easie. As for Setons *Logique*, trulie I never looke on it but it makes my head ache!" (lines 324–29). The Ramists made a special point of illustrating the principles of logic by examples from literature. Fraunce, for instance, uses Spenser's *Shepheardes Calender*. See Part Three.

husbands . . . the true use of Logike is as well apparant in simple playne and easie explication, as in subtile, strict, and concised probation. Reade *Homer,* reade *Demosthenes,* reade *Virgill,* read *Cicero,* reade *Bartas,* reade *Torquato Tasso,* reade that most worthie ornament of our English tongue, the *Countess of Penbrookes Arcadia* and therein see the true effectes of natural Logike which is the ground of artificiall . . . (fol. 3 $^{r-v}$) Let no day passe without some practice, either in making, framing, and inventing of our selves, or in resolving & dissolving of things doone by others, for the triall of their skil, and confirmation of our owne. Neither would I have this practise continued onely in reading, or writing, but in every civill assembly or meeting: wherein yet I will not bee so severe a censor, as to exact every speech to the formall rules of axiomes, syllogismes, &c. It shall be sufficient for us to folow a more easie and elegant kinde of disputation, joyning Rhetorike with Logike, and referring that precise straitnesse unto Philosophicall exercises.

Neyther let any man thinke, that because in common meetings and assemblies the woordes and tearmes of Logike bee not named, therefore the force and operation of Logike is not there used and apparent. For, as in Grammer wee name neyther Noune, Pronoune, Verbe, nor any other parte of speech: and as in Rhetorike, we make mention neyther of *Metonymia, Synecdoche, Exclamatio,* nor any other Rhetoricall figure or trope: yet use in our speech the helpe of the one in speaking grammatically, and the direction of the other in talking eloquently: so, although in common conference wee never name syllogismes, axiomes, propositions, assumptions, & other woords of art, yet doo wee secretly practise them in our disputations, the vertue whereof is, to make our discourses seeme true to the simple, and probable to the wise. (120 ^{r})

Despite differences as to the allocation of the topics of invention and their precise number, the traditionalists and Ramists clearly agreed on their importance and their vital function in providing matter for discourse. Both groups considered the general topics of logic the more fundamental, even for rhetorical use, and with minor exceptions and divergences accepted Cicero's seventeen topics.

6. Elocution or Style

The rhetoricians of the sixteenth century agreed in conceiving elocution or style as concerned mainly with the figures of speech, but they differed as to the scope of the figures and their number. The figures have a long history. Plato and Aristotle reprehended the excessive ornateness of Gorgias. Isocrates, the pupil of Gorgias, reduced this extravagance of ornament and used figures with more art. In the third book of his *Rhetoric* Aristotle took up the discussion of style, for, as he remarked,

The arts of language cannot help having a small but real importance, whatever it is we have to expound to others: the way in which a thing is said does
affect its intelligibility. (1404 ᵃ 8)

With regard to style Aristotle was concerned principally with lucidity,
vividness, appropriateness, structure, and prose rhythm, but he devoted
some attention to figures. He did not name many of those which he
described, but he favored metaphor, simile, synecdoche, prosopopoeia,
antonomasia, periphrasis, all of which tend to promote vividness; likewise antithesis, isocolon, homoioteleuton, anaphora, epistrophe, polysyndeton, and asyndeton, figures which emphasize balance in periodic
structure and affect prose rhythm. He counseled the avoidance of
zeugma, parenthesis, and in general whatever tends to ambiguity and
obscurity, although he liked antanaclasis and paronomasia, which are
figures of deliberate ambiguity. Nearly half of the *Rhetorica ad C.
Herennium*, contemporary with Cicero and influential as a school text
throughout the Middle Ages and the Renaissance, was devoted to style,
chiefly the figures. Cicero treated the same elements of style as did Aristotle, but he was more hospitable to the figures, enumerating them in
De oratore and again, reducing their number, in *Orator*. He used them
extensively in his orations, especially those which rise to the lofty style.
Quintilian reviewed Cicero's presentation of the figures before giving
his own more detailed treatment, and he told why he excluded some
which Cicero had included. He stated clearly his own concept of figures.

Consider what we are to understand by the word figure; for it is used in two
senses; signifying, in the one, any form of words, whatever it may be, as bodies,
of whatever they be composed, have some certain shape; in the other, in which
it is *properly* termed a figure, any deviation, either in thought or expression,
from the ordinary and simple method of speaking, as our bodies assume different postures when we sit, lie, or look back. . . . If we adopt the first and
general sense, then, there will be no part of language that is not *figured*. . . .
But if particular habits, and, as it were, gestures of language, are to receive
this designation, that only must here be regarded as a figure, which deviates,
by poetical or oratorical phraseology, from the simple and ordinary modes of
speaking. Thus we shall be right in saying that one sort of style is . . . desti-
tute of figures, (and this is no small fault) and another . . . diversified with
figures. . . . Let the definition of a figure, then, be *a form of speech artfully
varied from common usage*.⁵²

⁵² Quare primum intuendum est, quid accipere debeamus figuram. Nam duobus modis dicitur: uno qualiscunque forma sententiae, sicut in corporibus, quibus, quoquo modo sunt

This definition was accepted by the Tudor rhetoricians of all three groups. For example, Puttenham analyzes the purpose and scope of figurative language.

Figurative speech is a noveltie of language evidently (and yet not absurdly) estranged from the ordinarie habite and manner of our dayly talke and writing and figure it selfe is a certaine lively or good grace set upon wordes, speaches and sentences to some purpose and not in vaine, giving them ornament or efficacie by many maner of alterations in shape, in sounde, and also in sence, sometime by way of surplusage, sometime by defect, sometime by disorder, or mutation, & also by putting into our speaches more pithe and substance, subtiltie, quicknesse, efficacie or moderation, in this or that sort tuning and tempring them, by amplification, abridgement, opening, closing, enforcing, meekening or otherwise disposing them to the best purpose. (p. 159)

With the exception of Hoskyns, the rhetoricians of the three Renaissance groups employed the traditional division of figures into tropes and schemes, and the further division of schemes into those that are grammatical and those that are rhetorical. A trope, such as a metaphor, turns the significance of a word or sentence from its proper meaning to another not proper, but yet near it in order to increase its force. Grammatical schemes were subdivided into orthographical and syntactical schemes; rhetorical schemes, into figures of words and figures of sentence or thought. The rhetorical figures of words were figures of repetition. Some authors gave the name figures of amplification to a certain group of the figures of thought. In *The Arcadian Rhetorike* Fraunce remarked that tropes confer on language a certain grace, figures of words a kind of delicacy fit to delight, and figures of thought a majesty and force apt to persuade. (Sig. E 4 ᵛ)

The table on page 35 shows how the figures in the Renaissance works [53] compare in number with those in the *Rhetorica ad C. Herennium*,[54] in Cicero's *De oratore*, and in Quintilian's *Institutio oratoria*.

composita, utique habitus est aliquis; altero, quo proprie schema dicitur, in sensu vel sermone aliqua a vulgari et simplici specie cum ratione mutatio, sicut nos sedemus, incumbimus, respicimus. . . . In quo ita loquimur, tanquam omnis sermo habeat figuram. . . . Sed si habitus quidam et quasi gestus sic appellandi sunt, id demum hoc loco accipi schema oportebit, quod sit a simplici atque in promptu posito dicendi modo poetice vel oratorie mutatum. Sic enim verum erit, aliam esse orationem . . . carentem figuris, quod vitium non inter minima est, aliam . . . est figuratam. . . . Ergo figura sit arte aliqua novata forma dicendi. (*Institutio oratoria*, 9.1.10–14 [Loeb Classical Library]. Translation by J. S. Watson [Bohn's Classical Library], II, 146.)

[53] Rainolde gives almost no attention to figures; Cox, none at all.

[54] Faral, *op. cit.*, pp. 52–54, presents a table showing the degree of correspondence of the

According to the number of figures dealt with, the Ramists represent one extreme and the figurists the other. Yet they are not so far apart as the difference in number might suggest, for the figurists incorporated in their figures much of what the Ramists treated in their logic texts, since, as the former often remarked, many of the figures are derived from the topics of invention. The figurists, like the traditionalists and the Ramists, had a high regard for invention. Sherry included a brief but pointed section on invention and proofs in his *Treatise of Schemes and Tropes* (1550). Angel Day speaks of

invention first, wherein plentifully is searched and considered, what kinde of matter, how much variety of sentences, what sorts of figures, how many similitudes, what approbations, diminutions, insinuations, and circumstances are presently needfull, or furthering to the matter in handling. (p. 14)

It would be a mistake to regard the treatises of the figurists as limited to a discussion of style in the narrow sense.[55] Puttenham, eager to bestow upon the poet the right to use the rhetorical figures of thought, which he considered pre-eminent, declared the poet to be the most ancient orator (p. 196). Peacham emphasized the value of the figures as means of persuasion, considering

the knowledge of them so necessary, that no man can read profytably, or understand perfectlye eyther Poets, Oratours, or the holy Scriptures, without them: nor any Oratoure able by the waight of his wordes, to perswade his hearers, having no helpe of them. (Epistle dedicatory, A. iii ᵗ, 1577 edition)

In terms of the three-fold means of persuasion basic in Aristotle's *Rhetoric*, namely, *logos*, *pathos*, and *ethos*, and of the aesthetic aspects of grammar such as are touched on in his discussion of style, the fundamental likeness among the three groups of sixteenth-century works becomes clear. When the approximately two hundred figures which the Tudor theorists distinguished are arranged under these four headings, it becomes evident that the work of the figurists covered practically the

---

figures in nine leading rhetorical works of the twelfth and thirteenth centuries to those in the *Rhetorica ad C. Herennium*.
[55] All the Renaissance groups valued the figures as means to enhance style. In the words of Puttenham's recent editors: "The figures are the sum of all the resources (other than metrical) by which poetry conveys its special overplus of excitement or stimulation; they are the sum, expressed in Elizabethan terms, of the types of ambiguity, the obliquities, the transferences, the echoes and controlled associations, which lift poetry above mere statement and by which the poet lets odd and unexpected lights into his subject, 'drawing it,' says Puttenham, 'from plainnesse and simplicitie to a certaine doublenesse.' " (p. lxxx)

FIGURES OF SPEECH [a]

	I. TROPES		II. SCHEMES GRAMMATICAL		III. SCHEMES RHETORICAL		TOTAL	VICES
	Of Words	Of Sentences	Orthographical	Syntactical	Of Words	Of Thought and Amplification		
1. *Rhet. ad. Her.*	10				35	20	65	
2. Cic. *De or.*	4				41	46	91	
3. Quintilian	14				29	38	89	
4. Wilson	8	1 (5)	6	8	24	41	80	14
5. Talaeus	4				9	10	23	
6. Fenner	4 (8)				9	10	23 (27)	2
7. Fraunce	4 (8)				9	10 (11)	23 (28)	
8. Butler	4 (11)		13		8 (10)	10 (31)	22 (65)	21
9. Hoskyns	6			3	13	28	50	
10. Susenbrotus	9	10	15	32	14	60	132	16
11. Sherry 1550	7	8	11	12	41	25	104	
12. Sherry 1555	7	8	12	12	20	60	119	22
13. Peacham 1577	9	10	14	42	24	85	184	
14. Peacham 1593	8	10			24	123	165	10
15. Puttenham	10	12	6	18	9	52	107	15
16. Day	7	9		21	12	44	93	

[a] Because some authors list separately figures which others treat as subdivisions, a comparison of mere numbers is misleading. The same figure is sometimes treated in more than one section of a work and counted each time. For example, Wilson names five tropes of sentences but prefers to treat four of them under other classifications. In his table of figures Butler agrees with the other Ramists, but in his text he introduces additional figures which bring the number up to the totals indicated in parentheses. Similar additions of other writers are similarly indicated. Because Hoskyns uses a different and original classification, his figures have been reclassified here in the traditional groupings for purposes of comparison. The classification by Puttenham is novel in words rather than in meaning. He himself says (pp. 160, 163) that his auricular figures are orthographical and syntactical, his sensable figures are tropes, and his sententious figures, with some exceptions, are figures of thought. (For a more precise comment on Puttenham's classification in relation to the traditional one, especially Quintilian's, and for parallels with Quintilian see La Rue Van Hook, "Greek Rhetorical Terminology in Puttenham's The Arte of English Poesie,'" in *Transactions of the American Philological Association*, XLV [1914], 113, note 9). The vices of speech are listed above only where they are distinguished from the figures, not where they themselves are called figures, as in the work of Susenbrotus, of Day, and of Peacham in 1577.

same ground as the combined works on logic and rhetoric, whether traditionalist or Ramist. The figures under *logos*, constituting by far the most numerous and the most important group, best illustrate the parallel between the works of the logicians and the figurists, for many of the examples cited by the logicians to illustrate the topics and forms of logic are exactly parallel to those cited by the figurists as figures. Some of the figures are identical with logical forms, for example, the dilemma, which was regarded as both a figure and a form of reasoning. That the figures of thought were understood to function under *logos* is clear from the fact that the Ramists treated the substance of them in their logic texts and the figurists frequently mentioned the topics and forms of logic on which they are based. The tropes likewise function under *logos*, as the Ramists recognized, for although they treated them in their rhetoric texts, they related them strictly to the logical topics from which they are derived.[56] The figures may accordingly be reorganized as follows:

Grammar: schemes of words; of construction
the vices of language
figures of repetition

Logos: the figures related to
(*a*) logical topics: testimony, definition, division, genus, species, adjunct, contrary, contradictory, similarity, dissimilarity, comparison, cause, effect, antecedent, consequent, notation, conjugates
(*b*) logical forms, as the syllogism, enthymeme, sorites, dilemma
(*c*) the devices of disputation

Pathos: the figures of affection and vehemence

Ethos: the figures revealing courtesy, gratitude, commendation, forgiveness of injury

This reorganization makes the numerous figures more significant by ordering them in groups fulfilling four fundamental functions, somewhat as the periodic table makes the chemical elements more significant by ordering them in families having similar properties. By thus correlating the figures with the whole body of theory in logic and in the parts of rhetoric other than elocution this reorganization emphasizes the completeness of the pattern and the interdependence of its parts, for

[56] The Ramists admitted four tropes. They distinguished metonymy of cause, of effect, of subject, of adjunct; synecdoche of genus, of species, of the whole, of the parts. They explained that irony is based on the contrary; metaphor, on similitude.

every part gains meaning from its relation to the other parts and to the whole.

The essential general theory of composition and of reading current in Shakespeare's England, as expressed in the definitions, illustrations, and comments of the Tudor logicians and rhetoricians, is presented at the end of this volume in an eclectic handbook constructed by selecting each item from the author who seems to have treated it best and by arranging the whole in the pattern outlined above. The entire theory, with a few negligible exceptions, is illustrated from Shakespeare's plays and poems in the following chapters.[57]

The Renaissance figures seem to us remarkable for their inclusiveness. They deal with words, in the figures of orthography; with grammar, in such matters as interrogation, exclamation, the unfinished sentence, the periodic sentence, ellipsis, rhythm, and the means of varying through them; with coherence, through figures of conjunction and transition; with emphasis, through word order and the figures of repetition; with clarity and obscurity; with amplification and condensation; with beauty, through exergasia and all the figures of exornation; with force, through vehemence (*pathos*); with proof, through *logos;* with *ethos;* even with gesture (mimesis and mycterismus), and voice (pathopopoeia and tasis). The Tudor rhetoricians were tireless in their distinctions, unflagging in their faith in art and artifice, eager to assist in transplanting to the vernacular the adornments of Latin, Greek, and Hebrew literatures assiduously noted in the grammar schools and the universities. They anatomized composition and reading in an age that delighted in anatomies, as of wit, of flattery, of absurdity, and they showed composition interpenetrated with logic.

The Tudor rhetoricians classified the figures in the traditional manner indicated by the table on page 35, not under grammar, *logos, pathos,* and *ethos.* There is warrant for the present reclassification, however, in Aristotle, who furnished the pattern, and in the Renaissance rhetoricians, who implicitly adapted it. Aristotle, discussing style in his *Rhetoric,* gave some attention to the figures of grammar and, in relation to them, to

[57] The reader may study the theory in Part Three (Chapters VI–IX) either a section at a time or a chapter at a time before he reads the illustration of it from Shakespeare in Part Two (Chapters II–V). He may even want to read all of Part Three before beginning Chapter II. The headings of sections and the order of topics within sections in Parts Two and Three are identical to facilitate reference. The reader who is not interested in the theory either for proof or for flavor may disregard Part III entirely, since the chapters on Shakespeare are intelligible without it.

figures of repetition. In discussing the substance of rhetorical discourse
he emphasized its function to effect an interrelated threefold persuasion:
by *logos*, the speaker convinces his hearers of the truth of his argument
by appealing to their reason; by *pathos* he puts them into a favorable,
not a hostile, frame of mind by appealing to the emotions which color
their judgment; by *ethos* he inspires their confidence in his own character and trustworthiness by convincing them of his honesty and goodness, his competence and judgment, and above all his good will toward
them. The importance which Aristotle attached to *ethos, logos,* and
pathos is indicated by the fact that his final words on the art of rhetoric
emphasize the necessity of including this threefold persuasion in the
epilogue of an oration:

The Epilogue has four parts. You must (1) make the audience well-disposed
towards yourself and ill-disposed towards your opponent, (2) magnify or
minimize the leading facts, (3) excite the required state of emotion in your
hearers, and (4) refresh their memories. (*Rhetoric*, 19, 1419 [b] 10)

Renaissance rhetoricians, although accepting the traditional classification of figures under schemes of grammar, tropes, rhetorical figures of
words, and rhetorical figures of thought, nevertheless did take account
of these three modes of persuasion. For example, in his revised and im-
proved work of 1593 Peacham subdivided his figures into those whose
function is: repetition, omission, conjunction, and separation (grammatical); distribution, description, comparison, collection (*logos*); the
stirring of affection and vehemence (*pathos*); nor is the hearer's impression of the speaker (*ethos*) left out of account, for some figures are
directly designed to win good will and a favorable hearing. In other
words, Peacham divides his figures of thought according to their functions into those of amplification (*logos*) and those of affection (*pathos*).
Some promote *ethos*. In his *Elementa rhetorices* (1531) Melanchthon
classified approximately forty of the figures of thought under selected
topics of logic (definition, division, cause, contraries, similitudes, genus,
circumstances and signs). The studious reader, he says, will observe that
these especially take their origin from the places of dialectic, for the same
places, when they are applied to proving or disproving a matter are called
sinews of argument; when they are applied to illuminating it, they are
called ornaments and many times add weight to the argument.[58] We

---

[58] Melanchthon, *Opera*, XIII, 479–80: "Observet autem studiosus lector figuras omnes,
praesertim has, quae augent orationem ex locis dialecticis oriri, ad quos si quis prudenter
sciet eas referre, pleraque in causis subtiliter et acute iudicare, et definitas negotii regiones

should not, however, be too exact and superstitious in comparing the places of dialectic and the figures of elocution. It is enough to employ a moderate prudence and to see some relation between them.[59]

Peacham's subdivisions and Melanchthon's classification furnish contemporary evidence indicating that the Renaissance rhetoricians would regard the reorganization of the figures under grammar, *logos, pathos,* and *ethos* as a clarification of what is partly explicit and partly implicit in their work. The present study undertakes to reclassify not merely the figures of thought, which have long been recognized as related to dialectic, but all of the two hundred Tudor figures, in terms of these four functions, and that without resorting to a miscellaneous catch-all such as Melanchthon's circumstances and signs. This reclassification of the figures makes no claim to apodictic exactitude. Their classification, by whatever method, has always proved baffling, for one figure may fit into any one of a number of classes, and some figures may not fit precisely into any one. For instance, a figure of collection or summary does not precisely fit in with figures of division; yet it may reasonably be placed with them because it is understood in relation to division as a reverse process. In addition to making the figures more intelligible and significant, the reorganization here presented accentuates the basic agreement of the Renaissance rhetoricians and logicians among themselves and with the ancient tradition.

It is difficult for a modern to keep in mind the ancient and the Renaissance conception of ornament as something more integral than we conceive it to be. According to Aristotle,

Ornament is attained by induction and distinction of things closely akin . . . an instance of the kind of thing meant is . . . the distinction of sciences into speculative, practical, and productive. For everything of this kind lends additional ornament to the argument, though there is no necessity to say them, so far as the conclusion goes. (*Topics,* 8.1.157 ª 7)

Hermogenes constantly spoke of the enthymeme and the epicheirema as embellishments. Cicero also delighted in them and recognized that even

---

melius videre poterit. Nam iidem loci cum confirmandi aut confutandi causa adhibentur, argumenta sunt ac nervi, ut vocant. Cum adhibentur illuminandi causa, dicuntur ornamenta. Ac pleraque non tantum ad pugnae speciem comparata sunt, sed argumentis pondus addunt."

[59] *Ibid.,* p. 483: "Utimur autem in hac comparatione locorum dialecticorum et figurarum elocutionis non nimis subtili ac superstitiosa ratione. Satis est enim ad eam rem adhibere mediocrem quandam prudentiam, et aliqua ex parte cognationem videre, ut fontes ornamentorum et negociorum regiones animadverti queant."

to discuss style and ornament apart from thought involves an unnatural separation.

> It is impossible to achieve an ornate style without first procuring ideas and putting them into shape, and . . . no idea can possess distinction without lucidity of style.[60]

> This is the reason why that genuine and perfect eloquence we are speaking of, has been yet attained by no one; because the art of *reasoning* has been supposed to be one thing, and that of *speaking* another; and we have had recourse to different instructors for the knowledge of things and words.[61]

The figures of thought evoked great enthusiasm in the Renaissance, an age that delighted in logical exercise. As Sherry remarked at the close of his *Treatise of the Figures of Grammer and Rhetorike* (1555), they were called

> ornamentes of matter, because by them, not only the oration and wordes, but the body of the matter groweth and is increased. (fol. lvii ʳ)

Since the figures of thought bulk largest in both number and importance, logic emerges as the dominant factor in composition not only for the Ramists and the traditionalists but for the figurists as well. Elizabethan literature was produced by a technique which, while giving attention to patterns of sound and movement and heaping up a rich profusion of imagery, was deeply rooted in thought and emotion.

---

[60] ". . . tantum significabo brevi, neque verborum ornatum inveniri posse non partis expressisque sententiis, neque esse ullam sententiam illustrem sine luce verborum." (Cicero *De oratore* 3.6.24), tr. by E. W. Sutton and H. Rackham (Loeb Classical Library).

[61] ". . . quo fit ut veram illam et absolutam eloquentiam nemo consequatur, quod alia intelligendi alia dicendi disciplina est et ab aliis rerum ab aliis verborum doctrina quaeritur." (Cicero *Orator* 5.17); tr. by E. Jones, whose translation of this passage is preferable to that in the Loeb edition. An epicheirema is merely a syllogism in which either both premises or one is an enthymeme. If both are, it is a five-part argument which Cicero particularly favored. It is illustrated on p. 365 below.

PART TWO

SHAKESPEARE'S USE OF THE THEORY

CONCLUSION

CONCLUSION

Shakespeare knew the complete doctrine and method of composition regularly taught in the grammar schools of his day from a combination of Latin textbooks. He employed in his work the techniques prescribed in Cicero's *Topica*, the *Ad Herennium*, Susenbrotus' *Epitome troporum ac schematum*, Erasmus' *Copia* and *Modus conscribendi*, Aphthonius' *Progymnasmata*, Quintilian's *Institutio oratoria*, and a work on logic, perhaps Melanchthon's.[1] These techniques, comprising the core of grammar school discipline, were applied to both composition and the reading of classical Latin literature in a manner which formed the Renaissance creating and responding mind.

The Renaissance grammar school discipline justified itself by its results. Logic and rhetoric were, indeed, used too badly in Gascoigne's works, Lyly's *Euphues*, Sidney's *Arcadia*, and Greene's *Tritameron*, which reveal apprenticeship to art rather than achievement; and logic was employed in a too-obvious, even though interesting, way in the interludes of John Heywood and in the plays of Lyly, Jonson, Dekker, Chapman, and Massinger. Nevertheless, it is the work of the apprentice rather than that of the finished artist which shows most clearly the currents of the time, and one has only to remember Ben Jonson's "To Celia" to realize how an impression of creative spontaneity and ease can be wrested from borrowed material by one trained as the Elizabethans were in imitative synthesis.

Many of the great passages in Shakespeare similarly transfigured materials that were borrowed from the Latin literature studied in grammar school, for Shakespeare also pressed his school learning into service and his early work discloses his own apprenticeship to art. There is some evidence of his continued interest as an adult in theoretical works[2] and of his acquaintance with a number of the English works on rhetoric and logic that have furnished the selec-

[1] See T. W. Baldwin, *William Shakespere's Small Latine and Lesse Greeke*, 1944.
[2] See p. 44 above.

tions in Part III of the present study, which sets forth the Renaissance theory of composition. This theory was a penetrating and
comprehensive analysis of thought and its expression, and there can
be no doubt that formal training in it contributed vitally to the
development of Shakespeare's genius. An intensive and thorough
investigation of his use of any or all the features of this theory might
prove as instructive and rewarding as a study of his blank verse, for
verse was just one of many instruments of style carefully cultivated
by Renaissance writers and brought to unprecedented perfection by
Shakespeare. Verse was, in fact, a part of the theory, insofar as a
study of prosody and the composition of verse were important features of Tudor grammar school training.

Even though Shakespeare parodied the extremely narrow and
artificial style of *Euphues,* his own early work was marked by a
schematic use of the most obvious rhetorical and logical devices.
Like many of his contemporaries, he too seems often to have been
occupied in a pursuit of words rather than of ideas. In his mature
work he continues to use these devices and many more, but with a
delicate dramatic fitness and subtle inwardness adapted to minds and
moods of a range unmatched by any other dramatist. Each point of
view is fully entered into. Each person speaks in his own idiom, be it
that of king, scholar, pedant, or rogue. With equally authentic accent Shakespeare speaks the language appropriate to the garrulous,
the shallow, the ignorant, the grave. Mainly by a skillful use of
the vices of language, he travesties the verbal affectation of Osric,
the ineptitude of Dogberry, the misapprehension and confusion of
Bottom and Mistress Quickly, the scurrility of Thersites. By means
of fallacious and captious argument he creates the light sophistic of
Feste and Touchstone, the dodges and nimble wit of Falstaff, the
chicanery of Richard III, the cynical mockery of Apemantus, the
barbed shafts of the fool in *Lear.* Through complete mastery of
logos, pathos, and *ethos,* characters whom he has endowed with
natural eloquence full of personal and vivid touches engage both
the intellect and the feelings of the audience, whether they voice
with experienced tongue the cogent application of analytic thought
to grave affairs in public debate or in soliloquy unburden the heart
of poignant doubt or fear or grief. Thought and image commensurate with the genuine stress of a compelling problem or passion

forge language which by appealing simultaneously to the reason and the imagination confers beauty as well as vision. The style echoes the mood with sureness, though it shifts from unruffled deliberation to hysterical excitement, or from stern self-control to unbridled emotion in the movement of living drama. Shakespeare's creative art illustrates most fully the variety and compass of the Renaissance theory of composition.

In his best work Shakespeare employs the figures of repetition with easy mastery to achieve varied artistic effects. Yet even in his early plays he seldom uses them merely as verbal embroidery. When they are so used, they usually serve by that very fact to characterize the speaker. The repetition often accentuates an idea dramatically significant, as in *II Henry VI* (1.3), where the repetition of *Lord Protector* galls Queen Margaret, who wishes Henry to rule, and who accordingly schemes to get rid of the Lord Protector. In the scene in *King John* where Hubert, under orders from the king, comes to put out young Arthur's eyes with a heated iron (4.1), *iron* becomes symbolic through repetition and acquires a quality of reflection and meditation, which joined to the repetition of *eyes, see,* and *look,* communicates both dignity and pathos.

Even in the more external phases of his art Shakespeare is preeminent. Writing at a time which invited originality, distinction, and music of expression, he exhibits the ultimate in energy, verve, and daring creativeness. He uses every resource of language and imagination to give life, movement, and piquancy to his richly laden thought. Since the schemes of grammar owe much of their attractiveness to the very nearness of their approach to error, he likes to teeter on the brink of solecism and like a tightrope walker or an acrobatic dancer to display in the precariousness of balance such sureness, poise, agility, and consummate skill as to awaken tense admiration in the prosaic onlooker with two feet squarely on the ground. And all this he does within the scope of an approved tradition which sanctioned such deviations from pedestrian style. The very vices of language he employs with fine dramatic effect to portray the ignorance, affectation, scurrility, garrulity, and ineptitude of certain characters in his plays. The figures of repetition in his later works give beauty, emphasis, and strength to the thought and feeling.

Regarding invention in the contemporary and traditional sense of a systematic process for finding something to say, Shakespeare drew matter for his plays and poems from all the topics of invention including inartificial arguments, which were given an important place by the logicians and rhetoricians of his time. He employed all the rhetorical figures related to the several logical topics, sometimes adding comments which constitute a virtual definition of the figure. The characters in his plays manifest a knowledge and practice of logical and rhetorical theory, lively, concrete, specific, displayed in parody as well as in serious application, which were expected to win a commensurate response from an audience similarly disciplined and practiced in the arts of logic and rhetoric. The pedant Holofernes' question "What is the figure?" echoes the English schoolmaster's insistent and familiar *"Per quam figuram?"*

Equipped as every educated man of his time was with a thorough knowledge of the terms, the forms, and the processes of argumentation, Shakespeare skillfully adapts these devices to every conceivable dramatic purpose. Often the skirmish of wits is light and playful, as in *Twelfth Night, As You Like It, Much Ado About Nothing, Love's Labor's Lost, The Two Gentlemen of Verona, Romeo and Juliet,* displayed sometimes in a bandying of words, sometimes of ideas. An Elizabethan audience could be relied upon to follow the turns and twists of an argument, to note the skill, the adroitness, the fumbles, as readily as a modern crowd notes these points in a football game. Touchstone, Feste, and the other clowns, Rosalind, Beatrice, Benedick, Romeo, Juliet, Cressida are skillful fencers with words, adept at the quick retort, the pert reply. The gravediggers in *Hamlet* match Touchstone and Feste in light sophistic, even though the subject of their banter is grim. Richard III and Iago reason fallaciously, even falsely, in pursuit of deepest villainy. Despite his personal feeling and sympathies, York in *Richard II* upholds what reason tells him is the right. Desdemona and Hermione argue with dignity and cogency before judges at a public trial. Isabella contends with superb skill and honesty against the craft and deceit of Angelo, the reputed saint. Portia eloquently pleads that mercy temper justice; yet, upholding the literal application of the law, with consummate cunning she turns the tables on revenge-bent Shylock. Logic contributes much to the interest of *All's Well* and *Julius Caesar*. It is vital in the soliloquies of Hamlet.

In impregnating dramatic scenes of human urgency with the tension of genuine debate Shakespeare easily excels his contemporaries. Combining intellectual power with imaginative and emotional persuasion, he successfully blends logic, rhetoric, and poetic. He so fuses character and plot, thought and feeling, that they become almost indistinguishable and thereby more intense, more convincing, moving both mind and heart. This is particularly true of his great tragedies, *Othello, Macbeth, Hamlet, Lear, Coriolanus, Antony and Cleopatra*, and of the dark comedy *Troilus and Cressida*. In these he mirrors the whole of man's composite but integrated nature.

The formal training which Shakespeare received contributed not only to the breadth and stature of his thought but also to the richness of the gorgeous panoply with which he invested it. His language, fresh, vibrant, exuberant, and free, makes use of the schemes of words as well as the schemes of construction. He effects sudden and vivid concentrations of meaning by a poetically superb and daring use of anthimeria (nouns as verbs), catachresis (verbs and adjectives employed in a transferred sense), hypallage (the transferred epithet), the compound epithet, metaphor, metonymy, syllepsis of the sense, negative and privative terms.[3] He secures swiftness of movement, compactness, and emphasis through anastrophe (inverted word order), parenthesis, zeugma (one verb serving two or more subjects), brachylogia and asyndeton (omission of conjunctions).[4]

With figures of repetition, Shakespeare weaves a haunting harmony of sound; through the schemes of grammar he achieves such control over movement and rhythm that like a figure skater he may dart, poise, turn, plunge, go where he will, his words laden with penetrating thought and deep feeling—and all this but an art subservient to the larger art of the builder, to plot construction, character creation, and profound insight into human nature and its problems. Yet this myriad-minded man has time for fun and nonsense, for parody and foolery, for mere gleeful bandying of words.

One may read Shakespeare's plays, or see them produced, with attention to any or all these facets of his art. They give pleasure at many levels, as great music does. One who recognizes in the intricate web of harmonic and melodic progressions the chord structures and

---

[3] See below, pp. 299, 328, 295, 288, 328, 320 and 336, 341, 323.
[4] See below, pp. 294, 295, 296, 297.

rhythmic design, and notes the fine gradation and coloring, experiences a deeper and keener delight in music than one who does not perceive these things; he enjoys not only what the untrained listener enjoys but also a detailed intellectual perception of the relation of parts to parts and to the whole. Similarly, to cultivate the alert attentiveness to patterns of sound and movement and the expert analysis of thought-relations habitual to educated Elizabethans quickens the responsiveness requisite to a full appreciation of Shakespeare's plays.

PART THREE

THE GENERAL THEORY OF
COMPOSITION AND READING AS
DEFINED AND ILLUSTRATED
BY TUDOR LOGICIANS
AND RHETORICIANS

The following pages present a selection from the sixteenth-century English works on logic and rhetoric of what seemed to the compiler the best treatment of each item arranged under grammar, *logos*, *pathos*, and *ethos*—functions basic to Aristotle's conception of rhetoric. A few items from Aristotle are included because his work influenced Renaissance theory both directly and indirectly.

The essentially complete general theory of composition and reading thus set forth was universal in European countries during the Renaissance.

CHAPTER VI

SCHEMES OF GRAMMAR, VICES OF LANGUAGE, AND FIGURES OF REPETITION

THE SCHEMES of grammar represent deviations from ordinary expression to achieve swiftness, emphasis, rhythm, or some similar grace of style. If the deviation is excessive, lacking judgment or good taste, the language is faulty or vicious. When the repetition of words accentuates structure and rhythm, as it often does, the figures of repetition are seen to be related to those of grammatical construction, as Aristotle recognized in his discussion of style.

1. The Schemes of Grammar

The schemes of grammar are either of words or of construction.

a. Schemes of Words.—The orthographical schemes of words are devices for adapting words to meter and rhyme. The schemes may represent a choice among current forms of words or a variation introduced by the poet. After summarizing the types of variation Puttenham remarks:

These many wayes may our maker alter his wordes, and sometimes it is done for pleasure to give a better sound, sometimes upon necessitie, and to make up the rime. But our maker must take heed that he be not to bold . . . for unlesse usual speach and custome allow it, it is a fault and no figure . . . (p. 162)

Words may be varied by the addition, omission, or exchange of a syllable or letter. Butler and Susenbrotus illustrate the schemes of words from Latin literature. Wilson, Sherry, Peacham, and Puttenham explain them and give examples in English from which those in the following synopsis are selected.

Prosthesis is the addition of a syllable at the beginning of a word, as *embolden* for *bolden, berattle* for *rattle, ymade* for *made, adown* for *down.*

Epenthesis is the addition of a syllable or letter in the middle of a word, as *meeterly* for *meetly, goldylocks* for *goldlocks, relligion* for *religion.*

Proparalepsis, or paragoge, is the addition of a syllable at the end of a word, as *slacken* for *slack, spoken* for *spoke, hasten* for *haste.*

Aphaeresis is the omission of a syllable from the beginning of a word, as *'twixt* for *betwixt*.

Syncope is the omission of a letter or syllable from the middle of a word, as *tane* for *taken, idolatry* for *idololatry, prosprous* for *prosperous*.

Synaloepha is the omission or elision of one of two vowels coming together at the juncture of two words, as *thone* for *the one, t'attain* for *to attain*.

Apocope is the omission of the last syllable of a word, as *bet* for *better, morne* for *morning*.

Diastole, or eciasis, is the lengthening of a short syllable, or the stressing of an unstressed syllable, as to stress the first syllable of *endure,* the second of *possible,* or the third of *commendable*.

Systole is the shortening of a long syllable or the removal of stress from a stressed syllable as from *ve* in *perseverance*.

Metathesis is the exchange of letters in a word, as *brust* for *burst*.

Antisthecon is the exchange of one sound for another for the sake of rhyme, as *wrang* for *wrong*.

Tasis, though not strictly a figure, is mentioned by Sherry and Puttenham in close connection with the figures. Sherry describes it as

a swete and pleasaunte modulacion or tunableness . . . of the voyce in pleasaunte pronunciacion. (Sig. C iii ʳ)

b. Schemes of Construction.—Puttenham remarks of the schemes of grammatical construction:

As your single words may be many waies transfigured to make the meetre or verse more tunable and melodious, so also may your whole and entire clauses be in such sort contrived by the order of their construction as the eare may receive a certaine recreation, although the mind for any noveltie of sence be little or nothing affected. And therefore al your figures of *grammaticall* construction, I accompt them but merely *auricular* in that they reach no furder then the eare. (p. 163)

Puttenham discusses schemes of grammatical construction that work by disorder, by defect, by surplusage, and by exchange.[1]

Hyperbaton is the genus of the syntactical figures that work by disorder. The species include anastrophe, tmesis, hysterologia, hysteron proteron, hypallage, parenthesis, and epergesis. Anastrophe is a departure from the normal word order, often to secure a desired emphasis, as when we say,

faults, no man liveth without, when order requireth we should say, No man liveth without faults. (Day, p. 362)

[1] Puttenham includes some, however, which do not fit into these four groups.

Tmesis is the interjection of a phrase between the parts of a compound word, thus:

Hys saying was true, as here shal appere after, for hereafter. (Sherry, sig. B viii ʳ)

When a phrase is interposed between a preposition and its object and the preposition is thereby joined rather to the verb that precedes it, the scheme is called hysterologia.

I ran after with as much speede as I coulde, the theefe that had undone me. (Peacham, 1577, sig. F iiii ʳ) [2]

Hysteron proteron is a disorder of time,

where that which ought to bee in the first place is put in the second, as thus, After he had given saile to the wind, and taken the seas, for after he had taken the seas, and given saile to the wind. (Day, p. 362) [3]

Hypallage, or the changeling, as Puttenham calls it, perverts the sense by shifting the application of words,

as, he that should say, for . . . *come dine with me and stay not, come stay with me and dine not.* . . . A certaine piteous lover to move his mistres to compassion, wrote among other amorous verses, this one.
Madame, I set your eyes before mine woes.
For, mine woes before your eyes, spoken to th' intent to winne favour in her sight. (p. 171)

Hypallage need not, however, be so strange and far-fetched. Day gives as an example (adding the comment, "The use hereof in *Poesie* is rife"),

the wicked wound thus given, for having thus wickedly wounded him. (p. 363)

Parenthesis interrupts a sentence by interposing words. Peacham quotes Saint Paul.

They are the ministers of Christ (I speake as a foole) I am more, &c. (p. 198)

Epergesis interrupts by interposing a word in apposition as an added interpretation.

[2] No example of this scheme has been noted in Shakespeare.
[3] Puttenham makes hysteron proteron a shift in time order when he discusses it as a figure (p. 170); a shift in word order, apparently the same as anastrophe, which he nowhere names, when he discusses it as a tolerable vice (p. 255). The latter is the only meaning entertained by Veré L. Rubel, who states that the former is not considered in her study, *Poetic Diction in the English Renaissance*, p. 285.

I know that in me, that is to say, in my flesh, dwelleth no good thing. Rom. 7:18. (Peacham, p. 191)

Grammatical figures that work by defect and so represent short-cuts in expression include eclipsis, zeugma, syllepsis, scesis onomaton, and diazeugma. Eclipsis, or ellipsis, is the omission of a word easily supplied by ordinary understanding, as

You are not to answere or compare with him, for you are not meet, sufficient, or able, to answere or compare with him. (Day, p. 359)

Zeugma is the use of a word, usually a verb, to serve two or more others. If the verb is expressed in the first clause and understood in the others, the figure is called prozeugma.

> *Her beautie perst mine eye, her speach mine wofull hart:*
> *Her presence all the powers of my discourse.* (Puttenham, p. 164)

If it is expressed in the middle clause it is called mesozeugma; if in the last clause, hypozeugma. Syllepsis differs from zeugma in that the word which serves two or more others agrees grammatically with only the nearest.

> *Judge ye lovers, if it be strange or no:*
> *My Ladie laughs for joy, and I for wo.* (Ibid., p. 165)

If a verb is altogether lacking, and a saying is made up of only substantives and adjectives, the scheme is called scesis onomaton.[4]

A mayd in conversation chast, in speeche mylde, in countenaunce cheerefull, in behavioure modest, in bewty singuler, in heart humble and meeke, in honest myrth, merie with measure, in serving of God dilligent, to her parents obedient. (Peacham, 1577, sig. G iiii ᵛ)

Hypozeuxis is the contrary of zeugma, remarks Peacham, in that every clause has its own verb. To this characteristic Puttenham adds the iteration of the noun, thus:

> *My Ladie gave me, my Lady wist not what,*
> *Geving me leave to be her Soveraine . . .*

Here [*my Ladie gave*] and [*my Ladie wist*] be supplies with iteration, by vertue of this figure. (p. 166)

Also in contrast to zeugma, is diazeugma whereby one noun serves many verbs.

[4] No example of this scheme has been noted in Shakespeare.

The people of Rome destroyed Numance, overthrew Cartage, cast downe
Corinth, and raced Fregels. (Sherry, sig. B vii ᵛ)

The rhythm of language and its tempo are affected by the use of
brachylogia, asyndeton, polysyndeton, isocolon, homoioteleuton, and
hirmus. Brachylogia, or articulus, omits the conjunction between single
words, often imparting celerity and vehemence through brevity.

By sharpnes, voyce, countenaunce, thou madeste thyne enemyes afrayd.
(Sherry, sig. D v ʳ)

Asyndeton, or brachiepia, omits conjunctions between clauses, with like
effect.

The like brevitie *Simo* useth in *Terence:* The corps (saith he) goeth before, we
follow after, we come to the grave, it is put into the fire, a lamentation is made.
(Peacham, p. 182)

Polysyndeton, on the contrary, employs many conjunctions, producing
a slow, deliberate, impressive effect.

Ye observe dayes, and moneths, and times, and yeares. Gal. 4. (Peacham,
p. 53)

Isocolon is directly concerned with rhythm.

Compar, of the Grecians called *Isocolon* and *Parison,* is a figure . . . which
maketh the members of an oration to be almost of a just number of sillables, yet
the equalitie of those members or parts, are not to be measured upon our fingers
as if they were verses, but to bee tried by a secret sence of the eare: . . . First,
when the former parts of a sentence, or of an oration be answered by the later,
and that by proper words respecting the former . . . See that equitie flow as
the water, and righteousnesse as a mightie streame. Amos 5
Also it coupleth contraries, thus: An innocent, although hee be accused, he
may be acquited, but the guiltie except he be accused he cannot be condemned.
Also by this figure effects may be made to answer their efficients, consequents
their antecedents, habite privation: also contrariwise, and that by a very pleasant
forme and proportion. This ornament is very often used of *Solomon* in his
Proverbs and of *Esay* in his Prophesies. (*Ibid.,* p. 58) [5]

[5] Notice that Peacham shows how this figure can be used to emphasize the topics of logic.
The Tudor rhetoricians do not make the distinction between isocolon and parison, explained by Morris Croll, in Croll and Clemens, *Euphues: the Anatomy of Wit* and
Euphues and His England. London, 1916, Introduction, p. xvi. Peacham gives both these
names for the same figure. The definitions of parison by Puttenham and Day make it
identical with isocolon. This figure was in great favor among the Elizabethans as is
seen from its schematic use not only in *Euphues,* but in the work of Lyly's imitators.

Homoioteleuton, combined with isocolon and with alliteration (as in *Euphues*) accentuates the rhythm of the equal members by its own similar endings.[6] As Puttenham remarks, of all the figures of the ancients homoioteleuton approaches nearest to rhyme, which became important as a structural factor in English verse. In illustrating homoioteleuton Peacham incidentally expresses his own, and the traditional, conception of the functions of rhetoric.

He is esteemed eloquent which can invent wittily, remember perfectly, dispose orderly, figure diversly, pronounce aptly, confirme strongly, and conclude directly. (p. 54)

Hirmus, the periodic sentence, is a figure whereby "the whole sence . . . is suspended till ye come to the last . . . which finisheth . . . with a full and perfit sence" (Puttenham, p. 176). Day offers this example:

God in the beginning made heaven, earth, sea, firmament, sunne, moone, starres, and all things in them contained. (p. 364)

Metabasis is a figure of grammatical transition whereby the speaker

in a few words sheweth what hath bene alreadie said, and also what shalbe said next, and that divers waies. From the equall: The matters which you have alreadie heard, were wonderfull, and those that you shall heare are no lesse marvellous . . . From consequents: You have bene told how he promised, and now I will tell you, how he performed. (Peacham, p. 175)

The figures that work by exchange include enallage, hendiadys, Graecismus, and anthimeria. Concerning enallage Puttenham remarks:

Your figures that worke *auricularly* by exchange, were more observable to the Greekes and Latines . . . for the multiplicitie of their Grammaticall accidents, . . . that is to say, their divers cases, moodes, tenses, genders, with variable terminations, by reason whereof, they changed not the very word, but kept the word, and changed the shape of him onely, using one case for another, or tense, or person, or gender, or number, or moode. We, having no such varietie of accidents, have little or no use of this figure. They called it *Enallage*. (p. 171) [7]

[6] Since English is little varied by cases, the ancient distinction between homoioptoton, similar case endings, and homoioteleuton, similar endings of uninflected words, practically disappears in English. Although this figure could with justice be placed among the figures of repetition, it seems preferable to treat it with isocolon because its outstanding use in Elizabethan literature was to mark off rhythmic units.

[7] Veré L. Rubel, throughout her *Poetic Diction in the English Renaissance*, employs the word enallage to mean the exchange of parts of speech; this meaning is properly attached to anthimeria. Miss Rubel avowedly bases her terminology on Puttenham and on Warren Tay-

Puttenham offers no illustration, but Peacham gives this example of enallage of number:

Thus, *Plinie* in *Africke,* the greater part of wylde beastes doe not drink in Sommer for want of showres, here the plurall is put for the singuler, for the greater parte is the singuler number, and therefore so should the verbe be singuler also. (1577 ed., sig. H iii ᵛ)

Hendiadys substitutes two nouns for a noun modified by an adjective.

> *Not you coy dame your lowrs nor your lookes*

For [*your lowring lookes.*]   (Puttenham, p. 177)

Graecismus employs in another language a construction proper to the Greek. Butler quotes as not inelegant an example from Spenser's *Faerie Queene.*

> For not to have beene dipt in Lethe Lake,
> Could save the sonne of Thetis from to die. *Vid.* c. 13.[8]

Anthimeria is the substitution of one part of speech for another.

he spake very hote you all can tell, for, he spoke very hotely you all can tell, a nown [adjective] for an adverbe. (Peacham, 1577, sig., H iiii ᵛ)

2. *Vices of Language*

The line between the figures and the vices of language is sometimes not easy to draw, for blemishes of style result from excess or misuse of those very devices which, if used with taste and judgment, adorn it. Puttenham explains that

by ignorance of the maker a good figure may become a vice, and by his good discretion, a vicious speach go for a vertue in the Poeticall science. This saying is to be explaned and qualified, for some maner of speaches are alwayes intollerable and such as cannot be used with any decencie, but are ever undecent, namely barbarousnesse, incongruitie, ill disposition, fond affectation, rusticitie, and all extreme darknesse, such as it is not possible for a man to understand the matter without an interpretour . . . I see not but the rest of the common faultes may be borne with sometimes, or passe without any great reproofe, not being used overmuch or out of season . . . so as every surplusage or preposterous placing or undue iteration or darke word, or doubtfull speach are not

lor's "Dictionary of the Tudor Figures of Rhetoric," part of an unpublished dissertation presented to the University of Chicago in 1937, published and distributed by the University of Chicago Libraries. No justification for Miss Rubel's usage is to be found in either of them.

[8] Butler, *Rhetoricae libri duo,* I, 34.

so narrowly to be looked upon in a large poeme, nor specially in the pretie Poesies and devises of Ladies . . . whom we would not have too precise Poets least with their shrewd wits, when they were maried they might become a little too phantasticall wives, neverthelesse because we seem to promise an arte, which doth not justly admit any wilful errour in the teacher . . . I will speake somewhat touching these viciosities of language . . . (p. 249)

Solecismus, the most obvious vice of language, is related to the figure enallage, for it is the ignorant misuse of cases, genders, tenses. As Puttenham remarks, "every poore scholler knowes the fault, & cals it the breaking of *Priscians* head, for he was among the Latines a principall Grammarian" (p. 251). He gives no illustration.

Barbarismus, or foreign speech, is that

pronounced with straunge and ill-shapen accents, or written by wrong ortographie, as he that would say with us in England, a dousand for a thousand, isterday, for yesterday, as commonly the Dutch and French people do . . . (Puttenham, p. 250)

Soraismus, or the mingle-mangle, which Puttenham places among what he terms the intolerable vices,[9] consists in making

our speach or writinges of sundry languages using some Italian word, or French, or Spanish, or Dutch, or Scottish, not for the nonce or for any purpose (which were in part excusable) but ignorantly and affectedly as one that said using this French word *Roy,* to make ryme with another verse, thus,
       O mightie Lord of love, dame Venus onely joy,
       Whose Princely power exceedes each other heavenly roy.
The verse is good but the terme peevishly affected. (p. 252)

Heterogenium is a vice which consists in answering irrelevantly. Fenner explains it as a device of sophism.

Impertinent or not to the purpose is when any thing is brought for a proof, which is nothing neere to the matter in hand, whereunto the common proverb giveth answere: *I aske you of cheese, you answere mee of chauke.* (Sig. E 2 ᵛ)

Puttenham lists amphibologia, the ambiguous, among tolerable vices.

Then have ye one other vicious speach . . . and is when we speake or write doubtfully and that the sence may be taken two wayes . . . Thus said a gen-

---

[9] Puttenham's treatment of the vices, and Sherry's also, is similar to Quintilian's (8.3.44–61). A number of illustrations are identical. Puttenham's division of the vices into tolerable and intolerable seems, however, to be his own contribution to rhetorical theory.

tleman in our vulgar pretily notwithstanding because he did it not ignorantly, but for the nonce.

I sat by my Lady soundly sleeping,
My mistresse lay by me bitterly weeping.

No man can tell by this, whether the mistresse or the man, slept or wept: these doubtfull speaches were used much in the old times . . . by the Oracles of *Delphos* . . . and in effect all our old Brittish and Saxon prophesies be of the same sort, that turne them on which side ye will, the matter of them may be verified, neverthelesse carryeth generally such force in the heades of fonde people, that by the comfort of those blind prophecies many insurrections and rebellions have bene stirred up in this Realme, as that of *Jacke Straw,* & *Jacke Cade* in *Richard* the seconds time . . . which might be constred two or three wayes as well as that one whereunto the rebelles applied it . . . (p. 260)

Tapinosis is a vice whereby

the dignitie or majestie of a high matter is much defaced by the basenesse of a word, as to call . . . the Thames a brooke . . . great wisedome prettie witte . . . (Peacham, p. 168)

Puttenham cites the instance of a certain

Serjeant Bendlowes, when in a progresse time comming to salute the Queene . . . he said to her Cochman, stay thy cart good fellow, stay thy cart, that I may speake to the Queene, whereat her Majestie laughed . . . and all the rest of the company . . . (p. 259)

Puttenham attaches two meanings to cacemphaton, which he lists as a tolerable vice. The first meaning, the same as that which Sherry gives for aischrologia, is foul speech, often ambiguous, but permissible at times, thinks Puttenham, to move laughter, as do the jests of a buffoon or railing companion, whom the Latins called *Scurra* (p. 254). The second meaning of cacemphaton, according to Puttenham, is that of an unpleasant combination of sounds, as in rhyming too many like sounding words together, or as Sherry says, in using too many r's or t's, which cause a roughness or stammering (1555, fol. x ʳ), or as Peacham puts it, in

a contynuall jarring uppon one string, thus . . . your strength is not to strive, or stryke agaynste the streame so strong . . . (1577, sig. G iii ʳ)

Puttenham alone gives the name tautology to such overuse of alliteration.

Cacosyntheton, a vice related to the scheme anastrophe, is an intolerable departure from acceptable word order. It occurs especially, explains Puttenham, when an adjective is placed after a substantive,

as one that said ridiculously. In my yeares lustie, many a deed doughtie did I.
(p. 253)

The vices of verbosity include tautologia, perissologia or macrologia,
parelcon, pleonasmus, homiologia, and periergia. Tautologia is the wearisome repetition of the same thing in different words or in the same words.

If you have a friend, keepe your friend, for an old friend is to be preferred before a new friend, this I say to you as your friend. (Peacham, p. 49)

Perissologia or macrologia is the addition of a superfluous clause which
adds nothing to the sense, thus:

Men of so high and excellent vertue, let them ever live and never die. (Day,
p. 362)

Puttenham accounts this a tolerable vice and cites Turberville's use of it

to shew the great annoy and difficultie of those warres of Troy, caused for
Helenas sake.

> *Nor Menelaus was unwise,*
> *Or troupe of Trojans mad,*
> *When he with them and they with him,*
> *For her such combat had* . . .

Menelaus fighting with the Trojans, the Trojans must of necessitie fight with
him. (p. 257)

Parelcon is the addition of a superfluous word such as *that* in the following:

when that I call, I pray yee be ready. (Peacham, 1577, sig. F iii ʳ)

Pleonasmus is redundancy,

where, with words seeming, wee doe increase our reasons, as thus, *with these*
eares I heard him speake it. Or, with mine eyes I beheld him sorrowing, where
wee well know, that, without eares or eyes, we cannot well heare, or see, yet
carrieth this kind of speech, a *vehemency inforcing* the matter . . . (Day,
p. 361)

Homiologia offends by a monotony unpleasing to both mind and ear,

when the whole matter is all alyke, and hath no varietie to avoyde tediousnes,
as: He came thither to the bath, yet he saide afterwardes. Here one servaunt bet
me. Afterwardes he sayde unto hym: I wyll consider. Afterwardes he chyd
hym, & cryed more and more when manye were presente. Suche a folyshe tell-
yng of a tale shall you heare in many simple & halfe folyshe persons. (Sherry,
sig. C i ʳ)

Periergia, a vice related to the figure periphrasis, is superfluity resulting from overlabor to seem fine and eloquent by expressing oneself curiously. Quintilian remarks that such overlabor differs "from judicious care, just as a fidgety man differs from an industrious one." [10] Puttenham quotes Gascoigne in illustration, and comments:

His intent was to declare how upon the tenth day of March he crossed the river of Thames, to walke in Saint *Georges* field, the matter was not great as ye may suppose.

> *The tenth of March when Aries received*
> *Dan Phoebus raies into his horned head,*
> *And I my selfe by learned lore perceived*
> *That Ver approcht and frosty winter fled*
> *I crost the Thames to take the cheerefull aire,*
> *In open fields, the weather was so faire.*

First, the whole matter is not worth all this solemne circumstance to describe the tenth day of March, but if he had left at the two first verses, it had bene inough. But when he comes with two other verses to enlarge his description, it is not only more than needes, but also very ridiculous, for he makes wise, as if he had not bene a man learned in some of the mathematickes (by learned lore) that he could not have told that the x. of March had fallen in the spring of the yeare: which every carter, and also every child knoweth without any learning. (p. 258)

There is inflation of both words and matter in the vice bomphiologia,

when trifling matters be set out with semblaunt and blasing wordes, used of none but of such as be eyther smell feastes, and Parasites, which mayntayne their good cheere with counterfayted prayses, or of great bosters and craking Souldyours, as of *Thraso* in *Terence*, and such lyke persons in Comodyes . . . Sometyme beggers use this figure, when the Constable is having of them to the stockes, they thincke then the beste waye for them is, to speake fayre, and to lift up the Constable to a hygh dignitie . . . evermore when words be as unmeete for the matter, as a chayne of Golde for an Ape, and a silver saddle for a Sowe, then may it be called *Bomphilogia*. And also when by Eloquence, glorious persons would have there cunning blased abroade, in makyng trifles, treasures, cottages, castles, thistles, mightie Oakes, and peeble stones, precious pearles. (Peacham, 1577, sig. G ii ^r)

Cacozelia or fond affectation, according to Puttenham, is the coining of fine words out of Latin, and the use of newfangled speeches in order to appear learned (p. 252). Peacham accepts this meaning, but shows that

[10] . . . supervacua, ut sic dixerim, operositas, ut a diligenti curiosus et a religione superstitio distat (8.3.55), tr. by Watson, Bohn edition, II, 100.

such affectation on the part of the ignorant may deteriorate into that mis-application of words which we call malapropism.

Cacozelon, an ill imitation or affection, that is, when words be used over-thwartly, or contrarily for want of judgement, used of foolish folk, who covet-ing to tell an eloquent tale, doe deface that which they would fainest beautifie, men not being content to speake plaine english, doe desire to use wordes bor-owed of the latine tongue, imitatyng learned men, when they know no more their signification, then a Goose, and therefore many tymes they apply them so contrarily, that wyse men are enforced to laugh at their folly, and absurdi-tie . . . A man comming through a Gentlemans pastures, and seeing there a great number of Sheepe (as Mayster Wylson telleth the tale) and after speak-ing with the Gentleman, Syr, sayd he, your worship have goodly audience of sheepe, whereby the Gentleman perceyved that he was more fyt to talke amonge sheepe, then speake among men. On a time one was arrayned for steal-ing a Weather, and one of his neighboures, that was his friend, tooke upon him to intreate for him to the Judge . . . I beseech your Lordship, quoth he, be good Lord to my neighbour, for excessity distrainde him to steale, or else he would never have done it, and he that accuse, is an unrude fellow, and very contagious among his neighboures, and if he could conclare anye more, he would I am sure, . . . now if his wordes had bene such, as he himselfe had understood, he might have told a wyser tale, and have bene much lesse laughed at. (1577, sig. G ii ͮ) [11]

Acyron or impropriety is the use of a word opposite and utterly repug-nant to what we would express, as to say,

I hope I shall be hanged tomorrow. For [I *feare me*] *I shall be hanged,* . . . (Puttenham, p. 256)

or

you shall have six stripes whiche you long for: when thei long for them not one whit. (Sherry, 1555, fol. vi ͮ)

Aschematiston is the lack of figures, and this is no small fault, says Sherry, echoing Quintilian.[12]

---

[11] Peacham places malapropism also under cacosyntheton, which he defines as including not only words ill placed, as the other rhetoricians define it, but also words ill applied, thus: "there is (quoth one) small adversity betweene your Mare and mine, for deversity" (sig. G iiii ͬ). He remarks, however, that this misapplication is "much like to Cacozelon."
[12] Quintilian, 9.1.13, quoted on p. 32, above. Sherry, sig. C ii ͬ. This vice has not been observed in Shakespeare's work.

3. Figures of Repetition

Alliteration, or paroemion, is the only one of the figures of repetition concerned with the repetition of letters only. As Peacham remarks, this figure is used more in poetry than in prose. Yet it gives

a pleasant facilitie in a Proverbe . . . as, to hold with the hare, and hunt with the hound: soone ripe, soone rotten. (p. 49)

All the other figures of repetition involve the repetition of words. In a series of clauses or sentences, the repetition of a word at the beginning of each is anaphora; at the end, epistrophe; the combination of these is symploce. Peacham gives as an example of anaphora:

The Lord sitteth above the water floods. The Lord remaineth a king for ever. The Lord shall give strength unto his people. The Lord shall give his people the blessing of peace. Psalm 29. . . .

The use hereof is chiefly to repeate a word of importance, and effectuall signification, as to repeate the cause before his singular effects, or contrariwise the effect before his severall causes, or any other word of principall accompt. It serveth also pleasantly to the eare, both in the respects of the repetition, and also of the varietie of the new clause. (p. 41)

Peacham clearly subordinates sound to sense; he would have the repetition enforce the meaning, and he conceives the latter in the familiar terms of the topics of logic. Similarly, he adds to his example of epistrophe a comment which stresses the function of the repetition.

When I was a child, I spake as a child, I understood as a child, I imagined as a child. 1 Cor. 13. . . . it serveth to leave a word of importance in the ende of a sentence, that it may the longer hold the sound in the mind of the hearer. (p. 43)

Symploce combines the two preceding figures.

Him would you pardon and acquite by your sentence, whom the Senate hath condemned, whom the people of Rome have condemned, whom all men have condemned. (Peacham, p. 43)

Epanalepsis is the repetition at the end of a sentence of the word or words with which it begins. Fraunce quotes an example from Sidney's Sonnet 34.

They love indeed, who quake to say, they love. (AR, sig. D 3 ^{v})

Antimetabole is akin to logical conversion in that it repeats words in converse order, often thereby sharpening their sense.

We wish not peace to maintaine cruell warre,
But we make warre to maintaine us in peace.
(Puttenham, p. 208)

The repetition of the word ending one clause or sentence at the beginning of the next is called anadiplosis. Hoskyns quotes this example from Sidney's *Arcadia:*

why lived I alas? alas which loved I!

And Hoskyns adds: "as noe man is sicke in thought uppon one thinge, but for some vehemency or distress, Soe in speech there is noe repeticion without importance" (p. 126).

The same kind of repetition continued through three or more clauses or sentences is called climax, or gradatio.

Knowing that tribulations bring pacience, pacience bringeth experience, experience bringeth hope. Rom 5. (Peacham, p. 133)

The repetition of words which are derived from the same root, but have different endings or forms, is called polyptoton. This figure was a special favorite with Sidney, whom Fraunce quotes:

Thou art of blood, joy not to make things bleed:
Thou fearest death, thinke they are loth to dye. (*AR*, sig. D 6 ^{v})

Puttenham calls polyptoton the tranlacer, "when ye turne and tranlace a word into many sundry shapes as the Tailor doth his garment, and after that sort do play with him in your dittie" (p. 203).

Diaphora is the repetition of a common name, used first in extension to designate, second in comprehension to qualify, thus:

What man is there living but will pitie such a case: if he be a man, in the repetition man signifieth humanity, or compassion proper to mans nature. (Peacham, p. 45)

Similar to diaphora is ploce, which Peacham and Day define as the repetition of a proper name with a different signification.

Cicero continued *Cicero* unto the day of his death, meaning a lover of his countrey, and a most faithfull patrone of the commonwealth. (Peacham, p. 44)

Puttenham, however, gives the name ploce to the speedy iteration of one word at frequent intervals. He offers this illustration from Sir Walter Raleigh.

Yet when I sawe my selfe to you was true,
I loved my selfe, bycause my selfe loved you. (p. 201)

Other rhetoricians call this epanodos or traductio. Peacham quotes this example:

To the weake I became as weake, to win the weake. 1 Cor. 9 (p. 49)

Diacope and epizeuxis express vehemence. Diacope is the repetition of a word with one or few between.

My heart is fixed, O God, my heart is fixed. Ps. 57 (Peacham, p. 48)

Epizeuxis is the repetition of words with none between.

Awake, awake and stand by O Jerusalem. Esay 46. (Peacham, p. 47)

In censuring the overuse of the figures of repetition, which were almost the sole stock in trade of certain versifiers of his day, Puttenham expresses his own theory regarding them.

These repetitions be not figurative but phantastical, for a figure is ever used to a purpose, either of beautie or of efficacie: and these last recited be to no purpose, for neither can ye say that it urges affection, nor that it beautifieth or enforceth the sence, nor hath any other subtiltie in it, and therefore is a very foolish impertinency of speech, and not a figure. (p. 202)

As Peacham most often points out, the figures of repetition in addition to pleasing the ear have the functional value of emphasizing ideas and the movement of thought, as, for instance, by accentuating parallel or antithetical structure. In an age when books like the *Arcadia* were read aloud in groups, the figures of repetition were especially valued. And, conversely, the use by Fraunce and Hoskyns of the exceedingly popular and highly regarded *Arcadia* to illustrate the figures quite naturally increased their vogue.

CHAPTER VII

LOGOS: THE TOPICS OF INVENTION

IN THE RENAISSANCE, as in earlier times, educated men amplified a
subject by drawing it as a matter of course through the topics of
invention.[1] The topics provide a systematic and exhaustive analysis.
A definition expresses the nature or essence of the subject under discussion
by telling to what class or genus it belongs and how it differs from other
species within that genus. The contrary or contradictory illuminates by
contrast. Comparison of the subject with members of the same species
shows it to be greater, equal, or less; with those of a different species,
similar or dissimilar. The subject may be considered in its parts, and in
relation to its characteristics or adjuncts. One may further consider its
causes, its effects, its antecedents, its consequents. Its name may reflect
its nature, and related names signify related realities, as for instance,
to act justly signifies that one is just or possesses justice.

From these sixteen topics intrinsic to the subject under dicussion—
definition, division, genus, species, contraries, contradictories, comparison,
similarity, dissimilarity, adjuncts, cause, effect, antecedent, consequent,
notation, and conjugates [2]—are drawn artificial arguments, so called because they are discoverable through the art of topical investigation. Besides these there are extrinsic arguments, which are called inartificial
because they do not depend upon the art of the investigator, but are
furnished to him by the testimony of others.

In the sections of this and the following chapter the theory of the
logicians is presented first, then that of the figurists. Through this co-
ordination of the topics and forms of logic with the figures related to
them it becomes clear that the analysis of composition by the Tudor
logicians and figurists was essentially the same. The last two sections
of the present chapter illustrate how the topics and figures were applied
in genesis or composition and in analysis or reading.

[1] Francis P. Donnelly, S.J., in *Persuasive Speech*, admirably presents the topics and the
entire rhetorical tradition in a modern manual of speech-composition, with ample attention to applying the same technique to the reading of speeches ancient and modern.
[2] Cicero considered this list of topics exhaustive. See p. 22, above.

1. Inartificial Arguments or Testimony

Inartificial arguments, which include all forms of testimony, occupy a place of importance in the work of logicians and rhetoricians from Aristotle through the Renaissance. The Tudor theorists explain them clearly.

The witnesses upon whose authoritie proofes are grounded, are either heavenly, earthly, or infernall. Gods word, his wonders, his miracles, and his message, sent to men by angels, and Prophetes, are alledged as heavenly witnesses: Law, custome, othe, bargain, writings, sayings, and so forth, are accompted as humaine witnesses, and such as are taken of the credite of man: Conjuring, witchcraft, appearing of ghostes, oracles and answeres of divels, are infernall and ungodlye witnesses, used onelye of the wicked, and suffered of God for a punishment to deceyve them, that will not beleeve the true meanes that God hath appoynted.

Witnesses are not so muche founde out by the arte and cunning of the spokesman: as they doe arise of the matter it selfe, and are ministred to him by the information of others. (Lever, p. 197)

To these he referred whych the Greekes cal *Symeia* or sygnes: For they also commonlye are not fet by the wytte of hym that disputeth but are ministred otherwyse. They be called signes properlye, whyche rysinge of the thynge it selfe that is in question come under the sences of menne, as threatninges, whych be of the time that is paste, cryinge herde oute of a place, whyche is of the tyme presente, palenesse of hym whyche is axed of the murther, whyche is of the tyme followynge, or that bloud leapte oute of the bodye latelye slayne, when he came that did the murther. Also of signes some bee necessary, as that he liveth whiche dothe breathe, and some probable, as bloude in the garmente, whych myghte also come oute of the nose, or otherwyse. (Sherry, sig. E viii ^r)

Mans testimony is eyther of one man, or of many. That of one is eyther obligation or confession. To obligation bee referred pledges or sureties. So in August the two sheepeheards, *Perigot* and *Willy*, for want of better arguments to proove their skill in singing, lay downe wagers, the one a cuppe, the other a spotted lambe . . . The offering of triall and proofe, belongeth to this place . . . (Fraunce, *LL.*, fol. 65 ᵛ, 66 ᵛ)

The testimony of many men, especially that of the wise men of old, was held in great esteem.

Al such testimonies may bee called, sentences of the sage, which are brought to confirme any thing, either taken out of olde Aucthors, or els such as have beene used in this common life. As the sentences of Noble men, the Lawes in any Realme, quicke sayinges, Proverbes, that either have been used heretofore, or bee now used. Histories of wise Philosophers, the judgements of learned men, the common opinion of the multitude, olde custome, auncient fashions, or any such like. (Wilson, *RR*, fol. 49 ʳ)

Fifteen figures related to inartificial arguments provide an analysis even more detailed than that accorded testimony treated as a topic of invention.

Apodixis grounds argument on general or common experience.

Salomon: Can a man take fire in his bosome, and his clothes not be burnt: or can a man go upon coles, and his feet not be burnt? (Peacham, p. 86)

Martyria confirms a statement by one's own experience.

The Evangelist *John* sayth: That which was from the beginning, which we have heard, which we have seene with our eies, which we have looked upon, &c. I Joh. 1.1. (*Ibid.*, p. 85)

Paroemia, better known as an adage or proverb, is a common saying of popular origin.

Whoso toucheth pitch shall be defiled therewith. (Day, p. 358)

Gnome, more frequently called an apothegm or sentence, is a notable saying declaring with apt brevity moral doctrine approved by the judgment of all men.[3] For example,

Prodigalitie is the mother of povertie. (Peacham, p. 190)

Four figures depend upon inartificial argument from authority.

Diatyposis . . . is a forme of speech by which the speaker or Orator commendeth certaine profitable rules and precepts to his hearers and to the posterity. . . . *Peter* geveth good precepts to wives concerning their subjection to their husbands, and their modestie in apparell. I Pet. 3. (Peacham, p. 92)

Apomnemonysis . . . is a forme of speech by which the Orator . . . for the cause of better confirmation, confutation, consolation, praise or reprehension reciteth some apt sentence, or fit testimonie of approved Authors, and applieth it to his purpose . . . An example of the Holy Scripture: O hypocrites *Esay*, prophecyed well of you, saying: This people draweth neere unto me with their mouth and honoureth me with their lippes, but their heart is far from me. Matt. 15.7; Esay 29.13. (*Ibid.*, p. 87)

---

[3] Such collections of apothegms and adages as those made by Erasmus went through edition after edition in the sixteenth century. The works of Montaigne, Elyot, Pettie, Lyly, Greene, Bacon, to mention but a few, illustrate their abundant use.

Epicrisis . . . is a forme of speech by which the Orator reciting a sentence or saying of some Authour, addeth and delivereth his opinion or judgement upon it and that either in the praise or dispraise of it, or in giving light to it, which is best performed in a short addition . . . whereby he maketh that plain and evident, which was before darke and hard to be understood. An example of our Saviour Christ saying: Ye have heard that it was sayd to them of old time, Thou shalt not commit adultery, but I say unto you, That whosoever looketh on a woman to lust after her, hath committed adultery with her alreadie in his heart Mat. 5.27 . . . *Philip* enterpreteth a place of *Esay* to the *Eunuch*. Act 8. 35. (*Ibid.*, p. 99)

Chria, a very short exposicion of any dede or saying, with the autours name beyng recited. This is well handled of Cicero in the preface of the third boke of his Offices: that Scipio was wont to saye, he was never lesse ydle then when he was voyde of the common wealthe matters, and never lesse alone, then when he was alone. (Sherry, 1555, fol. lv ᵛ)

Oaths, vows, and pledges are figures of testimony. Orcos is an oath confirming what one has affirmed or denied. "God is my witnesse . . . Rom. 1.9." (Peacham, p. 75). Euche is a solemn promise or vow, such as Jaçob made when he awoke from his vision (Gen. 28:21; *ibid.*, p. 67).

Eustathia . . . is a forme of speech by which . . . the speaker promiseth and protesteth his constancie concerning something. . . . An example of *Paul*: Who shall separat us from the love of Christ? shall tribulation, or anguish, or persecution, or famine, or nakednes, or perill, or sword. And by and by after he addeth: I am persuaded that neither death, nor life, nor angels, nor principalities, nor powers, neither things present, nor things to come, neyther height, nor depth, nor any other creature shalbe able to separate us from the love of God, which is in Christ Jesus our Lord. Rom 8. (*Ibid.*, p. 69)

Asphalia . . . is a forme of speech by which the speaker persuadeth a securitie and safetie to his hearer by offering himselfe a suretie for the confirmation of his warrant . . . to ad courage in dreadfull adventures, and to give comfort and assurance in doubtfull causes . . . An example of *Juda* persuading his father *Jacob* to let *Benjamin* . . . go into *Aegypt* with the rest of his brothers . . . saying: I will be suerty for him, of my hand shalt thou require him, if I bring him not to thee, then let me beare the blame for ever. Gen. 49.9. (*Ibid.*, p. 68)

Three figures of testimony prognosticate future events.

Euphemismus . . . is a Prognostication of good . . . the orator either interpreteth an uncertaine thing to the better part, or else declareth before that some good thing shall come to passe afterward, which he speaketh from divine revelation, or else collecteth it by some likely signes and tokens. . . . An example of the Apostle *Paul:* I exhort you to be of good courage, for there shalbe no losse of any mans life among you, but of the ship onely. Act 27.22. . . . But the most generall use of this figure is to collect by probable signes and tokens the likely effectes of good causes, and to foretell them, as by the good towardnesse of youth to prognosticate the vertue and felicity of the future age, for a good beginning doth promise a good end, a good cause a good effect . . . The greatest abuse that this figure may commit is . . . to deceave and seduce by flattery and malice or by the false interpretation of dreames. (*Ibid.*, p. 89)

Paraenesis . . . is a forme of speech by which the speaker expresseth an admonition, or warning to his hearers. . . . Hitherto doth belong . . . the admonition of the Angels to *Lot,* concerning the destruction of *Sodom.* Gen. 19.12, 13. (*Ibid.*, p. 78)

Ominatio . . . is a forme of speech, by which the Orator foretelleth the likeliest effect to follow of some evill cause. . . . By this figure the Orator foresheweth beggery to the slothfull, shame to the proud, mischiefe to the quareller, and the gallowes to the thiefe. (*Ibid.*, p. 90)

2. Definition

Of artificial arguments the most fundamental is definition, which is, as Hoskyns says, "the shortest & truest exposicion of the nature of any thinge" (p. 158). Fraunce explains more fully:

A Definition is that which declareth what a thing is: it consisteth of two parts, the generall and the difference. Whereof the first is common to the thing defined, and all his other fellow specials, but the difference is proper onely to the thing defined, and distinguisheth it from all other his fellow specials . . . as, A man is a sensible creature endued with reason, where sensible creature is the generall, and endued with reason is the difference. (*LL*, fol. 60 ͬ)

Lever calls attention to an important point in definition, namely, that

the nexte generall is rather to be answered then that which is further of. For when I am asked what a peach is, I shall come neerer to the matter, if I say it is a frute, then if I say it is a creature or a substance. (p. 159)

Blundeville makes clear how species, which is the term to be defined, differs from genus.

Species . . . of the Greeks . . . is called *Idea,* which is as much to say, as a common shape conceived in the minde, through some knowledge had before of one or two Individuums having that shape: so as after wee have seene one wolfe, or two, we beare the shape thereof continually in our mindes, and

thereby are able to know a wolfe whensoever we find him, or (if need be) to
paint him. But *genus* extendeth too farre, and comprehendeth too many speciall
kindes to bee so easily painted. And note that such shapes or *Ideas* are said also
to be perpetuall. . . . Because they continue in the minde, though the things
themselves cease to have any being: as the shape of a Rose continueth in our
mindes in the cold heart of Winter, when there is no Rose indeed. (p. 7)

Fraunce illustrates the use of definition from Spenser's *Shepheardes
Calender.*

By an argument from the definition, *Piers* in May proveth hyrelinges, to be no
shepheardes, because the true definition of a shepheard agreeth not with them.

> Thilke same bene shepheards for the Devils stead,
> That playen whilest their flockes be unfead.

Where after followeth a definition (a cuntrey definition) of an hirelyng, by
application whereof unto them, hee prooveth them to bee hyrelings.

> Well is it seene their sheepe be not their owne,
> That letten them run at randome alone:
> But they bene hyred, for little pay,
> Of others that caren as little as they,
> What fallen the flocke, so they han the fleece,
> And get all the gaine paying but a peece. (*LL,* fol. 60 ᵣ)

Puttenham explains the relation between logical definition and the
figure horismus, which defines a word by impugning its contrary.

The Logician useth a definition to express the truth or nature of every thing
by his true kinde and difference, as to say wisedome is a prudent and wittie fore-
sight and consideration of humane or worldly actions with their eventes. This
definition is Logicall. The Oratour useth another maner of definition, thus: Is
this wisedome? no it is a certaine subtill knavish craftie wit, it is no industrie as
ye call it, but a certaine busie brainsicknesse, for industrie is a lively and un-
weried search and occupation in honest things, egernesse is an appetite in base
and small matters. (p. 231)

Peacham describes another rhetorical figure of definition.

Systrophe . . . is when the Orator bringeth in many definitions of one thing,
yet not such definitions as do declare the substance of a thing by the general
kind, and the difference, which the art of reasoning doth prescribe, but others
of another kind all heaped together: such as these definitions of *Cicero* be in the
second booke of an Orator, where he amplifieth the dignitie of an hystory thus:
An historie saith he, is the testimony of times, the light of veritie, the main-
tenance of memorie, the scoolemistresse of life, and messenger of antiquitie.
(p. 153)

3. Division: Genus and Species, Whole and Parts

Wilson points out the relation between definition and division.

As a definition therefore doth declare what a thing is, so a devision sheweth how many thinges are contained in the same. (*RR*, fol. 14 ᵛ)

There are three kinds of division: the genus into its species, the whole into its parts, the subject into its adjuncts. The first is a classification, the second a partition, the third a distinction between substance and the accidents which inhere in it, as redness inheres in a rose. Fraunce notes that "*Socrates* in *Phaedro Platonis* sayth, that if he finde any man who can cunningly divide, he will follow his steps, and admire him for a God" (*LL*, fol. 57 ʳ).

The rules of good division require that the dividing members be mutually exclusive and that together they constitute the whole that is divided. A proposition which expresses the result of a logical division is called disjunctive. For example:

Whatsoever is a living creature, the same is a thing, that either hath reason, or els that lacketh reason. . . . Either it is day, or els it is night. (Wilson, *RR*, fol. 16 ᵛ, 22 ʳ)

One may argue validly that if the whole be good, the parts must be good, but not conversely, because

One or many parts, whether they be principall or of small importance, are not alwayes of force to prove or to prayse a whole. For a song that standeth of foure parts, that is to saye of the base, the meane, the triple, and the contratenor, is not therefore fine and good, because two or three partes be excellently well song. For in such whole things as song and melody are, all the partes are necessarily required to be good, otherwise there shalbe a discorde and a jarre in the whole. (Lever, p. 159)

The ends served by division are:

First, as *Cicero* saith, it helpeth greatly to teach plainly to define, and to make things that be compound, intricate, or confused, to appear simple, plaine, and certaine: Secondly, by dividing things orderly into their parts, it greatly helpeth memorie: and thirdly, it helpeth to amplifie any kind of speech, and to make it more copious. (Blundeville, p. 62)

Fraunce explains the relation between division and induction.

As the distinguishing of the whole into his parts, is called Distribution: so the

collection or gathering together of all the parts to make up the whole, is named
Induction. (*LL,* fol. 56 ᵛ)

The foregoing principles of logic are reflected in the eleven figures
related to division whereby they are applied to specific problems of composition. Hoskyns comments on the value of division,

which *Bacon* in his [fifth colour] tooke out of the *Rhetoritians,* a way to am-
plify anything (quoth he) is to breake it & make an *Anatomie* of it into severall
parts, & to examine it, according to severall circumstances, he said true, it is like
the shewe which Pedlers make of their Packes, when they display them contrary
to the German magnificence, that serves in all the good meate in one dish.
(p. 136)

The figure diaeresis corresponds to the first kind of division named
by the logicians, that of genus into species.

Diaeresis . . . is a forme of speech which divideth the generall kind into the
speciall kinds, yet not in a dialecticall forme, but in a rhetorical maner for
amplifications sake, whereof this saying of *Job* may be an example: Aske the
cattaile, and they shall inform thee, the fowles of the aire & they shal tel thee,
the increase of the earth, and it shall shew thee, or the fishes of the sea, and they
shal certifie thee, by which answere of *Job* to his frends, he declareth that their
wisedome was no other then such as the very brute beastes do daily teach, which
he divideth into sundry kinds, whereby he doth pithily & elegantly set forth &
amplifie their grosse ignorance. (Peacham, p. 123)

Synecdoche, a trope concerned with division, is of four kinds: the genus
is substituted for the species,

put upp your weapon, for your dagger, (Hoskyns, p. 124),

or the part for the whole,

my name is tost & censured by many tongues for manye men where the part
of an entire bodye goes for the whole (*Loc. cit.*),

or species may be put for genus, as in the Lord's prayer,

Bread one helpe of life is put for all helps (Fenner, sig. D 2 ᵛ),

or whole for part as,

nations for the Heathen. (*Loc. cit.*)

Merismus, or partitio, employs the second kind of division, distributing
the whole into its parts.

If in generality we said *hee hath consumed al his substance in ryot:* By distribution wee might amplifie thus, Whatsoever patrimony hee had from his father, what private inrichment by his deceased mother, what large assistance by his friends, whereat the world never barked, what dowry soever by his wife, which no doubt was very great, all this hath hee consumed by a most dissolute and wanton living. (Day, p. 385)

Eutrepismus is the arrangement of the parts in an appropriate order.

Eutrepismus . . . is a forme of speech, which doth not only number the partes before they be said, but also doth order those partes, and maketh them plaine by a kind of definition, or declaration. . . . There are three sorts of men which do dispose of all that a man hath, the Lawyer, the Phisition, and the Divine. The Lawyer disposeth of his goods, the Phisition of his bodie, and the divine of his soule. (Peacham, p. 129)

Enumeratio employs the third kind of division,

when the subject is divided into the accidents, the matter into the antecedents, the effect into the causes, and into things annexed and following after the effect. . . . Of the subject into accidents. An example: what may we thinke of man, when we consider the heavie burthen of his miserie, the weaknesse of his patience, the imperfection of his understanding, the conflicts of his counsels, the insatietie of his mind, the brevitie of his life, and the certaintie of his death? (*Ibid.*, p. 125)

The remaining figures represent various rhetorical adaptations of division.

Propositio, which comprehendeth in few words the summe of the matter whereof we presently intend to speake. *Cicero:* I have now to speake of the excellent and singular vertues of *Pompeius.* . . . Now in a proposition, there are three things to be considered . . . First that it absolutely containeth whatsoever pertaineth to the cause . . . Secondly, that it be well divided . . . Lastly that it be disposed in an order, most meete for the same cause. (*Ibid.*, p. 192)

Restrictio, when of the generall word going before, a part afterward is excepted, . . . An example of S. *Paul:* We are afflicted on everie side, yet are we not in distresse: in povertie, yet not overcome of povertie: we are persecuted, but not forsaken: cast downe but we perish not. . . . This exornation is evermore used to these effects, . . . to mingle and temper commodities with their discommodities, as felicitie with miserie, . . . And also to note imperfection, in things whiche seeme perfect. (*Ibid.*, p. 131)

Prolepsis, where something generally first spoken, is afterwardes drawne into parts, as thus, . . . *Men diversely do erre, some by an ignorant simplicity, others by a most perverse folly.* (Day, p. 361)

Puttenham explains that epanodos is similar to prolepsis, since in both there is

the resumption of a former proposition uttered in generalitie to explane the same better by a particular division. But their difference is, in that [prolepsis] resumes but the matter only. This resumes both the matter and the termes, and is therefore accompted one of the figures of repetition. . . . The use of this figure, is seen in this dittie following [from Gascoigne],

> *Love hope and death, do stirre in me such strife,*
> *As never man but I lead such a life:*
> *For burning love doth wound my heart to death:*
> *And when death comes at call of inward grief,*
> *And lingring hope doth feede my fainting breath:*
> *Against my will, and yeelds my wound relief,*
> *So that I live, but yet my life is such:*
> *As never death could greeve me halfe so much.* (p. 221)

Synathroesmus has two meanings. One is to heap together many words of different meaning, and this is also named congeries.

Hee was a man wholly malicious, exceedingly proud, utterly arrogant, altogether subtill, by nature cruell, and in speeches contentious. (Day, p. 377)

The second meaning is to gather together by way of recapitulation (the reverse of division) points that have been dispersed throughout the speech in order to give them greater weight and to refresh the memory of the hearers.

The conclusion or lapping up of matter, is an apt knitting together of that, which we have saied before. As thus. If reason can perswade, if examples may moove, if necessitie may helpe, if pitie may provoke, if daungers foreseene may stirre us to be wise: I doubt not but you will rather use sharpe lawes to represse offendours, then with dissolute negligence suffer all to perish. (Wilson, *AR*, p. 183)

Similar to this is epiphonema, a brief summary of what has gone before, often sententious, with a moral note, sometimes expressing joyful approbation as in Vergil's,

> Tanta molis erat Romanam condere gentem. 1 *Aeneid.*
>   (Fraunce, *AR*, sig. F 4 ʳ)

It is especially suited to the closing up of an epigram. As Puttenham remarks,

Sir *Philip Sidney* very pretily closed up a dittie in this sort.
> *What medcine then, can such disease remove,*
> *Where love breedes hate, and hate engenders love.* (p. 217)

4. Subject and Adjuncts

The distinction between adjuncts and the subject in which they inhere provides the basis for the third kind of division discussed by the logicians in the preceding section. Much more important, however, than the distinction that may be made between these topics is their relationship to each other. This is best understood from the fundamental instance of this relationship, namely, that of a substance and its accidents, which Blundeville explains with his usual clarity.

We cannot see the substance of anything with our bodily eies, but only with the eies of our minde and understanding; but we may see the shape, the quantitie, the colour and such like accidents cleaving to the substance, without the which these accidents have no being at all: and therefore in seeing such accidents, we may assure our selves that there is a substance sustaining those accidents, which doth alwaies remaine, though the accidents doe faile or change never so often. (p. 20)

Fraunce gives a brief but comprehensive explanation of the logical doctrine of subjects and adjuncts, defining subject as a wider term than substance.

[A subject is] not onely . . . an essence, or substance, as the common Logicians usually take it, but also whatsoever can bee imagined or fayned to have any thing adjoyned unto it, in it, or about it: so one quality may bee the subject to another, as in this axiome, Vertue is commendable, where commendation is adjoyned to vertue, being the subject thereof. (*LL*, fol. 39 ^{v})

The subject is that whereunto some thing is adjoyned. The subject receiveth the adjunct, eyther in it, as the minde learning, the place the thing placed: or to it: & this is either affected by the thing adjoyned, as the body receiveth garments to it, and is of them affected: or els it dooth affect the thing adjoyned, as a sicke man receyveth unto him the physitian, and dooth affect him, by occupying and busiying his heade and minde in inventing remedies for him. (38 ^{r})

Explications, illustrations, amplifications, and extenuations are fet from this place: So *Cicero* to his sonne, Thou art at *Athens,* therefore thou shouldest bee learned. . . . From hence are almost all poeticall epithetes deducted. (40 ^{r})

An adjunct is that whereunto something is subject. An adjunct is eyther In-herent in the subject, or adherent to it. The adherent adjunct dooth eyther af-fect the subject: or is affected by it. So vertues, vices, learning, and all such qualities are adjuncts to mans minde. And as every place is the subject of the thing placed: so, time, that is to say, the continuance of every thing, is the ad-junct of those thinges which doo continue in time. So all qualities which eyther bee proper, as laughing to a man: or common, as whitenesse to a stone, and a wall, are truely called adjuncts. Finally everything which agreeth unto an other, beeing neyther the cause, nor the effect thereof, is an adjunct of the thing, whereunto it dooth agree. . . .

In March *Thomalin* argueth the spring to bee at hand, by these adjunctes.

> The grasse now gins to bee refresht
> The swallow peepes out of her nest,
> And clowdy *Welkin* cleareth. (41 ʳ)

Hence are also fet prayses and disprayses, deliberations and consultations. Herein are contained all those Rhetoricall places concerning the giftes and qualities of body and soule, as also externall and those of fortune. (43 ᵛ)

Eighteen figures are derived from the relation of subject and adjuncts.

Peristasis, a forme of speech by which the Orator amplifieth by circum-stances . . . either of a person or of a thing, a person hath these: Parentage, nation, Countrie, kinde, age, education, discipline, habite of bodie, fortune, con-dition, nature of the minde, studie, foredeeds, name, &c. . . . Circumstances of things: Cause, Place, Time, Occasion: To watch the opportunitie of darke-nesse to do mischiefe . . . Instrument . . . to murder by poisoning or by strangling doth argue a deepe and cursed malice of the murderer. . . . *Cau-tion* . . . take heede of long and tedious stay in them, as about who, what, when, where, how, and such like, which by prolixitie is wont to make the ora-tion barren.[4] (Peacham, p. 164)

Encomion is a forme of speech by which the Orator doth highly commend to his hearers, some person or thing in respect of their worthy deserts & ver-tues . . . this [is] the only forme of speech, which both speaketh while the vertuous man doth live, and also liveth when the vertuous man is dead. (*Ibid.*, p. 155)

Taxis is a figure . . . which distributeth to everie subject his most proper & naturall adjunct. . . . The divine wisedome hath assigned Kings to raigne, Judges to heare causes & give sentence, Advocates to plead, subjects to obey, the wise to give counsell, and the rich to give almes. (*Ibid.*, p. 60)

Puttenham explains the difference between epitheton and antonomasia.

[4] Compare Wilson's list of the places of persons, p. 24, above.

Epitheton . . . giving every person or thing besides his proper name a qualitie by way of addition whether it be of good or of bad . . . as to say.

> *Fierce Achilles, wise Nestor, wilie Ulysses* . . .

But if we speake thus not expressing her proper name *Elizabeth*, videl.

> *The English Diana, the great Britton mayde.*

Then is it not by *Epitheton* . . . but by . . . *Antonomasia*, or *Periphrasis*. (p. 176)

This form of antonomasia substitutes for the proper name a descriptive phrase; another form represents the reverse process whereby a proper name is substituted for a quality associated with it.

> When we give to one man the name of another for the affinities sake of their maners or conditions. In praise thus, as when we call a grave man a *Cato* . . . In dispraise, to call . . . a tyrant a *Nero*. (Peacham, p. 23)

Similar to the first form of antonomasia is periphrasis, which substitutes a descriptive phrase for a common name.

> If a short ordinarie sence bee odly expressed . . . for kill any maryed man, make his sword accursed by any widdowe . . . (Hoskyns, p. 162)

Metonymy is a trope which sometimes substitutes subject for adjunct or adjunct for subject.

> The change of name or Metonymie, where the subject or that which hath anything adjoined, is put for the thing adjoined or adjoynt. So the place is put for those or that in the place . . . *It shalbe easier for Sodome and Gomorra,* that is, the people *in Sodome and Gomorra. So Moses chaire is put for the doctrine taught in Moses chaire.* . . .
> On the other side, the adjoint is put for the thing to whiche it is adjoyned. . . . So in the Epistle to the Ephesians. *The dayes are evil,* that is, the manner, conversation, and the deeds of men in the dayes. (Fenner, sig. D i ʳ)

Enargia and hypotyposis are generic names for a group of figures aiming at lively description and counterfeit representation,

> when the Orator by a diligent gathering together of circumstances, and by a fit and naturall application of them, doth expresse and set forth a thing so plainly and lively, that . . . the hearer . . . rather thinketh he seeth it then heareth it. . . . Now under the generall name of Description, I do not only reckon speciall kindes of description, but also all other figures, which do chiefly respect circumstances and adjuncts . . . (Peacham, p. 134)

The names of the species of counterfeit representation both factual and fictitious exemplify an unflagging zeal for making distinctions which seem to us mere hair-splitting or wearisome pedantry but which men of the Renaissance evidently found interesting and delightful. In *The Lawiers Logike* Fraunce mentions, with a hint of mild amusement, the species which some of the rhetoricians distinguished.

If any person be described, they call it *Prosopographia*, if a place, *Topographia*, if a nation, *Chorographia*, if the earth, *Geographia*, if the water, *hydrographia*, if the wind, *Anemographia*, if a tree, *Dendographia*, if the time *Chronographia*, &c. (fol. 63 ᵛ)

The Tudor figurists omit some in this list, but add others. Because these kinds of description, except for their names, are familiar to us, it will suffice to summarize the figures of this group briefly.

Prosopographia is the lively description of an absent person as if he were present, as when Homer describes Achilles or Chaucer the Pardoner and the rest of his pilgrims. Prosopopoeia is fictional and includes the feigning of persons and the attribution of human qualities to dumb or even to inanimate creatures, as when Cicero represents Rome as reproaching Catiline; another example is Vergil's description of Fame or Rumor. Characterismus is the description of the body or mind; ethopoeia, of natural propensity and affections, manners, arts, virtues, vices; mimesis, of gesture, pronunciation, and utterance; dialogismus, or sermocinatio, of speech, especially when the orator engages in counterfeit dialogue with the feigned person. Pragmatographia is the vivid representation of a counterfeit action, as of a battle, a feast, a marriage. Chronographia describes times; topographia, places. But if the places are fictional, such as the house of envy in Ovid's *Metamorphoses*, the figure is called topothesia. "All Logike," remarks Fraunce, "is generall, and applyable as well to thinges imagined, as things that bee extant in truth." (*Ibid.*, fol. 59 ᵛ).

These figures of counterfeit representations, whether of real or of imaginary persons, places, events, and times, are essentially poetic in the sense of communicating experience by creating an illusion of reality. Through them an author speaks to readers or listeners, not directly, but indirectly by interposing characters and situations which seem real and immediate. This imitation lies at the very heart of epic and of drama, as Aristotle points out in the *Poetics*.

The poet should say very little *in propria persona*, as he is no imitator when doing that. Whereas the other poets are perpetually coming forward in person, and say but little, and that only here and there, as imitators, Homer after a brief preface brings in forthwith a man, a woman, or some other Character—no one of them characterless, but each with distinctive characteristics. (24, 1460 ᵃ 7)

5. Contraries and Contradictories

Often a matter is more clearly understood in relation to its contrary, as Wilson observes.

> By contraries set together things oftentimes appear greater. . . . set a faire woman against a foule, and she shall seeme much the fairer, and the other much the fouler. (*AR*, p. 125)

In his "Apologie for Poetrie" Sidney also explains:

> Now, as in Geometry the oblique must bee knowne as wel as the right, and in Arithmetick the odde as wel as the even, so in the actions of our life who seeth not the filthines of evil wanteth a great foile to perceive the beauty of vertue. (Smith, I, 177)

Through contraries one may more readily recognize the ambiguity of words, as of *sharp* or *clear*.

> Sharp, is a word of double understanding: for his contrarie . . . in voyce is, flat: and in edge, dull. Therefore it must folow of necessitie that it is not one sharpnesse, which is contrarye to flatnes in voyce, and to dulnesse in edge . . . not one and the same clearenes that is sene & heard: the one consisting in colour and the other in sound. (Lever, p. 50)

The Tudor logicians distinguish four kinds of opposites: contraries, relatives, privatives, and contradictories. Contraries are called mediate if there are species between the extremes, as there are between black and white, for

> if a cloth be not white, it is no reason to call it blacke. For it may bee blewe, greene, redd, russett, tawnie, yealowe, or any other colour els, as it shall best please the Dyer. (Wilson, *RR*, fol. 52 ᵛ)

Contraries are called immediate if there are no species between, but one or the other must be affirmed, as faith or unbelief in a man. Relative terms are opposed to one another, yet each implies the other, as father and son, husband and wife, cause and effect, subject and adjunct. They cannot both be present at the same time and in the same respect: Socrates cannot be father and son to the same man. Yet

> that which agreeth with one of the Relatives, commonly agreeth with the other, as if it bee honest to teach, it is no shame to learne. (Fraunce, *LL*, fol. 49 ʳ)

Privative terms represent deprivations opposed to natural perfections, as blindness to sight; hence a stone cannot properly be called blind because sight does not belong to its nature. Of contradictory terms, one is positive, the other negative, as a stone, no stone; righteous, unrighteous. And since the negative term includes everything except its opposite positive, one term must always be affirmed, the other denied.

Besides contrary and contradictory terms, there are contrary and contradictory propositions. Of contradictory propositions, one must be true and the other false.

Therefore if this saying (All fayre women are good) be false: then this saying (Some faire women are not good) muste needes be true. (Lever, p. 206)

But of contraries, both may be false, as

All men are moved with glorie, No manne is moved with glorie. (Wilson, *RR*, fol. 20 ʳ)

but both cannot be true.

The Tudor rhetoricians treat eleven figures based on contraries and contradictories. Litotes is related to what the logicians call equipollence or obversion, which consists in expressing a thought by denying its contradictory. This figure may be used to dispraise another with less offense or to speak well of oneself with greater modesty.

Job saith, that he hath not eaten his meate alone, that he hath not seene any man perish for want of clothing, or any poore for lacke of covering. Here if *Job* had said that he had feasted many, that he had clothed every poore body that should otherwise have perished, he had not spoken so modestly, albeit that he had sayd as truly. (Peacham, p. 150)

Synoeciosis is a composition of contraries.

> *Thus for your sake I dayly dye*
> *And do but seeme to live in deede:*
> *Thus is my blisse but miserie,*
> *My lucre losse without your meede.* (Puttenham, p. 207)

Paradox in the sixteenth century had two meanings: (1) a statement contrary to received opinion, evoking wonder because it is marvelous, strange, incredible; (2) a statement apparently self-contradictory. In Puttenham's illustration of this figure which he calls the Wonderer, Cato, pointing out a young unthrift who had lately sold his patrimony for some salt marshes, seems to find the cause of wonder or incredibility in the apparent contradiction.

> *Now is it not, a wonder to behold,*
> *Yonder gallant skarce twenty winter old,*
> *By might (mark ye) able to doo more?*
> *Than the mayne sea that batters on his shore?*
> *For what the waves could never wash away,*
> *This proper youth hath wasted in a day.* (p. 226)

In contrast to synoeciosis, which is a composition of contrary terms, antithesis [5] is an opposition of them, giving greater light and perspicuity.

For he that alwayes wyll be an enemy to his owne rekenyngs, how should a man trust that he wold be a frind to other mens matters? (Sherry, sig. D iiii ᵛ)

Aristotle comments on the value of antithesis.

Such a form of speech is satisfying, because the significance of contrasted ideas is easily felt, especially when they are thus put side by side, and also because it has the effect of a logical argument; it is by putting two opposing conclusions side by side that you prove one of them false. (*Rhetoric*, 3.9.1410 ᵃ 20)

Syncrisis, is a comparison of contrary things, & diverse persons in one sentence. . . . Wise women uphold their house, but a foolish woman pulleth it downe. Prov. 14.1. (Peacham, p. 162)

Antanagoge is a figure whereby something spoken unfavorably is in a measure counteracted, though not denied, by the addition of something favorable which gives another color to the matter. For example, one wishing to encourage youth in study might remark:

> *Many are the paines and perils to be past,*
> *But great is the gaine and glorie at the last.*
> (Puttenham, p. 216)

Inter se pugnantia, is a forme of speech by which the orator reproveth his adversarie, or some other person of manifest unconstancie, open hypocrisie, or in-

---

[5] This is the figure, remarked Hoskyns (p. 151), which Ascham taught the Queen of England and in which she excelled. Writing to his friend Sturm on April 4, 1550, Ascham mentioned that his pupil, the Princess Elizabeth, then sixteen years old, particularly delighted in noting contraries: "She very much admires modest metaphors, and comparisons of contraries well put together and contrasting felicitously with one another. Her ears are so well practised in discriminating all these things, and her judgment is so good, that in all Greek, Latin, and English composition, there is nothing so loose on the one hand or so concise on the other, which she does not immediately attend to, and either reject with disgust or receive with pleasure, as the case may be." (Letter XCIX, translated and quoted in Berdan, *Early Tudor Poetry*, p. 340.)

solent arrogancie. . . . Thou therefore which teachest another, teachest not
thy selfe; thou that preachest a man should not steale, yet thou stealest: . . .
Rom. 2. (Peacham, p. 163)

Irony is a trope which by naming one contrary intends another. It is
used in derision, mockery, jesting, dissembling.

This trope is perceived either by the contrariety of the matter or the manner
of utterance, or both. . . . So the Jewes said unto Christe: Hayle king of the
Jewes. (Fenner, sig. D 2 ᵛ)

Antiphrasis is the irony of one word,

when we deride by plaine and flat contradiction, as he that saw a dwarfe go in
the streete said to his companion . . . See yonder gyant. (Puttenham, p. 191)

Paralipsis is a kind of irony which in the very show of pretending to
pass over a certain matter tells it nonetheless.

I urge not to yow the hope of your friends, though that should animate yow
to answer their expectacion, I lay not before yow the necessitie of the place
which yow are to furnish, wherein to be defective & insufficient were some
shame. I omit the envious concurrencies & some prepared comparisons in your
countrie, which have somé feeling with yonge men of fore-sight, I onelie say
howe our owne promises shall give Judgment against us . . . (Hoskyns,
p. 145)

Epitrope is an ironical permission, such as Dido scornfully uttered
to Aeneas.

I, sequere Italiam ventis: pete regna per undas.

Fraunce quotes this from Vergil, and also an example from Sidney's
Arcadia.

If you seeke the victorie take it, and if you list, triumph.
(Fraunce, *AR*, sig. H 5 ʳ)

6. Similarity and Dissimilarity

Contrariety clearly exists between species at opposite extremes within
the same genus, as black and white, but objects of different classes may
be similar or dissimilar in some respect. Consequently argument from
contrariety is fundamental and convincing; that from similarity or dissimilarity is superficial, often adventitious, illuminating rather than compelling. Blundeville observes that

this kinde of reasoning of Like, is more apt to teach and to print in the hearers
minde a lively representation of the thing, then to urge him by any necessitie

of due proofe to beleeve the same, because it is unpossible, that the two things which are to bee compared can be like in all points . . . (p. 111)

Sidney remarks that the force of a similitude is not "to proove anything to a contrary Disputer but onely to explane to a willing hearer" (Smith, I, 203). And Lever asserts:

Learned men in arguing, make small accompt of any similitude. For by a similitude you maye as soone prove a wrong matter as a righte: yet doe men of great judgement use it, but rather to perswade and leade the simple and the ignoraunt, then to force and overcome the wittie adversarie. . . . A similitude is well answered, when an unlikelinesse is shewed in that matter wherein divers things were sayde to bee like. (p. 196)

Induction is a method of argument which from like instances draws a general conclusion. In this manner Socrates, by questioning his adversaries, gathered instances from them and drew conclusions which confounded them. Argument by example is a form of induction.

An example, is a maner of argumentation, where one thyng is proved by an other, forthe likenesse that is founde to be in them both, as thus. If *Marcus Attilius Regulus* had rather lose his life then not keepe promise with his enemie, then should every man beeing taken prisoner, keepe promise with his enemie. (Wilson, *RR*, fol. 33ʳ)

One may argue also from dissimilitude as Colyn does in "June."

> O happy *Hobbinoll*, I blesse thy state,
> That Paradise hast found which *Adam* lost,
> Here wander may thy flocke early or late:
> Withouten dreade of woolves to beene ytost,
> Thy lovely layes here mayst thou freely boste:
> But I unhappy man whome cruell fate
> And angry Gods pursue from coaste to coaste,
> Can no where finde to shrowde my lucklesse pate.
>   (Fraunce, *LL*, fol. 75ʳ)

This illustration cited by Fraunce in his work on logic would serve perfectly for the figure dissimilitude, which Peacham, using a similar illustration, describes as

a forme of speech which compareth diverse things in a diverse qualitie. An example . . . of our Saviour Christ: The foxes have holes, and the fowles of the aire have nestes, but the sonne of man hath not where to laie his head. Luc. 9.58. (p. 160)

Nine figures are based on similitude. By homoeosis, or the figure of similitude,

> we not onely bewtifie our tale, but also very much inforce & inlarge it. I say inforce because no one thing more prevaileth with all ordinary judgements than perswasion by *similitude* . . . which may be thus spoken.
>
> > But as the watrie showres delay the raging wind,
> > So doeth good hope cleane put away dispaire out of my mind.
> > (Puttenham, p. 240)

Puttenham makes homoeosis the genus of icon, paradigma, parabola, and fable or apologue. Icon is the comparison of one person or thing with another, form with form, quality with quality, as

> he whets his teeth like a Bore . . . we might compare one man with another, as *Salust* compareth *Caesar* and *Cato* together, or wee might heape many men together, and prove by large rehearsall any thing that wee would, the which of the *Logicians* is called induction. (Wilson, *AR*, p. 207)

By paradigma or example one also proceeds by induction.

> We . . . liken one case to another . . . compare the past with the present, gathering probabilitie of like successe to come in the things wee have presently in hand: . . . as if one should say thus, *Alexander* the great in his expedition to Asia did thus, so did *Hanniball* comming into Spaine, so did *Caesar* in Egypt, therfore all great Captains & Generals ought to doe it. (Puttenham, p. 245)

A parable teaches a moral by metaphorical and dark speeches, such as the parable of the laborers in the vineyard. According to Puttenham,

> they may be fayned aswell as true: as those fables of *Aesope*, and other apologies invented for doctrine sake by wise and grave men. (p. 245)

Wilson comments on the value of fables.

> The feined Fables, such as are attributed unto brute beastes . . . not onely . . . delite the rude and ignorant, but also they helpe much for perswasion . . . because such as speake in open audience have ever mo fooles to heare them, then wisemen to give judgment . . . The multitude (as *Horace* doth say) is a beast . . . use the quiddities of *Dunce*, to set forth Gods misteries: and you shall see the ignorant (I warrant you) either fall a sleepe, or els bid you farewell. The multitude must needes be made merie: . . . The Romaine *Menenius Agrippa*, alledging upon a time, a Fable of the conflict made betwixt the parts of a mans bodie, and his bellie: quieted . . . the uprore of sedicious Rebelles . . . (*AR*, p. 197)

A metaphor is a trope based on similitude. Metaphors

give pleasant light to darke things . . . by the aptnesse of their proportion, and
nearnesse of affinitie, they worke in the hearer many effects, they obtaine al-
lowance of his judgement, they move his affections, and minister a pleasure to
his wit. . . . they are forcible to perswade. . . . they leave such a firme impression in the memory, as is not lightly forgotten. (Peacham, p. 13)

In Aristotle's opinion,

to be a master of metaphor . . . is . . . a sign of genius, since a good metaphor implies an intuitive perception of the similarity in dissimilars. (*Poetics*, 22,
1459 ᵃ 5)

The figure allegory is a metaphor continued through whole sentences
or even through a whole discourse.

The continuance of Tropes called an Allegorie, is when one kinde of Trope is
so continued: as, Looke with what kinde of matter it be begunne, with the same
it be ended. So in the 23. Psalme, *the care of God towardes his Churche, is set
foorth by the woordes proper to a shephearde.* So in the whole booke of Can-
ticles, *the sweete conference of Christe and his Church, is set downe by the
wordes proper to the husbande and the wife.* (Fenner, sig. D i ᵛ)

Peacham describes onomatopoeia as a figure whereby

we invent, devise, fayne, and make a name, immitating the sownd of that it
sygnifyeth, as hurliburly, for an uprore, and tumultuous stirre, thwick thwack,
that is blow, for blow, stroake for stroake, and one harder then an other, thwick
sygnifyeth the lesser, and thwack the greater, buzzing for the noyse of Bees,
. . . and fynally the mooting of beasts, the blating of sheepe, the neighing of
Horse, the scriking of Infantes, and al such voyces, as doe resemble the sound,
or be straungely fayned. (1577, sig. C iiii ᵛ)

Catachresis is the borrowing of a word from its own proper signification
to accommodate it to another not proper to it, but somewhat like it, as
to say that the sword shall devour, that men's powers are short, or their
counsels long, when there is literally no such measure of them. Or, explains Puttenham,

as one said very pretily in this verse.

I lent my love to losse. . . .

Whereas this worde *lent* is properly of mony or some such other thing, as men
do commonly borrow, for use to be repayed againe, and being applied to love
is utterly abused, and yet very commendably spoken by vertue of this figure.

For he that loveth and is not beloved againe, hath no lesse wrong, than he that lendeth and is never repayde. (p. 180)

7. Comparison: Greater, Equal, Less

Objects of different classes may be similar or dissimilar in some respect, usually in quality. Objects of the same class may be greater, equal, or less with respect to quantity.

This Logicall quantity . . . may bee attributed to any thing incident and convenient to our purpose, as, to dignitie, prayse, reproche, abilitie and power, greatnes, multitude, conveniency, commoditie, opportunitie, facilitie, difficultie, care, neglect, excellencie, vilenes, and in a woorde, to whatsoever may bee saide to bee equall, more, or lesse. (Fraunce, *LL*, fol. 78 ʳ)

Blundeville points out that

of substances one cannot be more or lesse then another; for the greatest Giant, as touching substance, is no more a man then the least Dwarfe that is; neither is a man full growne, more a man then a childe newly borne: for more or lesse appertaineth properly to quantitie, and not to substance. (p. 21)

Lever likewise explains:

Al specials ar partakers of their general indifferently, without respect of more or lesse. For an Egle is no rather nor no more a birde or a foule, then an Oule is, nor an Oule more or lesse then a Wrenne: but they and all other foules equally and indifferently, are named and be in deede birdes, without degree of more or lesse. (p. 151)

Fraunce cautions against fallacy in this kind of argument.

As when you take that for lesse which is not lesse. As if a boy can paynt, then a man can paynt, for although a boy bee lesse then a man, yet a boy may sometimes sooner paynt then a man. (*LL*, fol. 81 ʳ)

One may, however, argue validly from number, as

pardon mee this fault: it is the firste . . . forgeve this second trespasse; for twice is not often. (Lever, p. 164)

An argument may proceed from the greater in any respect, such as the greater in probability, in desirability, in difficulty, or efficacy, as this which Fraunce cites from Vergil.

Counterfayt teares circumvented them, whome neyther the cruell *Diomedes*, nor fierce *Achilles*, nor ten yeares warre, nor a thousand ships could overcome. (*LL*, fol. 79 ʳ)

As an argument from the equal he quotes from Terence.

Sith I meddle not with thine, meddle not thou with mine. (fol. 76 ᵛ)

He presents as an argument from the less:

If God doe not reject the sparrowes, much lesse you: But he contemneth not them: therefore not you. (fol. 80 ᵛ)

The parallelism between the works of the Ramists and the figurists is clearly seen in the similarity of Fraunce's treatment of the logical topics of comparison—greater, equal, less—and Peacham's account of the figure comparatio, whereby

like things are compared among themselves, unlike from the lesse to the greater in amplifying, and from the greater to the lesse in diminishing . . . Comparison of like things, as *Camillus* by his vertue did drive away the Barbarians and set up againe the Romane Empire, being sore opprest, and almost brought to utter destruction: even so *Laurentius Valla* restored the Latine tongue to the former puritie, which through the ignorance of the Barbarians was corrupted, suppressed, and almost quite extinct . . .

From the lesse to the greater: Wherefore if God so clothe the grasse of the field which is to day and to morrow is cast into the Oven: shall he not do much more for you, O ye of little faith? Mat. 6. . . . From the greater to the lesse . . . If God spared not the Angels that had sinned but cast them downe into hell . . . much lesse will he spare the wicked which walke after the flesh in the lusts of uncleannesse. (p. 156)

A number of figures convey a sense of the greater or the less although comparison in them is merely implicit, as in following an order from greater to less or from less to greater in a series; in exaggerating or extenuating; in substituting a stronger for a weaker word; and in iterating the same idea in different words and figures.

Auxesis, as Puttenham and Day call it, or progression, as Hoskyns names it, is a kind of amplification

which by stepps of comparison stores everie degree, till it come to the topp, & [to] make the matter seeme the higher advaunced, sometimes descends the lower; . . . In like sort is this example to abuse the name of god: to make table talke of a meane man's name [were] wrong, to run upon a noblemans tytle were a great scandall, to play with a Princes name were a treason, & what shall it bee to make a vanitie of that name, which is most terrible to tirants & divells, & most reverende even to Monarchs and Angells. (Hoskyns, p. 140)

Such mounting by degrees through words or sentences of increasing weight we would call climactic word order. Peacham names it incrementum, and gives to auxesis a different meaning, that of augmentation accomplished chiefly through hyperbole.

Auxesis is a forme of speech by which the Orator amplifieth by putting a greatter word for a lesse, as to call a proude man *Lucifer*, a dronkard a swine, an angrie man mad, a covetous man a cutthroate: In praising, as to call an honest man a Saint, a faire Virgin an Angell, good musicke heavenly harmonie. This figure is chiefly set forth by tropes of words . . . but chieflie by *Hyperbole*, which maketh a large and most ample comparison. (p. 167)

That hyperbole exceeds the truth both the speaker and the hearer well know, and therefore its intention is not to deceive but to exaggerate the greatness or the smallness of things by an excessive similitude, as to call an extortioner a wolf, to speak of streams of tears, or to say that a cry reaches to heaven.

The opposite of auxesis is meiosis, whereby one makes a thing appear less than it is by putting a less word for a greater, for various reasons: to bring one's adversaries into contempt, as Hannibal did in his speech to his soldiers; to excuse a fault or an offense, as to call robbery pilfering or a great wound a scratch; to belittle through implication, as to speak of fantastical-minded people whom children and musicians call lovers. When such extenuation tends to flattery or soothing, it is named para-diastole, as for instance to call a prodigal man a liberal gentleman, a miser thrifty, drunkenness good fellowship, insatiable avarice good husbandry, craft and deceit wisdom and policy.

Charientismus mitigates with pleasant words or mocks under smooth and lowly words, as when

wee scoffe a man in his threatning mood, to say, *O good words, I pray you,* or, *Kill us not at the first dash,* or, *Bite not my nose off I pray you,* and such like. (Day, p. 359)

Catacosmesis, like auxesis, expresses degree through word order, but whereas auxesis sets the weightiest word last, catacosmesis sets the word greatest in dignity first, as God and man, sun and moon, life and death.

Epanorthosis, or correction,

is a figure which taketh away that that is said, and putteth a more meet word in the place, . . . written not with inke, but with the spirite of the living God, not in tables of stone, but in the fleshly tables of the heart. 2 Cor. 3.3. (Peacham, p. 172)

Similar to this is dirimens copulatio,

when we bring forth one sentence with an exception before it, and immediately joyne another after it that seemeth greater . . . Wherefore you must needes obey, not onely for feare of vengeance, but also for conscience sake. (*Ibid.*, p. 171)

The figure emphasis, as described by Puttenham, derives its force from substituting for a concrete quality that same quality regarded in its universal abstract essence.

One notable meane to affect the minde, is to inforce the sence of any thing by a word of more than ordinary efficacie, and nevertheles is not apparant, but as it were, secretly implyed, as he that said thus . . .
            O sinne it selfe, not wretch, but wretchednes
Whereas if he had said thus . . . *O sinfull and wretched man,* it had bene all to one effect, yet not with such force and efficacie, to speake by the denominative, as by the thing it selfe. (p. 184)

Mere repetition adds weight to an idea, as through the figure synonymia,

when by a variation and change of words that be of like signification we iterat one thing diverse times. An example . . . of *Virgil:* How doth the child *Ascanius?* is he yet alive? doth he eate the etheral foode? and lieth he not yet under the cruell shades? Here through affection he expresseth one thing thrise: for all that he demaundeth is no more but this, is *Ascanius* alive. (Peacham, p. 149)

Exergasia,[6] or expolitio, may be regarded as a figure of augmentation as well as of garnishing,

when we abide still in one place, and yet seeme to speake diverse things, many times repeating one sentence, but yet with other words, sentences, exornations, and figures: it differeth, saith *Melancton* from *Sinonimia,* forasmuch as that repeateth a sentence or thing onely with changed wordes: but this both with like wordes, like sentences, and like things, having also many exornations to the garnishing thereof. (*Ibid.*, p. 193)

In view of their function, three other figures may be regarded as forms of augmentation: an introductory narrative which opens a speech, a digression, and a return from digression.

[6] La Rue Van Hook pointed out in "Greek Rhetorical Terminology in Puttenham's 'The Arte of English Poesie,'" *Transactions of the American Philological Association,* XLV (1914), 120, that Puttenham is inaccurate in his definition of exergasia and in some other points. Nevertheless, inasmuch as Puttenham's work had a considerable circulation, his definitions and illustrations, even when inaccurate, represent to some extent contemporary opinion. Puttenham's definition agrees in substance with Peacham's quoted above.

Paradiegesis . . . a form of speech by which the Orator telleth or maketh mention of some thing, that it may be a fit occasion or introduction to declare his further meaning, or principall purpose, which is a speciall and artificiall forme of insinuation. A verie apt example we have in the 17. of the Acts, of *Paul* who tooke an occasion by the Aultar which he saw in *Athens* as he passed by, both to reprove the idolatry of the Athenians, and also to teach them the true worship of the living God . . . (*Ibid.*, p. 94)

By parecbasis, or digression,

we swarve sometimes from the matter, upon just considerations, making the same to serve for our purpose, as well as if we had kept the matter still. As . . . when I shall . . . declame against an hainous murtherer, I may digresse from the offence done, and enter in praise of the dead man, declaring his vertues in most ample wise, that the offence done may be thought so much the greater, the more honest he was, that hath thus bene slaine. (Wilson, *AR*, p. 181)

Concerning *reditus ad propositum*, coming again to the matter, Wilson remarks:

When we have made a digression, wee may declare our returne. . . . I knewe a Preacher that was a whole hower out of his matter, and at length remembring himself, saied well, now to the purpose, as though all that he had spoken before, had beene little to the purpose, whereat many laughed, and some for starke wearinesse were faine to goe away. (*Ibid.*, p. 182)

8. Cause and Effect, Antecedent and Consequent

The causes include whatever contributes in any way to produce the effect. Logicians distinguish four causes: the efficient, the material, the formal, and the final. Their importance is such that

no man is saide to knowe anye thing throughly afore he know the causes thereof. (Lever, p. 174)

This is pre-eminently true of the formal cause.

The efficient cause is constituted of the agent, for instance, a carpenter, and his instruments, such as axe, hammer, saw. Wilson explains how the efficient cause may be multiple.

In battaille, the Captaine is the efficient commaunder: the Soldiour the efficient obeier: Gunnes, Darts, Bowes and Billes, the instrumentes of doing. (*RR*, fol. 44 ʳ)

Fraunce cites an illustration of the efficient cause from Spenser's *Shepheardes Calender*.

Collyn in the first Egloge maketh loove the efficient of his weale and woe.

A thousand sithes I cursse that carefull howre,
Wherein I lov'de the neighbour towne to see,
And eke ten thousand siths I blesse the stowre
Wherein I saw so faire a sight as shee.
Yet all for naught, such sight hath bred my bayne,
Ah God, that love should breede both joy and payne.
(*LL*, fol. 12 r)

The material cause is that out of which the thing is made, as wood and stone in a house. It is not, however, limited to the corporeal.

The materiall causes, as also all other arguments Logicall, are not to be tied onely to sensible or bodily matters: but generally to bee applyed to any whatsoever, bee it subject to sence, or conceived by reason. As, a man conceiveth in his mind or memory the Art of Logike or any other science, the matter whereof is their severall rules and preceptes, the forme, the due disposition of the same: and yet neither first nor last is subject to sence, but onely understoode by reason, and imprinted in the inward power of mans soule. (*Ibid.*, fol. 22 r)

The formal cause is that which makes a thing to be what it is. Therefore, explains Fraunce,

hath *Aristotle* in the first of his *Topiks* assigned it two properties; The one for giving essence and knowledge of the same essence, the other for causing difference . . . for that especially by the forme things differ one from another . . . So every naturall thing hath his peculiar forme, as a lyon, a horse, a tree, &c. so every artificiall thing also, as a house, a shippe, &c. So things incorporall, as vertue, vice, &c. So in a woord, whatsoever is, by the formall cause it is that which it is, and is different from all other things that it is not. . . .

The forme is eyther internall, or externall: Internall which is not perceived by sence. Externall, which is subject to sence. Externall is eyther naturall, which is ingraven in every thing naturally: or Artificiall, which Art hath framed and performed. The naturall and internall formes of things bee hardly either known and understoode, or expressed and made plaine. The artificiall and externall is much more easily both conceived in reason, and expressed by worde. . . . But now, as the understanding of the formall cause causeth surest knowledge, so hardly can wee understand what the formall cause is . . . So that for the most part things bee not knowne . . . (*Ibid.*, fol. 24 r, 22 v)

The form is at the root of both identity and change.

The alteration of the forme chaungeth the thing formed, and maketh it another thing: but heere wee must distinguish betweene the universall chaunging of the forme, and the particuler alteration thereof. For if a house bee utterly defaced, though it bee reedified of the selfe same timber and stone, yet it is not the same house, but if it bee but a little decayed and so repayred in part, it remayneth the same house still, though in continuance of time, every stick and stone bee altered by often repayring of it. (*Ibid.*, fol. 24 ᵛ)

The final cause is the purpose of the agent which leads him to undertake the enterprise, that is, to produce the effect. Hence it is first in intention, but last in realization.

For first, the finall cause, the end, purpose, intent, drift, marke, or scope, as it were of the whole action, is propounded to the efficient, and so urgeth and moveth him to prepare the matter, and apply the forme thereunto for the full accomplishing of the enterprise: which beeing once performed, the efficient cause now ceaseth, as having obteined that it sought for. As for example, I purpose to sweate, and therefore I daunse: wee neede not take this woord, purpose or deliberation so strictly, as to apply it onely to reasonable creatures, but generally say, that every thing woorketh for some end and purpose whether it bee by nature's instinct, or voluntary consultation. . . . the cause finall is the purpose of God in naturall thinges, and the intent of the artificer in things that bee artificiall. (*Ibid.*, fol. 25 ʳ⁻ᵛ)

The first of the following illustrations of final cause has its end in the nature of the thing considered, the second in the purpose of the agent.

Palinode in the fift *Aegloge*,
            Good is not good, but if it bee spend:
            God giveth good for none other end.
Thenot in the second *Aegloge*.
            It chaunced after upon a day
            Th'usbandman self to come that way.
            Of custome for to survey his ground,
            And his trees of state in compasse round.
The ende of goodes is to be spent: the ende of the husbandmans going abroad, was to view his ground. (*Ibid.*, fol. 23 ʳ)

The effect is that which is produced by the operation of all the causes.

Howsoever any thing bee altered, mooved, or changed, the motion, and the thing mooved, or chaunged, belong to this place, and are called effects, or thinges caused: as also sayinges and writinges, thoughtes and all cogitations, although neither uttered nor accomplished. . . . [Thus] were *Lentulus*, *Cethegus* and other complices of *Catyline* brought to confusion. . . .
Matter of praysing and dispraysing commonly is fet from this place. . . .

Wee commend men . . . especially by reason of their effectes, as for that they
did this or this &c . . .

In July, *Thomalin* prayseth Christ the great sheepheard, by his effectes.

> O blessed sheepe, O sheepheard great,
> that bought his flocke so deare,
> And them did save with bloudy sweat
> from Wolves that would them teare.
>
> (*Ibid.*, fol. 29 ^{r-v}, 31 ^r)

The Ramists carefully distinguish between metonymy of the cause and
of the effect, as well as between that of the subject and of the adjunct, discussed above. They subdivide metonymy of the cause into that of the efficient cause and of the material cause. Fenner accordingly explains that
the change of name, called metonymy, may be put for the name of either
the maker, the matter, or the thing made.

Of the maker, when the finder out, or the author of the thing, or the instrument
whereby the thing is done, is put for the thing made. So *Moses is put for his
writinges.* . . . So *faith the cause is put for religious serving for God, the thing
caused. Rom.* 1. So *the tounge the instrument of speeche, is put for speech it
selfe. Rule thy tongue. James* 3.

Of the matter: *Thou art dust, and to dust shalt thou returne, that is, one
made of dust.*

Now on the other side, when the thing caused or the effect is put for any of
these causes. So *the Gospel of God is called the power of God to salvation,* that
is, the instrument of the power of God. So *Love is saide to be bountifull, because
it causeth one to bee bountifull.* (*Sig.* D 1 ^r)

Metalepsis is a figure which signifies a present effect by a remote cause,

as *Medea* cursing hir first acquaintance with prince *Jason,* who had very un-
kindly forsaken her, said:

> *Woe worth the mountaine that the maste bare*
> *Which was the first causer of all my care.*

Where she might aswell have said, woe worth . . . the time that *Jason*
arrived with his ship at my fathers cittie in *Colchos,* when he tooke me away
with him, & not so farre off as to curse the mountaine that bare the pinetree,
that made the mast, that bare the sailes, that the ship sailed with, which caried
her away. (Puttenham, p. 183)

Cause and effect are related productively, antecedent and consequent
temporally. The conditional or hypothetical proposition states the relation of antecedent and consequent.

If you marry my Daughter I make you myne heire: . . . if you will have warre, looke for cost, trouble, and daunger, for these are incident, and cleave to every person, that will live in warres. (Lever, pp. 69, 192)

Fenner explains important points regarding a hypothetical proposition, or axiom, as the Ramists call it—how it is contradicted and by what principles it is judged true or false or doubtful. The Ramists call a proposition an axiom.

If you were the children of Abraham you would do the workes of Abraham. Whose contradiction is, If the first be, yet the seconde doth not followe. So that when we judge this axiome to bee true, wee must judge the partes to be truly and necessarilye knit together. Whiche may be though the partes be both false: as in this example. The Jewes neither were Abrahams children, neither did the workes of Abraham. This axiome is doubtfull, when the parts and the folowing are doubtfull: As Paule in the shippe: *If you obey my counsell, you shall not perishe* . . . (Sig. C 3 ᵛ)

Fraunce states more forcefully than Fenner that when we judge a conditional proposition to be absolutely true,

wee judge it also to bee necessary. Albeit the necessitie ariseth onely of, or dependeth upon the necessary coupling together of the parts: which may bee when as, notwithstanding, both the parts . . . are false . . . The judgement . . . is certeine knowledge, when the connexion of the parts is necessary, but if the parts be variable, and the connexion onely probable, then our judgement thereof is onely an opinion. (*LL,* fol. 94 ʳ)

Necessity and contingency (which includes the doubtful and the probable) are important logical concepts that have a bearing not only on conditional propositions but on all, for logicians frequently call the subject of any proposition the antecedent, and the predicate, the consequent. If the predicate is the definition of the subject, or a part of the definition, namely, genus or difference, or if it is a property, that is, an invariable characteristic of that subject only, it is necessarily affirmed of the subject. Any other predicate affirmed of a subject is affirmed contingently, as when one says, The servant is crafty. For, as Wilson remarks, "a servaunt maie be, and yet not craftie. Again one maie be craftie, and yet not a servaunt" (*RR,* fol. 48 ʳ), thereby clearly explaining contingency, which he lists among his twenty-four places of logical invention.

Fraunce tells an amusing incident illustrating the status of the contingent in law.

Concerning casuall homicide, I remember an odde historie of a certaine man who falling from the top of a house, lighted on an other mans necke, and crushing him to death, preserved himselfe. The sonne of the dead man, procuring the revenge of his fathers death, caused him that fell to bee had before the Judge: Where hee no lesse pretily then reasonably, offered him this faire play: gett thee up, quoth he, to the top of the same house: I will stand where thy father did: and if by falling upon mee thou bruse me to death, and save thy selfe, I promise thee, my sonne shal never seeke to revenge my death. (*LL*, fol. 20 ʳ)

One figure, antisagoge, depends on the relation of antecedent and consequent.

The Orator joyneth to a precept, of virtue, a promise of reward, and to the contempt of a precept, he denounceth a punishment, whereof this example of *Moses* may sufficiently shew the forme, where he saith: If thou shalt obey the voyce of the Lord thy God, and observe and do all his commandements, which I command thee this day, then the Lord thy God wil set thee on hye above all the nations of the earth. And all these blessings shall come upon thee, &c. But if thou wilt not obey . . . then all these curses shal come upon thee, &c. Deut. 28.1, 2; 15, 16. (Peacham, p. 93)

9. Notation and Conjugates

The two topics notation and conjugates are concerned with words as words in relation to realities and to each other.

Words related to each other by derivation from the same root but differing in termination, as *justice, just, justly,* are called conjugates. Plato's dialogues often show Socrates skillfully arguing from conjugates. As Fraunce remarks, Aristotle highly commends this place as a source of argument in his *Topics*. In his *Rhetoric* he clearly illustrates how argument from conjugates clarifies meanings.

'Just' does not always mean 'beneficial,' or 'justly' would always mean 'beneficially,' whereas it is *not* desirable to be justly put to death. (2.23.1397 ᵃ 20)

Thomas Wilson explains:

I may reason from this place bothe affirmatively, and negatively. If one be not wise, he hath no wisedome, if one be wise, he hath wisedome . . . We may learne by this place, to knowe, what thinges are, being considered in other. . . . If I would knowe what wisedome is, best it were for me to marke their doinges, that are wise men. (*RR*, fol. 41 ʳ)

Despite Aristotle's authority and also that of Renaissance logicians, including Ramus, Fraunce does not admit conjugates among the topics of logic, but considers them to be in the province of grammar and rhetoric.

As for Conjugates, I see in them no new different force of arguing, as hee is just, for hee dealeth justly; heere is nothing in effect, but the cause and the effect. For as for the derivation of this woord Juste, from Justice, it seemeth altogether grammaticall: and whereas they both doo fitly allude in the ende and falling, thus, Justice, Just, Justly, that commeth from a Rhetoricall figure, called *Polyptoton*, which concerneth the elegancie that is in the divers fallinges and terminations of woords. (*LL*, fol. 50 ʳ)

Peacham recognizes the logical character of polyptoton, which he calls paregmenon, as is apparent in his comment on the use of the figure.

I will destroy the wisedome of the wise. Esay. . . . The use . . . is twofold, to delight the eare by the derived sound, and to move the mind with a consider- ation of the nigh affinitie and concord of the matter. (p. 55)

When a word is regarded as a word, it is called a notation, that is, a mark representing a sound. As such it may shed light on the thing it names through its etymology, or it may occasion ambiguity or obscurity. Fraunce quotes Aristotle's illustration of an argument from the name.

Dracoes lawes were a Dragons lawes, for their crueltie. (*LL*, fol. 51 ᵛ)

He gives as an example of false etymology a sixteenth-century favorite.

A woman is a woe man, because shee woorketh a man woe. (56 ᵛ)

To distinguish the various meanings of words was regarded by Renais- sance logicians as one of the kinds of division. Aristotle also had set high value on the ability to do this.

The means whereby we are to become well supplied with reasonings are four: (1) the securing of propositions; (2) the power to distinguish in how many senses a particular expression is used; (3) the discovery of the differences of things; (4) the investigation of likeness. (*Topics*, 1.13, 105 ᵃ 21)

From the fact that a word or notation may have a number of different meanings arises ambiguity, sometimes inadvertent, sometimes deliberate, for, says Fraunce,

Quips, taunts, jests, and conceipts are often fet hence. All *Platoes* Cratilus is spent in the interpretation of woords after this manner. (*LL*, fol. 51 ᵛ)

Fraunce, almost alone, denies notation a place among the topics of logic.

So in Notation, the interpretation of the name, seemeth rather the dutie of a dictionary, then of any Logicall institution . . . it seemeth also a Rhetoricall agnomination. (*LL*, fol. 50 ᵛ)

Agnomination, or paronomasia, is a form of pun. The word pun, according to the *Oxford English Dictionary*, appeared first about 1660.[7] What we call puns rhetoricians of the Renaissance subdivided into a number of figures which from ancient times were regarded as adornments. In the opinion of Aristotle,

The liveliness of epigrammatic remarks is due to the meaning not being just what the words say. . . . Well constructed riddles are attractive for the same reason. . . . The effect is produced even by jokes depending upon changes of the letters in a word; this too is a surprise . . . something that gives a twist to the word used. . . . Here again is the use of one word in different senses [as in] the much praised verse of Anaxandrides:

> Death is most fit before you do
> Deeds that would make death fit for you.

This amounts to saying . . . 'it is a fit thing to die when death is not fit for you,' i.e. when death is not the fit return for what you are doing . . . . but the more briefly and antithetically such sayings can be expressed, the more taking they are, for antithesis impresses the new idea more firmly and brevity more quickly. They should always have either some personal application or some merit of expression, if they are to be true without being commonplace— two requirements not always satisfied simultaneously. (*Rhetoric*, 3.11.1412 [a] 21–1412 [b] 26)

Aristotle refers here to paronomasia and antanaclasis, and further cites examples from Isocrates and other Greek writers. Aeschylus, Euripides, and Aristophanes used the figures of ambiguity. Cicero delighted in them, and his discussion in *De oratore* of their use in moving laughter was taken over by Castiglione in *Il libro del cortegiano* and thence by Wilson in *The Arte of Rhetorique*.

Antanaclasis depends for its effect on the two or more meanings attached to the same repeated word.

Care for those things which may discharge you from all care. . . . In thy youth learne some craft, that in thy age thou mayst get thy living without craft.

This figure as it uniteth two words of one sounde, so it distinguisheth them asunder by the diversitie of their sense, whereby it moveth many times a most pleasant kind of civile mirth . . . (Peacham, p. 56)

Peacham directs attention to two characteristics of this figure which caused it to be valued as one capable of dignity: its use in serious thought and its

---

[7] An earlier instance is noted in John Taylor's "Mercurius Aquaticus," 1643. See *Notes and Queries*, 11 Series, No. 1, p. 425, May 28, 1910.

nature as a form of logical distinction. Antanaclasis can also occasion the fallacy of equivocation.

Syllepsis of the sense, as distinguished from the syllepsis which lacks grammatical congruence in one member, is more subtle than antanaclasis, for in this figure one word serves a double sense but is expressed only once. For instance, in the following illustration concerning a young man who slew the murderer of his father and ravisher of his mother, the verb *requite* means both *to revenge* and *to satisfy*.

> *Thus valiantly and with a manly minde*
> *And by one feate of everlasting fame,*
> *This lustie lad fully requited kinde,*
> *His fathers death, and eke his mothers shame.*
> (Puttenham, p. 166)

Paronomasia, or agnomination, depends for its effect on the different meanings attached to words nearly alike. Wilson cites an interesting illustration of its use by William Somer, King Henry VIII's fool, who,

seeing much adoe for accomptes making, and that the Kinges Majestie . . . wanted money, such as was due unto him: and please your grace (quoth he) you have so many Frauditors, so many Conveighers, and so many Deceivers to get up your money, that they get all to themselves. . . . He should have saide Auditours, Surveighours, and Receivers. (*AR*, p. 201)

Asteismus, like syllepsis, is a subtle figure. It is more lively and witty than antanaclasis or paronomasia, for it is ·a figure of reply, returning a facetious or mocking answer,

when a saying is captiously taken, and turned to another sense, contrary or much differing from the meaning of the speaker, as in this example: To one demanding of *Diogenes* what he would take for a knocke upon his pate, he made this answer, that he would take an helmet. (Peacham, p. 34)

Cato said to one that had geven him a good knock on the head with a long piece of timber he bare on his shoulder, and then bad him beware: what (quoth *Cato*) wilt thou strike me againe? (Puttenham, p. 190)

Distinction is a figure whereby the ambiguity of words is taken away,

as being charged that yow have brought very light reasons, yow may answeare, if by light, yow meane cleare I am glad yow doe see them, if by light yow meane of noe weight, I am sorry yow doe not feele them. (Hoskyns, p. 156)

The figures of deliberate obscurity include enigma, noema, and schematismus. An enigma is a riddle, a covert and dark speech more obscure than an allegory. Peacham cites as examples the dreams of Pharaoh's butler and baker which were explained by Joseph. In noema the obscurity of the sense lies, not in a single word, but in an entire speech very subtle and dark,

as he that said by himselfe and his wife, I thanke God in fortie winters that we have lived together, never any of our neighbours set us at one, meaning that they never fell out in all that space, which had bene the directer speech and more apert. (Puttenham, p. 230)

The figure schematismus is used

when the Orator propoundeth his meaning by a circuite of speech, wherein he would have that understoode by a certaine suspicion which he doth not speake, and that for 3. special causes. 1. For safetie sake: As when it is dangerous to speake directly and openly. 2. For modestie and good manners sake: As when it is undecent to be spoken plainly. 3. For delectation sake and grace of the hearer, as when it may bring greater delight under the figurative shadow, then by the plaine report and open shew.

1. If some good man for the love of justice . . . should take upon him to reprehend a tirant . . . he should venture upon a verie dangerous enterprise . . . Except the manner and forme of his handling the cause be . . . circumspectly delivered. . . . The Orators speech may be shadowed two manner of waies, either by reproving another person, in whom the same evils are . . . or by commending such persons in whom the contraries are . . . by . . . reprehension of that crueltie and tirannie in *Phalaris*, he may make a most bright and resplendent glasse wherein *Dionysius* [the King of *Sicilia*,] must needes behold himselfe and his deformed tirannie. (Peacham, p. 196)

10. Genesis or Composition

Fraunce explains that the topics of invention provide writer and speaker with plentiful matter for composition, and reader or listener with a technique of analysis for the adequate understanding of what someone else has composed.

If we shall . . . draw any one woord through these generall places of invention, it will breede a great plentie and varietie of new argumentes, while wee marke what be the causes, effects, parts, whole, generall, speciall, subjectes, adjunctes thereof, and so foorth in all the rest: and this either in making and enditing our selves, or els in resolving, and as it were dismembring that which others have doone. (*LL*, fol. 81 ᵛ)

An example of genesis or composition is the following from Wilson, who derives from this process a series of notes rather than a finished composition on the chosen subject. Since a few of his names for the topics are strange, as *woordes yoked* for *conjugates,* the more familiar names used by other logicians have been substituted.

And to make this thing more plaine, I will goe through the places, with one certaine worde, and looke what helpe I shall finde there, for knowledge of the same. The worde shall bee (a Kyng) or (a Magistrate.)

The definition.

The definition of a Magistrate. Every King, or Magistrate, is the minister of God, for a good ende, to the punishing of naughtie persons, and the comforting of godly men.

The genus.

The Minister of God.

The Species.

Either a Tyraunt or a godly King, the one ruleth according to his lust, the other according to right and Justice.

Conjugates.

The Officer, the Office, to beare an Office, if the Office can not be spared, the Officer cannot be spared.

Adjuncts necessary.

Wisedome, earnest labour, cunnyng in sciences, skilfull both of warre and peace, these al must needes be in every Magistrate.

Adjuncts contingent.

To be liberall, to be frugall, to be of a temperate life, al these happen to be in good Magistrates.

Deedes necessary.

To defende Religion, to enact godly Lawes, to punish offenders, to defend the oppressed: all these are necessarie in a King, and are never found in a Tyraunt.

Subjects.

Moses, David, Salomon, Ezechias, Josias, Charles the Emperour, Edward the sixt of the name King of England.

The efficient cause remote.

God himselfe, or els the ordinaunce of God.

The efficient cause proximate.

Unquiet subjects, rebelles, disobedient people, are the cause why Magistrates are ordeined, that the rather they may bee ruled, and kept in good order.

The final cause of a Magistrate.

This ende he must needes observe, that alwaies the people live in quietnesse, & in honest conversation passe their whole life.

Effects.

Peace is made, the Realme enriched, all thynges plenteous, but where a Tyraunt ruleth, all thinges are contrary.

Testimony.

The xiii to the Romaines, let every soule be subject to the powers. 1 Peter. ii. Be subject to the King.

Adjuncts contingent.

The Scepter is a token of Justice, even as a Sworde is a signe of revengement, or wrathe, paying of Subsidies, Taxes, Tributes, Rent, or any suche like, Yeomen of the Garde, and al other waiters, Soldiours in warre, the obedience of the subjects, the honour given unto him, triumphes made, running at the Tilt, fighting at the Barriers, fighting at the Tourney. All these are *contingentia* to a King, that is, although these thinges bee not in a Common wealth, yet may there be a King, yea, and although there be no king in some Common weale, yet these thinges may be every ech one of them, as it was in *Athens,* where the people had the rule of the Common weale, and al was referred to their judgement.

Similitudes.

That which the Sheepeheard is to the Sheepe, the same is the Magistrate to his Subjects. That which the master of the Shippe, is to the Shippe, or the master of an household, to his house, or the head to the whole body; the same is the Magistrate to his Subjects.

Comparison.

Servantes must bee obedient, and subject to their Masters with all reverence, as we read in the Scripture: how much more then should the subjects be obedient to their king and soveraigne Lord, which by the ordinaunce of God, is appointed to rule, and to have governaunce over them. (fol. 54 ᵛ–55 ᵛ)

As Wilson remarks, he does not search all the places in this example, nor is it necessary to do so in every instance. One ought, however, to search most of them and select the arguments best suited to the purpose. Wilson stresses the fact that the value of this procedure is very great, for

the better able wee shalbe, to confirme our owne cause, and to avoyde all objections, where we knowe surely by this art, whereunto we may leane. For although other shall impeach our doinges, and wrest our wordes, yet we shall be able evermore to keepe our owne, when wee plainely perceive, whereof our argument hath his ground. Many speake wisely, whiche never read *Logike,* but to speake wisely with a judgement, and to know the very fountaine of thinges: that can none doe, except they have some skill in this art. . . .

Therefore, what diversitie there is betwixt a blind man, and him that seeth, the same difference is betwixt a wiseman unlearned, and a wiseman learned. (*RR,* fol. 54 ᵛ–56 ʳ)

11. Analysis or Reading

Fraunce presents an example of analysis or reading which is based on logic.

I have, for examples sake, put downe a Logicall *Analysis* of the second *Aegloge* in *Virgill* . . . I have attempted the interpreting of the same by a poeticall *Paraphrasis*, for the contentation of such as understand no Latine . . . (*LL*, fol. 120 ᵣ)

Fraunce's translation, which follows, besides supplying the matter for analysis, is in itself interesting as an illustration of the much discussed quantitative English hexameters, done by one associated with Sidney and Spenser.

Alexis 2. Aegloga Virgilii.

The same in English Hexameters,
verse for verse.

Seelly shepheard *Corydon* lov'd hartily faire lad *Alexis*,
His maisters dearling, but saw no matter of hoping.
Only amid the forest thick set with broad-shadoe beachtrees
daily resort did he make: thus alone to the woods, to the mountains
With broken speeches, fond thoughts most vainly revealing.
    O hardharted *Alexis:* I see my verse to be scorned,
My selfe not pitied, my death by thee lastly procured.
Now do the beasts even seeke for cooling shade to refresh them,
Grene lyzards now too in bushes thorny be lurking,
And for faint reapers by the suns rage, *Thestylis* hastning,
Strong-smelling wilde thime, and garlyke beates in a mortar.
But whilst I trace thee, with sun beams all to bescorched,
Groves by the hoarschirping grashoppers yeeld a resounding.
    Wast not far better t'have borne with surly *Menalcas*,
And sore displeased, disdainfull, prowd *Amaryllis*,
Although thou white were, although but swarty *Menalcas?*
    O thou faire white boy, trust not too much to thy whitnes:
Faire white flowers fall downe, black fruits are only reserved.
Thou carst not for mee, my state thou knowst not, *Alexis:*
What flocks of white sheepe I do keepe, of milke what abundance.
On *Sicil* high mountains my lambs feed more then a thousand:
New mylke in summer, new mylke in winter I want not.
My song's like *Thebane Amphions* song, when he called
His wandring bullocks, on Greekish mount *Aracynthus.*
Neyther am I so fowle: I saw my selfe by the seashore,
When seas al calme were: I doubt not, but by thy censure,
Daphnis I shall surpasse, unles my face do deceave mee.
    O, let this be thy will, to frequent my rustical harbors,
And simple cotages, and sticke in forkes to uphold them,
And drive on forward our flocke of kids to the mallowes:

Wee wil amid the forest contend *Pans* song to resemble:
Pan was first that quils with waxe ty'de joyntly together.
Pan is good to the sheepe, and *Pan* is good to the sheepsman.
Neither think it a shame to thy self t'have plaid on a cornpipe:
For, that he might do the same with skil, what did not *Amyntas?*
Damaetas long since did give me a pipe for a token,
Compact of seven reedes, all placed in order unaequall:
And thus sayd, when he dy'de: One used it onely beefore thee.
Thus sayd *Damaetas,* this greeved foolish *Amyntas.*
Also two pretty kids doe I keepe, late found in a valley
Dangerus: & their skins with mylke white spots be bedecked,
Of dams milke not a drop they leave; & for thee I keepe them.
Thestylis of long time hath these kids of me desired;
And they shalbe her own, for that thou skornst what I give thee.
Come neare, o faire boy, see the nymphs bring here to the lillies
With fullstuft baskets: faire *Nais* now to thy comfort
White violets gathering, and poppies daintily topping,
Daffadil ads to the same, & leaves late pluckt fro the sweete Dill.
Then mingling Casia with divers savory sweet flowrs,
With yelowish Marygold, she the tender Crowtoe bedecketh.
   Ile plucke hoare quinces, with soft downe all to besmeared,
And Chessnuts which were loved of my sweet *Amaryllis.*
Add wil I wheateplumbs too: for this fruit will be regarded,
And you laurell leaves wil I plucke, and thee, pretty myrtle
Next to the laurell leaves: for so plast yeeld ye the sweet sent.
   Th'art but a foole *Corydon,* for first gifts moove not *Alexis,*
Then, though thou give much, yet much more give wil *Iolas.*
But what alas did I mean, poore foole? I do let go the southwind
Into the flowrs, & boares send forward into the cleare springs.
Whom flyest thou mad man? Many gods have also resorted,
And *Paris* of olde *Troy,* to the woods. Let towers by *Minerva*
Built, by *Minerva* be kept; and woods of us onely regarded.
Grim Lionesse runneth to the wolfe, & wolfe to the yong gote,
And wanton yong gote to the flowring tetrisol hastneth,
And *Corydon* to *Alexis:* a selfe joy draweth on each man.
But see the plow come home hangd fast by the yoke, to the bullocks,
And shadoe by *Phoebus* declining double appeareth:
Yet do I burne with love: for what meane can be to loving?
Ah *Corydon, Corydon,* what mad rage hath thee bewitched?
Thy vin's scarse halfe cut, pestred with leaves of her elme tree:
Leave this churlish boy, and bend thy selfe to thy busnes,
With twigs and bulrush some needefull thing be a making:

Thou shalt find others though th'art disdaind of *Alexis*.

(fol. 121 ᵛ–122 ᵛ)

Fraunce borrows the following analysis of this eclogue from Freigius, a disciple of Ramus.[8]

There bee, saith *Freigius* 2. partes of the Aeglogue.

I. The propounding of the argument, which is of the incontinency of a lover lamenting his love in solitary places.

II. The complaint and lamentation of *Corydon* the lover, speaking

    A. To his love, and that by

        1. Accusing his crueltie, which is argued

            a. By comparison of the unlikes, the proposition consisteth of three unlikes, the beastes, Lysardes, and reapers seeke shade: the reddition is, but yet I burne with love.

            b. By the lesse *Amaryllis* and *Menalcas* are too cruell, but thou more cruel then they.

            c. By the cause of his pride, whiche was his beautie, and that is extenuated by a simily. As white primprint fales, but blacke Violets bee gathered, so beautie decayes, and blacknes remaines.

        2. Enticing him to come to his house to sing, to drive the kids to the Mallowes, &c. and that by praysing of himselfe by his adjunctes. *Corydons* adjuncts be these: he is

            a. Rich, and his riches be proved by specials

                (1) his lambs

                (2) his mylke

            b. Skilfull in singing, and this is prooved

                (1) By a comparison of the equall, in that hee is equall to *Amphion:*

                (2) And heere an objection is prevented by a comparison also of the equall: neither thinke it a shame to play on a pype, for *Amyntas* thought well of it.

                (3) Then the prayse of his singing is continued by his pype, and his pype by the autor that gave it, which was *Damaetas*, and another that envyed it, to wit *Amyntas*.

            c. Faire & comly: it is proved by

                (1) The adjunct of his image in the water

                (2) Comparison of the equall, as was Daphnis

            d. Franke and free, which is proved by his sundry giftes.

                (1) His Kydds, commended by their adjunctes, in that they were white spotted, well sucking, and desired of *Thestylis*.

[8] The analysis occupies folios 123 ʳ–124 ʳ of *The Lawiers Logike*. The tabular form has been changed to outline form, letters and numbers have been added, and slight changes in capitalization made to indicate co-ordination and subordination.

          (2)   His basket of sweete flowers gathered by the Nymphes, they be hearbs and also flowers, as, Lillyes, Violets, Poppy, Dylle, Daffadil, Casia, Marigold, Crowtoe.

          (3)   His diverse kindes of

               (a)   Fruits as Quinces, Chestnuts, wheatplums.

               (b)   Boughs as bee The Lawrell, The Myrtle.

   B. To himselfe, by resisting himselfe, as it were, and here is conteyned both a

       1. Doble correction or calling backe of himselfe, the first is

         a. Both of the

          (1)   Adjunct, pride, and contempt of hys gifts and here is

               (a)   A double exclamation: and here

                    i. Hee noteth *Alexis* his pride by two similies, the south winde, and the boare.

                    ii. he entreateth againe, by the equals, as *Paris,* and the gods &c.

               (b)   A permission by the unlike. Let *Pallace* keep her Pallaces, and wee the woodes which is our delight. The reddition is made playne by comparison of lykes: where also the generall is concluded by the specialles in a Clymax of three degrees, Grimme Lyonesse to the Wolfe &c.

          (2)   More, or greater, for *Iolas* gave mor largely then hee.

         b. Of the adjunctes both of

          (1)   The tyme, where there is a Periphrasis of night, and an argument of the divers, albeit the heate of the sunne is mitigated by the comming of the night, yet I burne still with love: the reason followeth of the adjunct of love: for love hath no meane.

          (2)   His businesse neglected, where is a double negligence: of

               (a)   His vine halfe cut   ⎫

                                     ⎬ for both be naught.

               (b)   His elme full of boughes ⎭

       2. Remedy of love by contraries which be:

         a. Businesse in making some needefull thinge of twigs and bulrush.

         b. And hope of some other lover, if *Alexis* should still thus disdaine him.

The figurists would have analyzed this poem with similar thoroughness, noting precisely the same points as Fraunce but in terms of the figures and their nomenclature.

The complete Ramist technique of reading, which combines logic and rhetoric, is exemplified in the analysis of Saint Paul's Epistle to Philemon, with which Dudley Fenner concludes his work on *The Artes of Logike and Rhetorike.*[9] In this analysis Fenner appears in a threefold role: as a logician exemplifying his precepts; as a rhetorician illustrating the figures; as a Puritan minister of the Gospel elucidating Holy Scripture by the enthusiastic application of the arts of reading.

The Epistle to Philemon

The entrance of this Epistle hath two partes,
{ The inscription or title.
{ Prayers.

The inscription setteth downe
{ The persons which doe write.
{ The persons to whom it is written.

The first person which doth write is *Paule* the principal writer, who is described by the adjoint *captive:* which adjoint is declared by the cause *Christ,* that is, by a change of name of the cause for the effect, *Christ leading him to prison by his spirit.* And the second person which doth write is also declared by his proper name, *Timothie:* and an adjoynt of relation, *a brother,* that is by a Metaphor *one of the same Christian religion.*

The persons to whom he writeth, are
first { The husband.
       { The wife.
Seconde { The Minister.
        { The Church.

The *man* is described by his proper name, *Philemon:* by his adjoint *beloved,* & by his effect, *worker togither with us.*

The *woman* is also described by her proper name, *Appia,* & her adjoint, *beloved.*

The *Minister* is also described by his proper name, *Archippus:* and his adjoint, *a fellow souldier:* that is, by a Metaphor, *a felow Minister.*

The *Church* is declared by the subject, which is at *thy house.*

The prayers are { The salutation
                 { Thankesgiving.

[9] This work, published in Middelburg in 1584, is attributed to Fenner, although his name does not appear in it. There were at least three editions, two in 1584 and another in 1588. The precepts are avowedly translated from sources unnamed, but they are clearly Ramus and Talaeus, at least ultimately. The illustrations from the Bible are probably Fenner's own selections, unless they owe something to Mulhemius, who, according to Miller (*The New England Mind,* p. 497), published at Frankfort, also in 1584, a Ramist logic with the topics and figures illustrated from the Bible. Miller does not mention Fenner in his brief survey of the literature of the Ramist logic in Europe, including England.

The terminology of Fenner requires a brief explanation: he calls a proposition an axiom; the major premise, the proposition; the minor premise, the assumption. Change of name is metonymy. Fenner is careful to note from which topic the matter for each syllogism is derived.

The *salutation* is set downe, first by the matter of it, which hee wisheth to them. Whereof the parts are *grace*, that is, *ful favour of God*, *peace*, that is by a Sinechdoche of the special for the general, *al prosperity both of soule and body*. Secondly, by the forme, *from God the father, and from Christ*. All whiche is disposed in a coupled axiome.

The *Thankesgiving* is described, first by the subject, *my God:* that is, *whom only I doe serve and hang upon*. Secondly by the adjoint, *alwaies making mention of you in my prayers*. Thirdly by the efficient cause, *hearing of your love and faith*. Both which are declared by their proper subjectes, *whiche you have towardes our Lorde Jesus Christ, and love towardes al Saintes*. And all these are disposed in a coupled axiome.

In the 6. ver. the adjoint *of thanksgiving, his mention making of them in his prayer*, is set forth by the matter, which he seeketh for in *praier, the communication of faith*, that is, which proceedeth from faith may be effectual, which is declared by the cause, *by the acknoweledging of al good: which good* is set forth by the subject *which is in you*, and by the cause, *by Christ Jesus*.

The principal matter of this Epistle, which is to intreat for, *Onesimus* is set downe in a simple axiome of the cause & the effect in the 10. ver. *I Paul pray thee for Onesimus*, where the antecedent *Paule*, is declared by the adjoint, *being such a one*, which is declared by the special, *even Paule an old man*, and increased by the greater, and made lightsome by the time, *yea now a bondman of Christ*. The first part of the consequent *pray thee*, is declared by a divers reason, *Although I have liberty to commaund thee, yet I pray thee:* where the first divers, *liberty of commaunding*, is declared by the adjoynt *great:* by the forme, *in Christ*, by the subject, *that which is thy duetie*. The second divers is declared by the moving cause *for loves sake:* and by a comparison of the greater, *rather I pray thee*. The laste part of the consequent, *Onesimus* is described: First by the relation of the cause to the effect, *my sonne*, that is, by a metaphor *one brought to the faith by my ministery:* which is declared by the formal cause, *Whome I begotte:* that is by a Sinecdoche of the part for the whole, and a metaphor *whom God by me did effectually call*, which is declared by the subject of the place, *in my bandes:* that is, by a Sinecdoche of the special for the general, *in prison*. Where in the beginning of the 9. *and* 10. verses, there is a repetition of the same sound in the beginning. *I pray thee, I pray thee*. Secondly, *Onesimus* is described by the adjoint, *unprofitable to thee:* which is made lightsome by the time *once*, and declared by the contrary, *but profitable:* which is declared by the adjoynt of time *now:* & enlarged by a comparison of the greater, *to me also*, and it is garnished by a redoubling of the same sound or Anadiplosis, *thee, me, and thee:* and by a little changing of the name called Paranomasia, *profitable, unprofitable*. This axiome *I pray thee*, beyng thus worthely declared, is confirmed in the 7. verse by the making cauſe, *bicause*

I have great joy and comfort in thy love, and is disposed in a connexive sillogisme of the first kind.

If I have great joy and comfort in thy love: then I may pray thee for
Onesimus:
But I have great joy and comfort in thy love,
Therefore I may pray thee for Onesimus.

The proposition is wanting, the assumption is in the 7. verse, & it is confirmed
by the effect of that love, wherein it doeth rejoyce, *because the bowels of the*
Saints have been refreshed by thee: And it is concluded in a lesse playne Syllogisme of the second kynd, affirmative speciall.

That love that doth refresh the bowels of the Saints, is to be rejoyced in:
But this love doth refresh the bowels of the Saintes.
Therfore this love is to be rejoyced in.

The bowels, that is by an excessive metaphor, *the inward affections of the*
Saintes. Here is set down the special of the former request, in a simple axiome
of the cause and the effect *receive thou him,* where the last parte of the conse-
quente *him,* is declared by the adjoynt, *my bowels,* that is, first by a Metaphor,
my love that is by a chaunge of name of the cause for the effect, *my beloved.*
Thys is confirmed by the cause which should move him, and it is concluded in
a connexive Sillogisme of the first kind.

If I have sent him for that purpose, receive him:
But I have sent him for that purpose.
Therefore receive him.

This is a preventing of an objection: The objection is wanting, and may be
supplied: *If he were so profitable, why diddest thou not keepe him.* The subjection or answere is from the divers reason, *Although I desired to keepe him,*
yet I would not doe it without thy consent.

The first divers is declared by the moving cause, *That instead of thee he*
might minister unto me in the bandes of the Gospel, that is by a Sinecdoche, in
the *afflictions which the Gospel hath brought me.*

The second divers is also declared by the moving cause, *That thy benefits*
should not be by necessity: where *necessitie* is declared by the contrary, *but*
willingly or freely.

Here is another preventing of an objection, The objection is wanting, & is
thus to be supplied, *He was a run away:* The answeare is by the adjoynt of the
time, *He went away but for a little time:* which is increased by the moving
cause, *But that thou shouldest receive him for ever:* Which is enlarged by a
comparison of the lesse, *not so much as a servant, but as more than a servant:*
which is garnished by a redoubling or Anadiplosis.

The second part of the comparison, called reddition, is declared by the
speciall, *a beloved brother, more then a servant:* which is enlarged by the
greater, *especially to me:* which is amplified also by the greater, *much more*

to thee: whiche is declared by a distribution of the subject, wherein he was more bound unto *Philemon,* then to *Paule* himselfe, *both in the flesh, and in the Lord,* that is, *things appertayning unto this life, to the Lorde:* By a chaunge of name of the subject for the adjoynt.

Here is a new reason to prove that he should receive him, drawne from the working cause, in a connexive Sillogisme.

If we have fellowship togither in any common blessings, then receive him:
But we have felowship togither in common blessings,
Therefore receive him.

The proposition is the 17. verse, the assumption is wanting: the conclusion is made manifest by a comparison of the like, *receive him as me.*

Here is a preventing of an objection, the objection is wanting, and is thus to be supplied: *He hath hurt me, or done somewhat to me.* The answere is from the divers, *If he owe thee any thing, impute it to me:* which is increased by the greater, *I will pay it:* which is confirmed by a testimony, *I Paule have written it with mine owne hand.*

The last part of the 19. verse is a confyrmation of the second answere from a comparison of the more to the lesse, and is concluded in a connexive sillogisme of the first kind.

If thou doest owe me thy very selfe: then much more thou maiest forgive
 him this debt for my sake.
But thou owest me thy very selfe,
Therefore thou maiest forgive him this debt for my sake.

The proposition is wanting, the assumption is in the end of the 19. verse.

Here is another confirmation drawn from the effects, and is concluded in a connexive Sillogisme of the first kind.

If by this I shal obteine fruite of thee in the Lord, and if thou doest refresh
 my bowels in the Lord: then thou shouldest receive him:
But I shal obteine fruite, &c.
Therefore thou shouldest receive him.

The proposition is wanting, the assumption is in the 20. ver. & is garnished with a crying out of a wishing, *yea, my brother, I would I might obteine.*

Here is an answering of an objection, which might be made against the whole Epistle. The objection is wanting, & must be thus supplied: *why write you so earnestly?* The answere is from the cause, *The perswasion I had of thy readinesse to obey it caused me:* which is proved by a comparison of the lesse to the greater, in a connexive Sillogisme of the first kind.

If thou wouldest do more then this: then thou wouldest do this.
But thou wouldest doe more then this:
Therefore thou wouldest do this.

The proposition is wanting, the assumption is in the 21. ver. and is confirmed by a testimony of *Paule* his owne knowledge, *I know it.*

Here is set downne *a commandement to prepare him hostage*, whereunto is a briefe transition in this word, *Also*, it is confirmed by a reason drawn from the working cause, in a connexive sillogisme of the first kind.

If I hope to be given unto you by your prayers: then prepare hostage:
But I hope to be given unto you by your praiers,
Therefore prepare hostage.

The proposition is wanting, the assumption is in the 22. vers.

Certaine *salutations* are set downe in the 23.24. vers. in a gathering axiome of the cause and the effect.

Epaphras, Marcus, Aristarchus, Demas, and Luke salute thee: whereof the first is set forth by an adjoint, *my fellow prisoner:* which is declared by the cause, for *Christ Jesus,* their other by their adjoints, *my helpers.*

The salutation is set down in a simple axiome affirmative, of the subjecte and adjoynt, *grace be with your spirit,* that is by a Synecdoche, *with you:* The antecedent *grace* is declared by the efficient cause, *Christ,* and is garnished wyth a certaine crying out of wishing. *Amen.*

And this is the particular resolution of this Epistle.

If it makes us somewhat dizzy to follow Fenner through these analytical gymnastics, we must remember that such exercise, like parsing in grammar or noting rhetorical features such as loose and periodic sentences, parallel structure, balance and rhythm, establishes habits of subconscious observation and appreciation which contribute greatly to mature reading even when rapid and preoccupied with content. A habit of logical analysis subconsciously associates itself with one's reading even more deeply than a grammatical or rhetorical analysis, for it is more closely related to the thought itself.

There is ample evidence that boys in the Tudor grammar schools were systematically trained to note both the topics and the figures in their reading. For example, even in a work commonly used as early as the third form, attention was directed to the figures. In the epistle to his edition of *The Floures of Terence* (1533) Nicholas Udall announces:

Where any outstanding or elegant metaphor is used, I have indicated it. Where any figure occurs, I have noted it. Where any fable comes along I am not bored to narrate it rather at length. . . . If any proverb is interspersed, I have exposed it.[10]

[10] Quoted by T. W. Baldwin, *William Shakspere's Small Latine and Lesse Greeke,* I, 745.

CHAPTER VIII

LOGOS: ARGUMENTATION

ARGUMENTATION consists in the orderly disposition of the ideas which have been derived from invention or exposition. In explaining the relation of the two parts of logic Fraunce uses an analogy.

> As in Grammer, *Aetymologie* concerneth severall woords, and *Syntaxis* the due coherence of the same, so Exposition the first part of Logike, declareth the particular affection and nature of every severall argument, and Disposition the second part, by ordering and setling the same, causeth judgement and understanding. (*LL*, fol. 6 ʳ)

According to Ramist terminology, every proposition is an axiom, and every term an argument. The relation of terms in a proposition is axiomatical; that of propositions to one another is dianoetical. The simplest way to relate propositions is merely to join two or more of them. Drawing his illustrations from *The Shepheardes Calender* by Spenser, Fraunce states the principles governing the truth or falsity of such conjunction.

> Hereunto must be referred full comparisons and similitudes, wherein the conjunction is the very relation itselfe, as, *Colyn* in January.
> > And from mine eyes the drizling teares descend,
> > As on your boughs the ysicles depend.
>
> Heere the judgement is compound, as if hee had sayd, *the ysicles depend on your boughs, and the teares fall from myne eyes.*
> The true judgement of this copulative axiome dependeth on the truth of every part: for if all the partes bee true, it is then a true axiome: false, if any bee false. . . . The contradiction of these, are the denials to every part. . . . The negation in a copulative axiome is not the denying of the partes conjoyned; but the denying of the conjoyning of the partes. (*Ibid.*, fol. 93 ʳ)

Much more important than the mere conjunction of propositions is their coherence and consequence, true or apparent. Accordingly, first to be considered is valid syllogistic reasoning; next fallacious reasoning; and lastly disputation, which may employ either or both in the give and take of argument. The figures related to reasoning and disputation are treated in connection with the logical processes to which they correspond.

1. Syllogistic Reasoning

Fraunce makes clear how syllogistic reasoning derives its matter from the topics of invention.

The arguments in Invention must bee considered severally, singlely, and alone, then after to bee disposed and ordered by certeine precepts, thereby to judge of the truth or falsenesse of the same: as for example.

Paris. A good sheepheard.

These two singly put downe as two arguments, to wit, the subject and the adjunct, are afterwards disposed in an axiome, to judge of the truth thereof, as thus:

Paris is no good sheepheard.

But because this proposition is contingent and doubtfull . . . it is confirmed by another argument, that is to say, by an effect and working of *Paris*, I meane that which *Thomalin* putteth downe in July, in these words.

But nothing such thylk sheepheard was

whome *Ida* hill did beare:

That left his flocke to fetch a lasse,

whose love he bought too deare.

So then, heere bee three severall arguments, or two joyned in the axiome before, and the third following in these verses of *Thomalin;* which third they call, *Medium,* or third argument,

1 *Paris:* 2 A good sheepheard.

3 To leave his flocke to fetch a lasse.

Whereof it is concluded in this wise syllogistically, by disjoyning the two first arguments, the subject and adjunct, *Paris*, and, The good sheepheard.

Hee that leaveth his flocke to fetch a lasse, is no good sheepheard:

But *Paris* did leave his flocke to fetch a lasse,

Therefore *Paris* is no good sheepheard.

That which they call *Medium,* and third argument, is, as it were, an *Arbiter honorarius,* a determiner, a reconciler a daies man: which if it agree with both the other arguments, maketh the conclusion affirmative: but negative, if with one onely, as in the former example of *Paris,* the *Medium,* the arbiter, the determiner, is that effect of *Paris.* To leave his flocke to fetch a lasse: which because it is agreeable with the nature of *Paris,* but is flatly repugnant to the dutie of a good sheepheard, therefore is the conclusion negative, *Paris* is no good sheepeheard. (*LL,* fol. 6 ⱽ)

Fraunce discusses the value of syllogistic reasoning.

In this order, first of single arguments wee make axioms: which axioms, if of themselves they bee perceived and graunted, they bee straightway judged as true or false. . . . if these propositions bee doubtfull, then therof be made questions, which are to bee proved by third arguments, set from the affections of the other two which were joyned in the axiome, and lastly are to be concluded by syllogisme, the onely judge of all coherence and consequence . . . syllogismes, and onely syllogismes are the true and onely rules of consequence and inconsequence. . . . (fol. 7 ʳ⁻ᵛ) Syllogisme is onely proper and peculiar to man; whereof, no beast dooth in any respect participate. (fol. 112 ᵛ)

A syllogism is the relation of three terms in three propositions. The propositions are the major premise, called the proposition; the minor premise, called the assumption; and the conclusion, called the question, because it is that which is to be proved. The subject of the conclusion is the minor term, or antecedent; the predicate of the conclusion is the major term, or consequent. The middle term is that which appears in both premises but not in the conclusion. The relation of the minor term and the major term in the conclusion is determined in consequence of the relation of each of them to the middle term as stated in the premises; in other words, their relation to the middle term determines their relation to each other. It is therefore of the utmost importance that the middle term, the yardstick of reasoning, be understood in its full extension in at least one of the premises. Blundeville emphasizes this fundamental point when he explains the two principles regulative of all syllogistic reasoning, called *dictum de omni et nullo*. The first rule is concerned with affirming the predicate of all the subject (the middle term); the second with denying it of all.

The first rule is, whatsoever is truely affirmed of his naturall and proper Subject, is also affirmed of all those things which are contained under the said Subject: the second rule is thus, whatsoever is denied to bee spoken of any Subject, is also denied to bee spoken of every thing contained under the said Subject. The first rule confirmeth all Syllogismes affirmative, the second confirmeth all Syllogismes negative. (p. 135)

A number of the general and special rules of the syllogism are designed to safeguard the basic rule that the middle term be understood in its full extension in at least one of the premises. Thus it is a corollary that one premise must be a universal proposition, for from two particular premises no conclusion can be drawn. At least one premise must be affirmative, for from two negative premises no conclusion can be drawn, since, obviously, if neither term of the conclusion is related to the middle term in the premises, one cannot thereby determine their relation to each other. Another principle of syllogistic reasoning is that the conclusion follows the weaker part: if one premise is particular, or negative, or contingent, the conclusion can be no stronger than that premise. Moreover, no term may be used in the conclusion in a wider extension than in its own premise, for one cannot validly draw from premises more than is in them; the attempt to do so is an illicit process. There are special rules for each figure of the syllogism, having the same purpose as the general rules, to insure valid reasoning.

A syllogism may be either simple or compound. According to Renaissance logicians, the simple syllogism has three figures, determined by the position of the middle term in the premises. If the middle term is the subject of the major premise, and the predicate of the minor, the syllogism is in the first figure.

> That which bringeth to good, is good.
> Death bringeth to good,
> Therefore Death is good.

Thus Fraunce states in strict logical form the essential thought in the following stanza of Colin's song in "November."

> Unwise and wretched men to weete what's good or ill,
> Wee deeme of death as doome of ill desert:
> But knew wee fooles what it brings us untill,
> Dye would wee daily once it to expert.
>> Faire fields and pleasant layes there beene,
>> The fields ay fresh, the grasse ay greene.
>>> o happy hearse:
>> Make hast ye shepheards thither to revert,
>>> o joyfull verse. (*LL*, fol. 107 ^{r})

In the second figure the middle term is predicate of both premises, as in this syllogism from "May."

> The hyreling letteth his sheepe run at randon:
> The good shepheard letteth not his sheepe run at randon,
> Therefore the good shepheard is not a hyreling. (*Ibid.*, fol. 106 ^{r})

In the third figure the middle term is subject of both premises. The Ramists make a special point of showing that a syllogism in this figure is clearer in the contracted form in which it is used in daily life than in the full form, and therefore they call this form the contracted syllogism. Fraunce gives as an example of this contracted form:

Some confidence is not vertue, as Rashnes.

He then expands it and adds his comment.

> Rashnes to bee no vertue, yet a kind of confidency,
> Therefore some confidency to bee no vertue.

And after this manner, Use, the mayster of syllogisticall judgement, dooth alwaies contract it, and never otherwise expresse it. (fol. 104 ^{r})

Of greatest practical importance is the enthymeme, which although described by Aristotle as the rhetorical counterpart of the dialectical syllogism is nevertheless regularly treated by the Renaissance logicians. Blundeville and Wilson follow Aristotle in their account of its matter and its form. As to its matter, the enthymeme is based on signs or on probabilities. The signs may be infallible, as: He has a fever; therefore he is ill. Or fallible, as: This man is a night-gadder; therefore he is a thief. Probabilities include generally received opinions which in the form of maxims provide a favorite source of matter for enthymemes. As Aristotle remarks, maxims invest a speech with moral character, and people love to hear general statements about practical conduct which voice opinions they themselves hold regarding particular cases. Aristotle explains at length the relation of the maxim to the enthymeme.

> A maxim . . . is a statement; not about a particular fact . . . but of a general kind . . . about questions of practical conduct, courses of conduct to be chosen or avoided. Now an Enthymeme is a syllogism dealing with such practical subjects. It is therefore roughly true that the premisses or conclusions of Enthymemes, considered apart from the rest of the argument, are Maxims: . . . add the reason or explanation, and the whole thing is an Enthymeme; thus . . .
>
> > There is no man among us all is free,
>
> [is a maxim]; but . . . taken with what follows it, is an Enthymeme—
>
> > For all are slaves of money or of chance.
> > [Euripides, *Hecuba*, 864 f]
>
> . . . the maxim may or may not have a supplement. Proof is needed where the statement is paradoxical or disputable; no supplement is wanted where . . . the view expressed is already a known truth . . . or [where] as soon as the view is stated, it is clear at a glance, e.g.
>
> > No love is true save that which loves for ever.
> > [Euripides, *Troades*, 1051]
>
> . . . the best . . . are those in which the reason for the view expressed is simply implied, e.g.
>
> > O mortal man, nurse not immortal wrath.

To say 'it is not right to nurse immortal wrath' is a maxim; the added words 'O mortal man' give the reason. (*Rhetoric*, 2.21, 1394 ª 21- ᵇ 23)

As to its form, Aristotle asserts:

The enthymeme must consist of few propositions, fewer often than those which make up the normal syllogism. For if any of these propositions is a familiar fact, there is no need even to mention it; the hearer adds it himself. (*Rhetoric*, 1.2. 1357 ª 16)

Fraunce agrees.

Strict syllogismes bee never lightly used among authors, but eyther contracted or amplified, or els inverted, . . . The quicknes of mans wit is such, that it conceaveth the whole sometimes without any proposition, another while without any assumption, and now and then it preventeth and foretaketh the conclusion. (*LL*, fol. 112 ᵛ)

In the first of the following enthymemes the minor premise is omitted; in the second, the major.

That is not good whiche bringeth a man to mischief. Therefore money is not good. Pleasure bringeth endlesse paine after it. *Ergo* pleasure is to be eschued. (Wilson, *RR*, fol. 31 ʳ)

The figure which the rhetoricians call aetiologia is identical with what the logicians call an enthymeme. It is a cause given to a sentence uttered:

I mistrust not the Judges, because they are just. (Wilson, *AR*, p. 205)

Puttenham calls aetiologia the Reason rendrer, and composes a

dittie . . . where the lover complaines of his Ladies crueltie, rendring for every surmise a reason, and by telling the cause, seeketh (as it were) to get credit, thus.

> *Cruel you be who can say nay,*
> *Since ye delight in others wo:*
> *Unwise am I, ye may well say,*
> *For that I have, honourd you so.*
> *But blamelesse I, who could not chuse,*
> *To be enchaunted by your eye:*
> *But ye to blame, thus to refuse*
> *My service, and to let me die.* (p. 229)

The rhetoricians reserve the name enthymeme for a figure whereby a cause is given to things contrary. Their limitation of the word enthy-

meme to a striking antithesis of thoughts in opposition is apparently due
to the fact that Cicero and Quintilian (8.5.9) regarded this as the pre-
eminent type of enthymeme. But Aristotle too recognized its outstanding
character.

The Refutative Enthymeme has a greater reputation than the Demonstrative,
because within a small space it works out two opposing arguments, and arguments put side by side are clearer to the audience. (*Rhetoric,* 2.23, 1400 ᵇ 25)

Sherry and Peacham offer these examples of the figure enthymeme.

If it be a great praise to please good men, surely to please evyl men it is a greate
shame. (Sherry, sig. F vii ʳ)

They which may do me good, wil not, and they which are willing cannot,
therefore my distresse remaineth. (Peacham, p. 163)

Syllogismus is a figure even more contracted than the enthymeme. According to Peacham it expresses a sign or token from which the whole
meaning is gathered.

Virgill speaking of *Poliphemus,* saith he held a pine tree in his hand to stay himselfe, and walked through the sea: by this we conjecture what a great bodie
he had. (p. 180)

The full syllogism implicit in this single proposition may be stated thus:

Whoever walks through the sea holding a pine tree in his hand to stay him-
self has a great body.
But Poliphemus does this.
Therefore Poliphemus has a great body.

Hoskyns calls this figure intimation, because it suggests more to the mind
than to the ears.

It exceedeth speech in silence, & makes our meaning more palpable by a touch,
then by a direct handling, as he that should say (yow must live many yeares in
his companie, whome yow shall accompt for your friend) sayth well, but he that
saith yow had need eate a bushell of sault with him, saith more, & gives yow
to reckon more then many yeares. (p. 139)

This figure of intimation by vivid detail is essential to poetic composition
in the Aristotelian sense as contrasted with exposition. A man who is
frightened trembles; he who repents weeps. Given the situation, only
the action need be stated. The reader or listener supplies the rest.

A sorites is a chain of enthymemes. Fraunce cites one attributed to
Themistocles.

My sonne ruleth my wife; my wife commaundeth mee: I the Athenians; the Athenians all Graece: Therefore my sonne ruleth all Graece. (*LL*, fol. 99ᵛ)

Two figures of repetition are frequently employed in syllogistic reasoning.[1] Anadiplosis may express an enthymeme and climax or gradatio a sorites. In his work on rhetoric, Hoskyns explains:

> *Climax* is a kinde of *Anadiplosis* leadinge by degrees and makynge the last word a stepp to the further meaninge, if it be turned to an Argument it is a Sorites . . . yow could not injoy your goodnes without government, nor goverment without a magistrate, nor a magistrate without obedience, & noe obedience where every one uppon his private passion doth interpret the doeings of the Rulers, Nowe to make it a *Sorites* or Clyming Argument, joyne the first & last with an *Ergo*, as *Ergo* yow cannot enjoy your goods where every man uppon his private passion doth &c: this in pennd speech is too Accademicall, but in discource more passible & plausible. (p. 126)[2]

Discussing sorites in *The Arte of Logick*, Blundeville observes:

> The Rhetoricians use another kinde of Argument, called *Gradatio*, which is much like to *Sorites*, saving that the Subject of the first Proposition is not rehearsed in the Conclusion, for they use it rather as an ornament of speech, then as a proofe. (p. 177)

The compound syllogism is either hypothetical or disjunctive, or a combination of these called the dilemma.

The sign of the hypothetical or conditional proposition is *if, unless,* or an adverb of time, such as *when.* A hypothetical syllogism is valid if the minor premise either affirms the antecedent or denies the consequent of the major premise, which is a hypothetical proposition. Fraunce quotes from Spenser:

> *Willy* in March.
>
>> But see, the Welkin thicks apace,
>> And stouping *Phebus* steepes his face,
>> It's time to haste us homeward.

He then formalizes the argument.

---

[1] See above, p. 306, where anadiplosis and climax are discussed among the figures of repetition.

[2] Hoyt Hudson, in the notes to his edition of Hoskyns, *Directions for Speech and Style,* Princeton, 1935, states: "This relation between the figure of climax and the sorites . . . is mentioned in Claude Minos's gloss to Talaeus (*Rhetorica*, Frankfort, 1587, p. 109) with a reference to the *Rhetorica ad Herennium*, lib. 4."

When night drawes on, it's time to goe homeward,
But now night drawes on,
Therefore it's now time to get homeward. (*LL,* fol. 109 ᵛ)

The figure epilogus is related to the hypothetical syllogism. Sherry explains it as a figure

which by a brief argumentacion of these thinges that be spoken before or done, inferreth that thynge that necessarilye shulde folowe, thus: And if a revelacion wer geven to the Trojanes, that Troy myght not be taken without the arowes of Philectetes, and thei did nothing else but strike Alexander, to kyl him, that in dede was Troy to be taken. (Sig. D iiii ʳ)

In a disjunctive syllogism the minor premise affirms one of the two alternatives presented in the disjunctive major premise, and the conclusion denies the other, or contrariwise. Thus:

He is eyther good or evill;
but he is good:
Ergo not evill. (Blundeville, p. 157)

The figure apophasis, or expeditio, is equivalent to the disjunctive syllogism of the logicians and is consequently grounded upon division. It is used

when many reasons being reckoned by which somthing may be done or not done, one reason is left which the Orator standeth unto & concludeth upon, and the other are taken away, thus: Seeing this ground was mine, thou must needes shew, that either thou diddest possesse it being void, or made it thine by use, or bought it, or else that it came to thee by heritage: Thou couldest not possesse it voide when I was in possession: also thou canst not make it thine by use: Thou hast not to shew that thou diddest buy it, it could not come to thee by inheritance, and I alive: it followeth then that thou wouldest put me from mine owne ground, before I be dead. (Peacham, p. 186)

Prosapodosis, which also depends on a disjunction of alternatives, differs from apophasis in that it

overthroweth noe parte of the *Division*, but returneth some reason to each member . . . affirmes & keepes all sides upp . . . your silence must carrie with it a construccion of contempt, unkindness or displeasure, If yow take me not for your friend, yow offer unkindnes, if you deeme me unworthie of an answeare it comes of contempt, if your passion differrs a reply, it argues your displeasure. (Hoskyns, p. 160)

In its full form the dilemma consists of a compound hypothetical proposition as the major premise, a disjunctive proposition as the minor, and a simple or a disjunctive proposition as the conclusion. Fraunce gives as an example of the dilemma and its rebuttal the oft-repeated one concerning the rhetorician Protagoras and his pupil Euathlus.

Euathlus gave some money in hande to his Rhetoricall Doctor *Protagoras*, and covenanted to pay the rest when *Euathlus* should win the first cause that ever hee pleaded for. *Protagoras* suing *Euathlus* for his money, saide, if *Euathlus* overcome mee, then by bargaine & composition hee must pay mee the money; if hee loose, then by the course of Law. Nay quoth *Euathlus*, if I loose, then by covenant you get nothing: if I winne, then will the judgement discharge mee. (fol. 99 ᵛ)

Such rebuttal is possible when each of two opposites has both a good and a bad consequence opposite, respectively, to each other. A dilemma open to rebuttal is an invalid argument. A correct dilemma is, however, a valid form of reasoning.

The figure dialysis or dilemma is like the dilemma of the logicians except that it usually states only the major premise and leaves the rest to be understood. According to Sherry, this figure by

dividing one thyng, from another, endeth them both by shewing a reason, thus . . . what shuld I speake of myne owne good turnes towarde the. If thou do remember them, I shuld not trouble you: If you have forgotten them, when by deede I have profited nothyng, what good can I do in wordes? (Sig. D iiii ʳ)

Fraunce insists that all argumentation is syllogistic.

The schoolemen have commonly foure kindes of Argumentations, Syllogisme, Enthymeme, Induction, Example, to the which some adde *Sorites* and *Dilemma* . . . and all these, . . . come all to one. For an Enthymeme is but a contracted and short syllogisme: An example, but an argument from the like or equall . . . and no argumentation of it selfe without the helpe of a syllogisme: An Induction, which is called the *Socraticall* Argumentation, is but an argument concluded by a syllogisme, from the enumeration of the partes: A *Sorites*, but an Enthymematicall progression by certainy [*sic*] degrees. (*LL*, fol. 99 ʳ)

The relation between the example, induction, and the syllogism is clearly explained by Blundeville.

An Example is a kind of Argument, wherein wee proceed from one particular
to prove another particular, by reason of some likenes that is betwixt them . . .
an Induction out of many particularities gathereth an universalitie . . . Notwithstanding *Aristotle* saith, that it may be reduced partly to an Induction, and
partly to a Syllogisme: for in taking the first particular, you may by an unperfect
induction imply an universal Proposition. And so from that universall Proposition to proceed by order of Syllogisme unto the other particular implyed in the
conclusion of the Example, as in this Example: *Judas* died evill; *Ergo, Pilate*
also died evill: it may be first reduced to an unperfect Induction thus: *Judas*
dyed evill, because hee was the author of Christs death, and did not repent:
Ergo, Every man that was author of Christs death, and did not repent, died
evill. Into a Syllogisme thus: Every man that was author of Christs death, and
did not repent, died evil; but *Pilat* was author of Christs death, and did not
repent: *Ergo, Pilate* died evill. (p. 175)

Blundeville warns that for validity in this kind of argument the similitude of the particulars must be the very cause why the predicate of the antecedent belongs to its subject. And Lever remarks:

A reason by example allureth the ignorant: a reason by rule forceth the learned.
(p. 102)

The method of applying syllogistic reasoning to the writing of themes as practiced in Tudor grammar schools is exemplified in the instructions dictated by Christopher Johnson, master of Winchester school, in the autumn of 1566. These instructions were recorded in the notebook of William Badger, a pupil in the sixth form.[3]

He who is about to treat a theme, ought at the very beginning to examine thor-
oughly what is its *sententia*, to what common place it must especially be referred, and whether it must be restricted by some added word. (185 ͮ) . . .
in proof two kinds of arguments are used: either enthymeme or syllogism. Of
the enthymeme the parts are the proposition, the reason, the confirmation of the
reason, the embellishing, the conclusion. Of the proposition and conclusion the
sententia should be the same with the theme itself. The embellishing serves
rather for ornament than proof. The confirmation of the reason is not of the
form of the enthymeme, but proves its assumption. For example, let the theme
be this, "Virtue being praised increases."
    By love of praise all things are governed and especially stimulated, therefore
virtue also.
    There is no animal so stupid which does not permit itself to be petted, there

---

[3] Quoted by T. W. Baldwin, *William Shakspere's Small Latine and Lesse Greeke*, 1944,
I, 334 ff. Badger here exemplifies the five-part double epicheirema; the Conclusion
merely repeats the Proposition.

is no man so barbarous who does not permit himself to be praised, therefore all are captivated, etc. Here now the oration should run on into similitudes, examples, apothegms, and other ornaments, and thence concludes (186 ʳ).

Of the rhetorical syllogism, which is the other part of explaining the theme, six parts are enumerated, the proposition, the major, the proof of the major, the minor, the proof of the minor, and the conclusion. Let the theme be, "A philosopher should never be an avaricious person."

Proposition	No one doubts, I think, that especially disgraceful in a philosopher is that avidity for riches which we call avarice. For avarice
Major	rice (that I may say it in one word) as it is the contrary of virtue, so certainly it fights directly against wisdom. For wisdom
Proof of the major	is a kind of right habit of the mind lifting itself to celestial and eternal things. But avarice is what other than depravity depressing the mind in itself immortal to the enfeebled members of this money, that is, earthly dregs? So that no one does not clearly see what is the difference between avarice and wisdom.
Minor	Further, since the philosopher teaches others wisdom, so too he himself should also be a participator of the same in his life. For
Proof of the minor	wherefore that boast, wherefore the name of philosopher unless as he professes to love wisdom, so also he can follow it and live according to its prescript? Wherefore, since this is now manifest that wisdom does not at all couple with avarice, but a philosopher both in fact and in name is a wise man, how disgrace-
Conclusion	ful in a man of this kind would even a slight suspicion of avarice be. Those of whom I speak this ought to appear wise (186 ᵛ).

What in the proof of themes we have omitted must here be added that nothing may be lacking. For there are certain propositions so general and universal that it is possible for each one to be demonstrated a priori (as they say). These are to be proved by enumeration, which is accustomed to be called induction by the dialecticians, and confirmed by multitude. Let the proposition be one in Aristophanes that all obey money. But this, what enthymeme? What syllogism? will so appositely establish it as if one by running through all orders of men, arts, inventions, labors should show with Chremulus that nothing is done except for money? Therefore in these three ways all themes must be treated, by enthymeme, syllogism, and enumeration (188 ʳ).

2. Fallacious Reasoning

Sophistry ostentatiously employs the forms of reasoning but hides underneath them a fallacy which must be detected by the art that teaches true reasoning. The sophist wishes to appear wise, to win an argument, to put down his adversary. He is little concerned with truth. Aristotle

ARGUMENTATION

describes him as one who asks as if for information while he draws from
his adversary statements against which he himself is well supplied with
arguments; he shows the discrepancy between his opponent's hidden and
professed opinions; he puts to him many questions at once. As Blundeville observes,

Aristotle saith, that the fraudulent disputation of the Sophister, tendeth alwayes
to one of these five Ends or Marks; that is, either by force of argument, to bring
you into some absurditie, which he calleth Elench; that is to say, a reprehension
or reproofe, or else to make you to confesse that which is manifestly false, or to
grant some Paradox, which is asmuch to say as an opinion contrary to all mens
opinions: or to allow of incongrue speech contrarie to the rules of Grammar,
called in Latine, *Solecismus,* or to admit some vaine repetition, called in Latine,
Nugatio.

Of the first marke, let this be your example: If in disputing of Vertue, you
have perhaps granted, that the meditation of Vertue doth make a man sad, the
Sophister will force you by argument, to denie againe that which you before
granted, thus: all things that bee contrarie, have contrarie effects: but it is
proper to vice to make the minde of man sad: *Ergo,* vertue maketh his minde
glad . . .

Of the second Marke, let this be your example: Every Dog hath power to
barke; but there is a certaine Starre called the Dog: *Ergo,* that starre hath
power to barke. . . .

Of the Paradox: . . . Whosoever is subject to sin, is wretched: but all rich
and happy Kings are subject to sinne: *Ergo,* all rich and happy Kings are
wretched and miserable . . .

Of the fourth . . . The Sophister will make you to allow of this false
Latine, *mulier est candidus,* by force of argument, thus: *Omnis homo est candidus, at mulier est homo, ergo mulier est candidus* . . .

Of the fift . . . The Sophister will make you to allow of this vaine repetition . . . *Plato* is learned, but *Plato* is a man learned: *Ergo, Plato* is learned;
a man learned: heere the premisses and the conclusion are all one thing, and
therefore contrarie to the rules of Logick. (p. 188)

Aristotle explains the value of knowing how to deal with sophistic arguments.

The use of them, then, is, for philosophy, two-fold. For in the first place, since
for the most part they depend upon the expression, they put us in a better condi-
tion for seeing in how many senses any term is used, and what kind of resem-
blances and what kind of differences occur between things and between their
names. In the second place they are useful for one's own personal researches;
for the man who is easily committed to a fallacy by some one else, and does not

perceive it, is likely to incur this fate of himself also on many occasions. (*De sophisticis elenchis*, ch. 16, 175ᵃ5)

Falsity arises from an erroneous relation of terms; a fallacy from an erroneous relation of propositions. A premise may be false; a syllogism may be fallacious. One may flatly deny a premise as false

by shewyng the faulte to bee in the definition, in the devision, in the causes, or in some other place: As thus.

> I had good cheere in suche a mans house.
>
> *Ergo,* he is an honest man.

Here the fault is in the definition, for, if I would goe about to define an honest man, every bodie would laugh me to scorne if I would thus define him. That man, whosoever he be, that maketh mee good cheere at his house, is a very honest man. . . . For vertue is gotten by long practise, and by well doing of many good thinges, not by making a good dinner. (Wilson, *RR*, fol. 83ʳ)

A syllogism is fallacious when the conclusion does not follow from the premises, even though both premises may be true; their lack of coherence may be due to a formal or to a material fallacy.

The fallacy is formal if it violates a rule of the syllogism. For example:

Every covetous man doth violate the lawes of liberalitie; but every prodigall man doth violate the lawes of liberalitie; therefore every prodigall man is a covetous man. (Blundeville, p. 184)

Here the middle term is not understood in its full extension in either premise, since it is predicate in both of them and both are affirmative. Consequently the conclusion does not follow from the premises and in this instance it is false. Wilson offers an example of another formal fallacy.

> All ryot is an offence.
>
> No covetousnesse is riot.
>
> *Ergo,* no covetousnesse is any offence.

Thus we see a false conclusion, made of two undoubted true propositions . . . (fol. 85ʳ)

In this syllogism there is an illicit process of the major term: *offence* is used in its full extension in the conclusion and in only part of its extension in the major premise.

A material fallacy is one that vitiates an argument which on the surface appears to be formally correct. Blundeville and Wilson, following Aristotle, group material fallacies into two classes: those arising from ambiguity in the language, and those arising from a hidden assumption in the matter.

Six material fallacies have their root in ambiguity of language and therefore common to all of them is the formal fallacy of four terms; for if the middle term has a different meaning in each premise, it merely appears to be one term whereas it is really two and consequently cannot serve to establish a true coherence between the premises. The ambiguity may be in one word or in a conjunction of words.

The fallacy of equivocation arises from the ambiguity of one word.

The Prophet saith that there is no evill in the Citie, but God doth it; but there be horrible evils in the Citie; *Ergo,* God is the Author of evill: the Conclusion is to be denied, because in the Major this word evill signifieth punishment, and in the Minor it signifieth sinne: (Blundeville, p. 190)

Wilson remarks:

Of no one thyng riseth so muche controversie, as of the doubtfulnesse, and dubble taking of a worde. Scholars dispute, wise men fall out, Lawyers agree not, Preachers waxe hot, Gentlemen strive, the people mutter, good men give counsaile, women have their wordes, this man affirmeth, the other denieth, and yet at length, the dubble meaning being once knowne (when al things are quiet) endes the whole matter. (*RR,* fol. 65 ᵛ)

He cites as an amusing instance of equivocation the story of Will Somer, King Henry VIII's fool, who

in commending a bishop of his acquaintaunce, declared to a noble personage, that this Bishop had a goodly base voice, and made at one time (quoth he) as base a Sermon, as he never heard the like in all his life before, and therefore, worthie to be coumpted a great Clerke, in his foolish judgement. Who will not say, that this Bishop was basely praised. (66 ʳ)

Amphibology is ambiguity in construction, as in the oracle prophesying that

Craesus going over the flood *Halim,* shal overthrow a great Empire. Here is not mentioned, whether he shal overthrow his owne, or an other mans. By the which Oracle in deed, he being deceived, lost his owne Kingdome, when he thought to subdue his enemies, and bring them under subjection. (Wilson, *RR,* fol. 66 ᵛ)

Wilson also quotes in full, with evident relish, the two love letters from Nicholas Udall's *Ralph Roister Doister* in which meanings quite opposite are given by different punctuations. He himself composes two verses to illustrate the same point.

> A robberie doe not feare: thy God, thy maker
> Will punish not one: God spareth, be thou sure.
> *Otherwise*
> A robberie doe not: feare thy God, thy maker
> Will punishe, not one God spareth, be thou sure.
> (*Ibid.*, fol. 66 ⸗)

The fallacies of composition and division are the reverse of each other.

Composition or conjunction, is the joyning together of things that are to be severed. As for example, two and three be even and odde, but five maketh two and three, therefore five is both even and odde:

Division is, when things are severed, which should be joyned together, as, all the wise men of Greece are seven; *Solon* and *Periander* are wise men of Greece, therefore *Solon* and *Periander* are seven: heere the Consequent is to be denied, because *Solon* and *Periander* are severed from the rest whereunto they should be joyned. (Blundeville, p. 191)

The fallacy of form of speech results

when words are falsely supposed to be like either in signification, in Case, or in Gender, or to be of one selfe Predicament, because they are like in termination . . . coloured and numbred are like in termination: *Ergo,* they are of one selfe Predicament, and yet the first belongeth to the Predicament of Qualitie, and the other to Quantitie. . . . when a word hath not his proper signification, or is not used according to the true phrase of speech in which it is uttered, as thus: Whatsoever thou hast not lost, thou hast still, but thou hast lost no hornes: *Ergo,* thou hast hornes. Heere this word, to lose, hath not his proper signification, for wee are said to lose properly that which we had, and not that which we never had. (*Ibid.*, p. 192)

As an example of the fallacy of accent whereby the true signification of a word is altered, Blundeville, as a true Englishman, offers

this old jest of a Master that said to his servant: Go heate this Capons legge, who immediately did eate it: then his Master being angry, said, I bade thee heate it, with an h: no Sir (said the servant) I did eate it with bread. (p. 191)

Seven fallacies have their source outside the language in a hidden assumption.

In the fallacy of accident it is falsely assumed that whatever is attributed to the substance of some thing, is attributed also to some accident of the said substance, and contrariwise, as thus: Whatsoever thou hast bought, thou hast eaten, but thou hast bought rawe flesh: *Ergo,* thou hast eaten rawe flesh: heere the Consequent is to be denied, because the Major hath respect to the substance, and the Conclusion to the qualitie. Another example, What I am, thou art not, but I am a man: *Ergo,* thou art none. (*Ibid.,* p. 193)

Wilson gives this illustration of the fallacy of accident.

> This man is a wittie fellowe.
> This man is lame.
> *Ergo* this same man hath a lame wit.

This is evidently false, because the accidentes of the bodie are referred to the substaunce of the mynde. (*RR,* fol. 71 ᵛ)

The fallacy of speech respective instead of speech absolute rests on the false assumption that what is true in a qualified sense is true absolutely.

The Fallax *A dicto secundum quid ad dictum Simpliciter,* chanceth when we goe about to make a thing to seeme absolute, that is spoken in some respect . . . by reason of time, place, person, comparison, and such like. Of time, as thus: I saw *John* yesterday, but I saw him not today: *Ergo,* I did see him, and not see him. Of place thus: It is not good to buy and sell in the Church: *Ergo,* it is not good to buy and sell. Of person thus: A Magistrate may kill a theefe: *Ergo,* every man may kill a theefe. Of comparison, thus: Riches are not good to him that cannot use them: *Ergo,* Riches are not good. (Blundeville, p. 194)

Wilson explains how hyperbole may have a bearing on the fallacy of *secundum quid.*

There is a figure in Rhetorike, called *Hyperbole,* that is to say, when a thing is spoken beyond measure uncredibly, and yet is not so largely meant. . . . Therefore, we must diligently take heede, when such speaches are used, that we take not them as they bee spoken, but as they are ment. . . . A noble man had a childe, which was very towarde in learnyng, and partly for such worthinesse as was in the childe, and partly to get favour of such a Peere, as the father was, divers commended the childe wonderfully well, and one above all other, thinking to say the most, not content with right excellent, or marveilous wittie, or toward, sayd thus after other mens judgement, and report given: Surely in my mynd, the childe is even a very monster. With that the noble man laughed, to heare his folly, and all the other likewise that were there. (*RR,* fol. 74 ʳ)

The fallacy of ignorance of the elench differs little, in Blundeville's opinion, from that of *secundum quid*, except that it is more general and inclusive.

An Elench . . . is a Syllogisme rightly gathering a Conclusion contrary to the assertion of the respondent, which contrarietie consisteth of foure principall points or respects, whereof, if any be wanting, then the contrarietie is not perfect. . . . First, that it be one selfe thing. Secondly, in one selfe respect. Thirdly, in one selfe manner. And fourthly, in or at one selfe time: for if you be deceived at any time by some false Elench, in thinking that it rightly gathereth a Conclusion meere contrarie to your assertion, when it is not so indeed, by reason that it faileth in some part requisite and incident to a true Elench: then it may be rightly said that you are deceived by ignorance of the Elench . . . Of the first, let this bee your example: foure is double to two, but not to three: *Ergo*, foure is double and not double; this is not to one selfe thing. . . . Of the third thus: This Prince ruleth mightily, but not mercifully: *Ergo*, he ruleth, and not ruleth; this is not in like manner. . . . (p. 194)

The fallacy of consequent arises from the assumption that a proposition is convertible when it is not. A universal affirmative proposition is convertible only when the predicate is the definition or a property of the subject. In the following argument the implicit major premise, Whoever is pale is in love, is not convertible.

> He is pale in countenaunce.
> *Ergo* he is in love.

Palenesse may come of studie, or care, and thought, of abstinence, of watching, of some distemperature in the body, and manie other wayes besides. (Wilson, *RR*, fol. 78 ^{r})

The fallacy of consequent also occurs when one thinks that upon the contrary of the antecedent the contrary of the consequent must needs follow.

It is a man: *Ergo*, It is a sensible body. It is no man: *Ergo*, it is no sensible body. Heere you see that this Proposition, It is no man, is the contrary of the first Antecedent, which saith, It is a man. Of which contrary, the contrary of the Consequent doth not necessarily follow: for though it bee no man, yet it may be some other sensible bodie. (Blundeville, p. 196)

The fallacy of false cause results

when a cause that is not able to prove the matter, is brought in, as though it were of force and strength, but the grounde being considered the faulte easely espied,

> Dronkenesse is evill:
> *Ergo* wine is naught. . . .

In all such argumentes, wherein good thinges are reproved, because evil bodies abuse the same, the evill will and the naughtie enclination of the man, which abused, such thynges is to bee rebuked: and therefore when it is otherwise, it may be saied, that a cause which is not, is put for a cause. . . .

Now a daies they will say, I cannot tell, here is much preaching, much teachyng of Gods word, but I see fewe folowers of it, it was a better worlde, when we had not halfe so many preachers, Heresies were never more ripe, naughtinesse never more abounded, therefore geve us the old learning again, and take you the newe.

This reason is not worthe a strawe. The wickednesse of the Preachers cometh not of their learning, but of their vicious natures, and naughtie desires: for out of one and the same flower the Bee sucketh Hony, and the Spider draweth poyson. . . .

This deceiptfull argument is much used in this our life, & made a buckler for divers maters. . . . when one that is rich should helpe a poore man, to say: God helpe you sir I have a great charge my self, I can not doe for you. . . . And the using of such excuses among the Rhetoricians, is called *translatio*, that is to say a shifting of the fault from one to an other. As we reade that *Demades* used a wonderfull good shift, when it was laied sore to his charge, that he had written a verie naughtie decree and unhonest, for the obteyning of the peace at *Alexanders* hand. He answered that the same decree was not written with his owne writing penne but with *Alexanders* warring speare, which is asmuch to say, feare did drive him to take such, & such condicions of peace. (Wilson, fol. 76 ^{r}–77 ^{r})

The fallacy of begging the question is present when the proof is as little known as the thing to be proved, or when it is less known, or when the proof is the same as the conclusion.

Every sensible bodie sometime sleepeth: *Ergo*, Man sometime sleepeth. Heere it is more to be doubted whether all sensible Bodies, all Beastes, Fowles and Fishes, doe sometimes sleepe or not, then whether man doth sometime sleepe: for it is an easier matter to know the nature and propertie of one speciall kinde, then of all, or many kindes. Of the third way, thus . . . The soule doth live ever: *Ergo*, it is immortall. (Blundeville, p. 195)

Wilson calls the first kind utis, and the last kind the "Cuckoes song," of which he remarks:

Self willed folke that followe lust, and forsake reason, use oft the Cuckowes song. As being asked why they will do this and that, they answere streight, Mary, because I will doe it, or because it pleaseth me best so to doe: . . . Some women are subject to this aunswere, which in wit doe excell, though in the eight partes of reason, fewe Schollers can hardly finde them. (*RR*, fol. 80 ^{r})

The fallacy of many questions consists in demanding a simple answer to a complex question.

The seventh and last Fallax, is when unadvisedly, and without using any distinction, you make an answere to manie questions, as though they were but one; as for example, The Sophister, seeing two men standing together, whereof the one is blinde, and the other hath his sight, will aske you, perhaps, whether they see, or not; whereunto if you answere directly, either yea, or no, you are by and by taken: for if you say that they see, then you grant that the blind man also seeth, and if you say, that they doe not see, then you grant, that he which seeth, is blinde; but if you answere, that the one seeth, and the other not, you shall by such distinction easily avoid the Sophisters cavillation: for divers questions hudled up in one, doe alwayes require divers answeres. (Blundeville, p. 196)

The fallacies lend themselves to jesting, of which Aristotle remarks:

As to jests. These are supposed to be of some service in controversy: Gorgias says that you should kill your opponents' earnestness with jesting and their jesting with earnestness; in which he was right. (*Rhetoric*, 3.18, 1419 ^{b} 3)

Wilson concludes his treatment of the fallacies with a group of seven captious arguments which he introduces zestfully.

And nowe the rather to delight the Reader, I will ad here certaine wittie questions and arguments, which can hardly be avoyded, being very pleasant, & therfore not unworthie to be knowne.

They are called trapping arguments, because fewe that aunswered unto them, can avoyde daunger, and thus they are named in straunge wordes. *Crocodilites, Antistrephon, Ceratinae, Asistaton, Cacosistaton, Utis, Pseudomenos.* (*RR*, fol. 85 ^{r})

Utis, an argument in which the proof is as uncertain as the thing to be proved, is identical with the first form of begging the question illustrated above.

Antistrephon, is nothing els, then to turne a mans saying into his owne necke againe, and to make that which hee bringeth for his owne purpose, to serve for our purpose . . . There is in *Aristophanes* a wonderfull pretie talke, betwixt the father and the sonne . . . For where as the sonne had beaten his father, contrary to all order and honestie: yet notwithstanding, the soonne thought he had as good authoritie to beate his father, if he did amisse, as the father had to beate him. And therefore he sayd, wherefore should my father beate me? His father made answere. Mary (quoth he) because I love thee, and would thou shouldest do wel. Mary therfore (quoth the sonne) will I beate thee to, because I love thee also good father, and would thou shouldest doe well: & with that

layd on strokes surely, till he made his father graunt that it was as lawfull foɪ
the sonne to beate his father, as for the father to beate his soone. (Wilson,
RR, 85 ᵛ)

As another example of antistrephon, Wilson cites Euathlus' reply to
Protagoras, the rebuttal which has been quoted on p. 363.

Cacosistata are such arguments, that being proponed betwene two persons, they
serve aswell for the one part, as the other, as thus. . . . Alas, saith one, it is
pitie such a man should be hanged, considering he is a gentleman. And why not
gentlemen, aswel as other poore men, if they deserve it? Yea, why not they
rather then any other, if they more deserve it then any other. (*Ibid.*, fol. 87 ᵛ)

Of the four remaining captious arguments Blundeville remarks that
they are intricate kinds of reasoning comprehended under dilemma.[4] He
and Wilson illustrate them with the same examples.

Pseudomonos. This is called a lying argument, for whatsoever ye shall say, must
needes say amisse. *Epimenides* a man borne in *Crete*, sayd that the people borne
in *Crete*, were lyers, sayd he true or no? (Wilson, fol. 87 ᵛ)

Assistation, is a kinde of cavelling, not consisting of any sure ground, as if a man
did say, that he doth hold his peace . . . another by and by might cavill thereof
in this sort: *Ergo*, He that holdeth his peace, speaketh . . . (Blundeville,
p. 179)

[Ceratin or] The horned Argument is, when by some subtile and craftie manner of questioning, we seeke to have such an answere, as we may take vantage
therof, as the Pharises did, when they questioned with Christ touching the pay-
ment of Tribute to *Caesar*. (Blundeville, p. 179)

Crocodilites, is such a kinde of subtiltie, that when we have graunted a thing
to our adversarie, being asked before what he will say: the same turneth to our
harme afterward, and causeth an inconveniencie, thereupon to ensue. Aucthours doe feigne, that the Crocodile . . . did take a womans childe from her,
and spake with the mother in this wise: woman, I will give thee thy childe
againe, if thou wilt say trueth to me, and tell me assuredly, whether I will give
thee thy child againe or no: She aunswered, I know assuredly, thou wilt not
give me my childe againe, and therefore it is reason I have my childe againe,
because I have sayd trueth. Nay, sayd the Crocodile, I will not give thee thy
childe againe, because thou mayst be seene to have sayd trueth: least that if I
give thee thy childe again, thou shouldest have made a lye: neither yet would
I have given thee thy child again, if thou haddest not sayd otherwise, because
then thou haddest not sayd trueth. And hereof this argument hath his name,
called *Crocodilites*. (Wilson, fol. 85 ᵛ)

[4] Blundeville makes no mention of utis, antistrephon, and cacosistaton.

3. Disputation

In distinguishing four kinds of disputation Blundeville follows Aristotle.

Disputation is a contention about some question taken in hand, either for finding out of truth, or else for exercise sake, and there be foure kindes of disputation, whereof the first is called doctrinall, because it appertayneth to Science.

The second is called Dialecticall, which belongeth to probable opinion.

The third is called Tentative, which serveth to trie another mans knowledge, in any kinde of Science. The fourth is Sophisticall, which tendeth onely to deceive. (p. 187)

Disputation most often deals with the probable, which has the inherent capacity to generate arguments on both sides of a question. There are five ways in which a proposition may be probable.

Things probable, according to *Aristotle*, are these that seeme true to all men, or to the most part of men, or to all wise men, or to the most part of wise men, or else to the most approved wise men. (*Ibid.*, p. 169)

Because dialectic and rhetoric have as their subject matter the probable, they are by that very fact arts of disputation, as Aristotle explains:

No other of the arts draws opposite conclusions: dialectic and rhetoric alone do this. Both these arts draw opposite conclusions impartially. Nevertheless, the underlying facts do not lend themselves equally well to the contrary views. No; things that are true and things that are better are, by their nature, practically always easier to prove and easier to believe in. (*Rhetoric*, 1.1., 1355 [a] 34)

Fraunce gives this brief picture of the ancient seeker after truth.

Socrates in this sort cogged with the olde *Graecian* Sophisters, making them say and unsay, and therefore say this, that hee was a wrangler, an inchaunter, a dissembler, a deceiver. (*LL*, fol. 114 [r])

One savors a keen relish of disputation in Wilson's account of it.

That is called a disputation, or reasoning of matters, when certaine persons debate a cause together . . . whereupon after harde holde and long debating, the trueth either appeareth, or els they rest both upon one point, leaving the matter to bee adjudged of the hearers . . .

In al debating of causes, warines is ever thought great wisedome. And therefore, he that wil shew wit and learning, must . . . evermore have some cheefe ground in his head, whereunto he mindeth to leavell all his reasons before hand,

that upon the graunt of them, a weightier matter may evermore be obteyned.
And whereas the aunswerer perhapps shall smell where aboutes he goeth, and
therfore will seeke starting holes to escape, and flee such daunger: The disputer
must alwaies keepe him in, and suffer him at no hand to slippe away, but force
him still, to aunswere the propouned argument directly, that either he graunt
the argument to be true, or denigh it to be good, or els shewe wherein the fault
is, by either opening the doubtfulnesse of some worde, or declaring plainely the
wrong knitting and lapping up of the whole reason. (fol. 61 $^{r\text{-}v}$)

The maner of confutation, two waies considered.

For the first, either we purpose by disputation, to aunswere fully to the matter, or els secondly (if power want to compasse that) we seeke some other
meanes, to satisfie the man, and that three maner of waies, either by making
the objection seeme lesse then it is, or by bringing some other example against it,
or els by seeking some meanes, to goe from the matter.

We make the argument appear slender, when we receive it laughingly, and
declare by wordes, even at the first, that it is nothyng to the purpose, and so
abash the opponent.

Again, we turne an other argument in our adversaries neck, when we bring
an other example against him. Or els when wee charge him, with a like fault,
and lay some greater matter in his dish. Lastly, wee shift away from the violence
of our adversarie, by making some digression, or giving occasion of some other
talke, whereby the adversarie, either is driven to forget his argument, or els
being blinded with too much matter, is forced either to goe no further, or els
to thinke himself content. (63 ^{v})

Objections are then used, when wee doe not dissolve the argument, by the
rules of Logicke, or directly avoyde the daunger, but bryng an other thing, as
an example, to overthrowe that, which was spoken before, and this maner is
fower waies used.

i. By takyng occasion of the selfe same thyng, that is put forth and wresting
it otherwise . . . riches are good, because they bring pleasure. The answere:
Nay Marie, richesse are evill, because they bring woe. . . .

ii. By using the same example in an other matter . . . Such a one is an
honest man, for, I saw him once give almes to the poore: I aunswere: Such a
one is no dronkard, for I sawe him once sober. . . .

iii. By makyng a cleane contrary example. . . . Such an honest man hath
once received a great displeasure, of his frend and neighbour. *Ergo,* he may
hate him deadly for ever. Nay, not so, for the wicked man will sometimes forgive, receiving displeasure, and therfore, the good man must much more forgive. . . .

iiii. By standing to authoritie, or using sentences of the sage. . . . Forgive
him, because he is a childe. Nay, not so, for *Salomon* biddeth, that the rodde
should not goe from the childe, therefore, it is good to beate him, when he of-
fendeth. (82 $^{r\text{-}v}$)

Fraunce gives a more detailed outline of the technique of disputation, after warning against faults manifest in Vergil's clowns.

In every syllogisticall conflict and controversie, there is a defendant & an opponent. The first is to urge, prove, conclude; the other to repell, avoyd, and drive backe. The disputation being once begon, it is an unorderly confusion for the same man sometimes to aunswere, sometimes to reply, and never constantly to playe out his owne parte: much like the two clownes in *Virgill*, which, when they could not aunswere what was propounded, begin a freshe with a new doubt on the necke of the olde: *Dic, quibus in terris,* quoth the one, and *Dic, quibus in terris,* quoth the other, Arreede me a riddle, sayth *Damaetas:* and Arreede me a riddle replyeth *Menalcas,* thincking it a faire conquest, to have taken and given blowe for blowe, as Bakers and Butchers use to doe, who never care for any curious wardes, but lay on loade like good fellowes, one for one, till both begin to stagger, with their valiant blood about their brused pates. I have therefore in a word or two, layd downe some generall instructions and directions for orderly disputations.[5]

Logicall exercise is that which expresseth that in particular practise which is generally put downe in art. For as art followeth nature, so exercise followeth art. Herein let us consider

  I. The adjuncts & affections of it, for it is performed either by
      A. Writing, or
      B. Speaking, & eyther of these is eyther
          1. Continued as in long discourses & tractates, or
          2. Interrupted as, in
              a. Dialogues
              b. Disputations. Vide B B.
  II. The specials of it. Vide A A.

  B B. Disputation is an argumentable discussing of a doubtfull proposition, where note.
      1. The Disputers
          a. The proponent, who defendeth the proposition or position: whereunto also the moderator and determiner of the disputation is referred, who commonly mainteineth the position.
          b. The opponent, whoe defendeth the contrary.
      2. The duties of the disputers, eyther,
          a. Common to both of them as in
              (1) preparation and furniture

[5] What follows has been changed from tabular to outline form by supplying numbers and letters in place of braces to indicate subordination and co-ordination. Fraunce here outlines his whole theory of composition and of reading. Although *logos* naturally predominates, he gives some attention to *ethos* (by recommending courtesy) and to *pathos* (by remarks on scorning).

        (a) of instruments for the disputation, as bee
           i. Logike
           ii. Rhetorike
        (b) things requisite for the same, it must be noted there-fore.
           i. What may confirme or confute the position.
           ii. What sect of philosophy the adversary followeth.
           iii. They must have in memory the generall heades of artes, which are commonly used in disputations.

(2) Conflict and assault: they must neither
    (a) Wrangle about trifling wordes,
    (b) Nor make long and impertinent excursion and va-garies.
    (c) Nor seeke starting holes.
    (d) Nor bring in any such thing as may rather make against them, then with them.
    (e) Nor seeke to supplant or circumvent one another in-juriously.
    (f) Nor overweene themselves, or be obstinate and singu-lar in conceipt.
    (g) Nor fal to threatning and railing with undecent tearmes.

b. Proper to eyther of them.

C C. The proper dueties of the
  1. Opponent be
    a. To have his weapons in a readines, that is, to have his objections framed artificially with syllogisticall disposition.
    b. Not to cast his argumentes confusedly on a heape, but to use them distinctly, one after another.
    c. To have Prosyllogismes in a readynes, for the confirmation of such parts of his syllogismes, as may by likelyhood, be denied.
    d. To bring in nothing which hath not some probabilitie or shew of truth in it.
    e. Sometimes to deale directly & openly: sometimes covertly, and by bringing his adversary to an absurditie or impossibilitie.
    f. Never to choppe in impertinent matters, which make nothing at all to the matter in controversie.
  2. Defendent be
    a. In choise of his position, that it be not
      (1) Repugnant to sence.
      (2) Contrary to equity & honesty.

(3) Too hard and difficult.
  b. Both in
    (1) Repetitions of the objections made, & that either by the selfesame words, or with the selfe same sence, in the like order as they were propounded: with a kind of courteous preface: that both himselfe may have some meane-space of conceaving a solution, and the auditors better understand what was objected.
    (2) And also in aunswering of the same.

D D. The objections be aunswered
  1. Either
    a. By skorning, and rejecting, if absurd fooleries be objected, or such as no man understandeth.
    b. By graunting and confessing, when such thinges bee brought in, as make nothing against the position.
    c. By affirming or denying, when any interrogation is made: or els by asking what he meaneth by his interrogation, if it be ambiguous and sophisticall
  2. Or by direct solution, & that either
    a. Perfect, when the very cause is shewd, why the conclusion is not sufficient, and it is
      (1) By denying either of
        (a) The premisses and prosyllogisms when they be false
        (b) Or the consecution & consequence, when the fault is in the forme of conclusion: for the conclusion it selfe must never be denied.
      (2) Eyther
        (a) By distinguishing when eyther
          i. The questions and interrogations be captious and doubtfull,
          ii. Or the premisses bee true not absolutely, but in part. And here fryvolous distinctions must be avoyded.
        (b) Or conditionall graunting, as I graunt, if you so understand it. Sometimes the defendent doubteth of the truth of some one of the premisses, and doth therefore leave it, of purpose to aunswere to the other that is more plaine, Thus, Let the Major passe for a whyle, I now aunswere to the minor.
    b. Imperfect by bringing in some instance, that is by taking a particular exception to a generall proposition.

A A. So much of the affections of this logicall exercise the specials now follow which bee
   1. Analysis, in undoing & examining that which is already made, & is
      a. eyther belonging to Invention: as
         (1) to search and invent the question it selfe.
         (2) to picke out the arguments and proofes.
         (3) to refer every one to their several heads, & there to inquire
             of their sufficiency, as whether that be used for a Cause
             which is no cause, &c
      b. or to Disposition & that either
         (1) Axiomaticall, where all the axiomes must be also brought
             to their heads, and their truth or falsnes diligently exam-
             ined.
         (2) Dianoeticall which is eyther
             (a) Syllogisticall, for the examination and triall of con-
                 seqution, what followeth or not followeth
             (b) Methodicall, for proofe of order and Methodicall
                 handling of the matter discoursed upon.
   2. Genesis, in making or framing of any thing by our owne industrie,
      & that eyther
      a. By way of imitation and that either
         (1) Of the whole worke ⎱
         (2) or of some part   ⎰ eyther of these is
             (a) in wordes, called Translation
             (b) in things called properly imitation. Wee must Imitate
                 i. neyther all autors, but the best of al:
                 ii. nor al things but the best, & that freely, not ser-
                     vilely, as bindyng our judgment to othermens
                     fancie.
      b. Or by proper Invention, where we must
                 (1) First peruse every place of Logicall invention
                     for the inventing of proofes and arguments.
                 (2) Then dispose them artificially both by judgment
                     (a) Axiomaticall
                     (b) and Dianoeticall & that both
                         i. Syllogisticall
                         ii. Methodicall
                                          (*LL*, fol. 101 ^{r}–103 ^{r})

   The twenty-one figures of disputation represent a rhetorical analysis
of its techniques which closely parallels the logical analysis. Among these
figures are included all that have any sort of reference to an opponent

or to judges, even when the speaker himself takes both parts, as in arguing with himself, or in anticipating and answering beforehand questions or objections which his adverasary may put to him.[6]

The figure aporia is a doubting or deliberating with oneself, when

the speaker sheweth that he doubteth, either where to begin for the multitude of matters, or what to do or say, in some strange and doubtfull thing. *Cicero* for *Roscius;* Of what shall I first complaine O Judges? or where shall I first begin? Of what or of whom shall I call for helpe, of the immortall gods, or of the Romane people? or shall I most pitifully crave your defence, who have the highest authoritie? (Peacham, p. 109)

Anthypophora is a reasoning with ourselves.

Then we reason the matter with our selves, when we aske questions of our selves, and aunswere thereunto. As thus. . . . Seing thou art so basely borne, so poore in state, so smally learned, so hard favoured, and hast no witte at al, what meanst thou to vaunt thy selfe so much, and to make such bragges as thou doest. What doth make thee to waxe so proud? Thy stocke whereof thou diddest come? Why man they are very base folke. Thine owne wealth? Tush, thou art as poore as *Job.* Thy learning? Marie thou never camst yet where any learning did growe. Thy beautie? Now in good soth, a worse favoured man can there not be upon earth againe. Thy witte? Now God he knoweth, it is as blunt as many bee. What other thing then is all this thy bragging, but plaine madnesse. (Wilson, *AR,* p. 207)

Anacoenosis is used when

the Orator seemeth to aske counsell of his adversary, or to deliberate with the Judges what is to be done, or what ought to have bene done. . . . the Apostle *Paul:* This would I learne of you, received ye the spirit by the workes of the law, or by hearing of faith preached? Gal. 3. (Peacham, p. 110)

By the figure synchoresis,

the Orator, trusting strongly to his cause, giveth leave to the Judges or to his adversaries, to consider of it with indifferencie, & so to judge of it, if it be found just and good, to allow it, if evil to condemne and punish it. . . . *Peter:* Whether it be right saith he in the sight of God, to hearken unto you more then unto God, judge ye. Acts 4. (*Ibid.,* p. 111)

Eight figures illustrate more specific methods of meeting an opponent's arguments than those outlined by logicians.

[6] These figures are concerned with points similar to those dealt with by Aristotle in his *Rhetoric,* Bk. III, ch. 15, and those dealt with by Wilson and Fraunce in their treatment of disputation quoted above.

By an apt similitude Puttenham conveys the spirit of the figure procatalepsis, which confutes what an adversary may object even before he
has uttered it:

for by reason we suppose before what may be said, or perchaunce would be said
by our adversary or any other, we do prevent them of their advantage, and do
catch the ball (as they are wont to say) before it come to the ground. (p. 232)

Puttenham offers no illustration. Fraunce quotes an example from Cleo-
phila's speech to the inconstant multitude, in Sidney's *Arcadia*.

An unused thing it is, and I thinke not heretofore seene, *Arcadians*, that a
woman should give publike counsaile to men, a stranger to the countrey people,
and that lastlie in such a presence a private person, as I am, should possesse the
regall throne. But the strangenes of your action makes that used for vertue,
which your violent necessitie imposeth. For certainlie a woman may well speake
to such men who have forgotten all manlike government; a straunger may with
reason instruct such subjects, that neglect due points of subjection, and is it
mervaile this place is entred into by an other, since your owne Duke, after
thirtie yeares government, dare not shewe his face to his faithfull people? (*AR*,
Sig. H 3 ᵛ)

Paromologia is a figure by which the speaker admits and grants to his
adversary many things unfavorable to his own position, and then sud-
denly brings in a point which overthrows all that was granted.

Suppose you have omitted nothing in your owne person, of a friend to be performed, that you were no partaker with him of these evill counsels, that you
abstained to accompany him in the execution of his mischiefes, yet are you not
therefore cleared: For it is not sufficient for a man not to do evill of himselfe,
but that by too much lenity he become not occasion of anothers mischiefe. (Day,
p. 384)

Concessio is used

when we jestinglie admit of anie speach or argument. . . . This figure de-
lighteth very much when we grant that which hurteth him to whom it is
graunted, as it manie times falleth out in contentious disputations. (Fraunce,
AR, Sig. H 5 ᵛ)

Fenner gives this example of concessio.

Eccle. 11. *Rejoyce young man in thy youth, and let thy heart cheare thee in the
dayes of thy youth, and walke in the wayes of thy hearte, and in the sight of
thine eies: but knowe that for al these thinges God will bring thee to judgement.*
(Sig. E 2 ᵛ)

Metastasis is a forme of speech by which we turne backe those thinges that are objected against us, to them which laid them to us . . . 1 Kings 18: When *Ahab* likewise charged *Elia,* that it was he which troubled all Israel, nay saith *Elia* it is not I that trouble Israel, but thou and thy fathers house, in that you have forsaken the commandements of the Lord, and thou hast followed Baal. (Peacham, p. 181)

Apodioxis, when the Orator rejecteth the objection or argument of his adversaries as thinges needlesse, absurde, false, or impertinent to the purpose, as proceeding from follie, or framed by malice, or invented by subtiltie. . . . To the Sadduces captiously inquiring of Christ, concerning the state of mariage in the resurrection, he answered: you do erre, not knowing the Scriptures, neither the power of God: by which answere he rejecteth their captious objection, by noting their ignorance. (*Ibid.,* p. 185)

Diasyrmus is a Trope by which the arguments of an adversarie are either depraved or rejected. . . . This figure is for the most part made either by some base similitude, or by some ridiculous example, to which the adversaries objection or argument is compared, whereby it is either made ridiculous, or at least much disgraced.

As for to shew examples of this figure I judge it needlesse and superfluous, considering the dayly plentie of them almost everie where, both private and publike. (*Ibid.,* p. 39)

The last two of these eight figures, namely, antirrhesis and aphorismus, involve reprehension. By antirrhesis,

the Orator rejecteth the authority, opinion or sentence of some person: for the error or wickednesse of it. . . . This same forme of speech Christ useth against Satan Mat. 4, where he rejecteth the subtil attempts and false allegations of Satan by the mightie power and truth of his answeres. (*Ibid.,* p. 88)

Aphorismus is a form of reprehension which raises a question about the proper application of a word, as,

your councellors, if such may be called counsellers as draw unto mischiefe, are utterlie unmeet to such kind of assemblies. (Day, p. 380)

Two figures of argument depend on an insistent return to one point. Commoratio consists in dwelling upon and frequently returning to one's strongest argument, supporting it with varied pleas or with varied expression.

When wee are earnest in a matter, and feele the weight of our cause, we rest upon some reason, which serveth best for our purpose. Wherin this figure appeareth most, and helpeth much to set forth our matter. For if we stil kepe us

to our strongest hold, and make often recourse thither, though we be driven
through bytalke to goe from it now and then: we shall force them at length,
either to avoyd our strong defence, or els to yeeld into our hands. (Wilson, *AR*,
p. 178)

Epimone is the persistent repetition of the same plea in much the same
words.

There is a good example hereof in *Abrahams* praier or sute to God for the
Sodomites, saying: if there be fiftie righteous within the Citie wilt thou destroy,
and not spare the place for the fiftie righteous that are therein? . . . and thus
he continueth perseverantly . . . Gen. 18. (Peacham, p. 70)

Puttenham describes epimone as a refrain in a poem, repeated often at
intervals. He calls it the Love-burden, because it bears the whole burden
of the song. A refrain obviously has the qualities of persistence and repetition, characteristics of this figure.

Apoplanesis is a figure of evasion through digression. The logicians
mention digression as one of the recognized forms of defense in disputation. By apoplanesis,

the speaker leadeth away the mind of his hearer, from the matter propounded
or question in hand, which maketh much against him. . . . when the cause
of the Orator is weake, and not able to abide the uttermost triall. . . . *Cicero*
when he should have answered to an accusation, in which it was objected that
Caelius poysoned *Metellus* . . . he digressed by and by to *Metellus* death
. . . he sigheth, weepeth and bewaileth that death, whereby he staieth and ap-
peaseth his adversaries, and causeth them to mourne with him . . . turneth
the mindes of the Judges from the cogitation of the fact . . . it may be compared to the subtiltyes of war called stratagems. (*Ibid.*, p. 117)

Three figures of excuse represent another refuge in disputation. By
proecthesis,

the speaker defendeth by his answere, conteining a reason of that which he hath
said or done, proving thereby that he ought not to be blamed. . . .
    In this forme of speech our Saviour Christ doth many times defend his doings
against the accusation of his enemies: as, for healing the man with the withered
hand on the Sabboth. (*Ibid.*, p. 102)

The figure dicaeologia, or anangeon, is used

when we confesse the thynge to be done, but excuse it by necessitye, eyther of
the person or tyme, thus: I confesse that thys I dyd. But the woman that thou
gavest me dyd deceyve me. (Sherry, Sig. D vi ᵛ)

By pareuresis,

the speaker alledgeth a premeditated excuse conteining reasons of such might as are able to vanquish all objections. A most artificiall example hereof is found in the answere of *Aeneas* to *Dido*, in the *4.* booke of *Aeneidos*, wherof I have gathered the summe both of the [3] objections of *Dido*, and of the [9] answeres & excuses of *Aeneas*. (Peacham, p. 95)

Questions should be used skillfully in disputation. Pysma is a figure by which

the Orator doth demaund many times together, and use many questions in one place, whereby he maketh his speech very sharpe and vehement . . . *Cicero* for *Roscius:* In what place did he speake with them? with whom did he speake? did he hire them? whom did he hire, and by whom? To what end, or how much did he give them? . . .

This figure . . . is mighty to confirme, to confute, to provoke, to cause attention, to moove affections. . . . Plaine meaning & just dealing would that this figure should not be used to deceave the hearer by the multitude of questions . . . as doth the fallace in Sophistrie, called *Plures interrogationes.* (*Ibid.*, p. 106)

Lastly there are two general figures of persuasion and dissuasion. Peacham asserts of these that dehortatio needs no further explanation than that it is the contrary of adhortatio, or protrope, of which he remarks,

that forme of speech which deserveth the name of *Protrope* or *Adhortatio*, hath not only the forme of a commandement or of a promise, but also sundry & mightie reasons to move the minde and understanding of man not only to a willing consent, but also to a fervent desire to performe the thing adhorted. . . . The greater power that this figure hath, the more mischiefe it may worke, if it be perverted and turned to abuse . . . as by moving of sedition, tumults, or rebellion. (p. 78)

CHAPTER IX

PATHOS AND ETHOS

1. Pathos

ARISTOTLE gave the name *pathos* to that form of persuasion which endeavors to put the audience into a certain frame of mind. He thus describes its importance.

When people are feeling friendly and placable, they think one sort of thing; when they are feeling angry or hostile, they think either something totally different or the same thing with a different intensity: when they feel friendly toward the man who comes before them for judgement, they regard him as having done little wrong, if any; when they feel hostile, they take the opposite view. Again, if they are eager for, and have good hopes of, a thing that will be pleasant if it happens, they think that it certainly will happen and be good for them: whereas if they are indifferent or annoyed, they do not think so. (*Rhetoric*, 2.1.1377 ^{b} 31)

The orator must accordingly know how to appeal to the emotions, which so change men as to affect their judgments. He must know how to arouse or quiet them according to his purpose, for the emotions or passions come and go, and therein lies his opportunity.

Passion is a sudden motion of the minde or body, that endureth not long, and therefore easie to be removed. Passion of the minde is a sudden feare or joy conceived of some evill or good that is offered: and of the body, as palenesse . . . blushing, or trembling. (Blundeville, p. 32)

It is particularly in the conclusion of a speech that the orator should

stirre the hearers to bee sorie, to bee glad, or to bee offended . . . vehemently enlarging that, which before was in fewe wordes spoken to set the Judge or hearers in a heate: or els to mittigate, & asswage displeasure conceived with much lamenting of the matter, and moving them thereby the rather to shewe mercie. (Wilson, *AR*, p. 114)

The response of the hearer is the effect at which every speaker aims; his efforts are vain if he does not put his audience into the frame of mind he desires.

And assuredly nothing is more needfull, then to quicken these heavie loden wittes of ours, and much to cherish these our lompish and unweldie Natures, for except men finde delite, they will not long abide: delite them, and winne them: wearie them and you lose them for ever. And that is the reason, that men commonly tarie the ende of a merie Play, and cannot abide the halfe hearing of a sower checking Sermon. . . . Thus we see, that to delite is needfull, without the which weightie matters will not be heard at all. (*Ibid.*, p. 3)

In *The Arte of Rhetorique* the traditionalist Wilson speaks of moving the affections, of moving to pity, and of moving to laughter. The moving of affections, he explains, is

none other thing, but a stirring or forsing of the minde, either to desire, or els to detest and loth any thing, more vehemently then by nature we are commonly wont to doe. . . . Neither onely are wee moved with those things, which wee thinke either hurtfull, or profitable for our selves, but also we rejoyce, we be sorie, or wee pittie an other mans happe. . . .

In mooving affections, and stirring the Judges to be greeved, the waight of the matter must be set forth, as though they sawe it plaine before their eyes, the report must be such, and the offence made so hainous, that the like hath not bene seen heretofore. (*Ibid.*, p. 130)

To move the hearers to pity, the speaker should feel in his own heart the sorrow he recounts, then lead them to share in it either through memory or through imagination.

Now in moving pitie, and stirring men to mercie . . . the best were to wil them, to remember their owne state . . . if the like hath not happened unto the hearers of this cause, yet it were meete to shewe them that the like may happen . . . Neither can any good bee done at all . . . except we bring the same affections in our own harte, the which we would the Judges should beare towards our owne matter. For how can he be greeved with the report of any hainous act . . . in bewayling the miserable misfortune of the thing, or in fearing much, the like evill hereafter: except the Oratour himselfe utter such passions outwardly, and from his heart fetch his complaints . . . such men . . . will force a man to be sory with them, and take part with their teares even against his wil. Notwithstanding when such affections are moved, it were good not to stand long in them. For though a vehement talke may moove teares, yet no arte can holde them. For as *Cicero* doth say, nothing drieth soner then teares, especially when we lament an other mans cause, and be sorie with him for his sake. (*Ibid.*, p. 133)

Moving the audience to laughter serves two purposes: it gains their attention and it puts them into a favorable frame of mind.[1]

[1] Wilson's discussion of moving to laughter is derived from *Il cortegiano* of Castiglione, who borrowed it from Cicero's *De oratore.*

Assuredly it behoveth a man . . . evermore to have regarde to his audience
. . . And now because our senses be such, that in hearing a right wholsome
matter, we either fall a sleepe . . . or els are wearied with still hearing one
thing, without any change . . . the wittie and learned have used delitefull
sayings, and quicke sentences, ever among their waightie causes, considering
that onely good will is got thereby (for what is he that loveth not mirth?) but
also men wonder at such a head, as hath mens hartes at his commaundement,
being able to make them merie when he list . . . Againe, we see that men are
full oft abashed, and put out of countenance by such taunting meanes, and those
that have so done are coumpted to be fine men, and pleasaunt fellowes. (*Ibid.*,
p. 136)

The figurists also understood the value of appealing to the feelings.
Concerning this form of persuasion, Peacham remarks:

the Orator . . . may prevaile much in drawing the mindes of his hearers to
his owne will and affection: he may winde them from their former opinions,
and quite alter the former state of their mindes, he may move them to be of his
side, to hold with him, to be led by him, as to mourne or to marvel, to love or
to hate, to be pleased or to be angry, to favour, to desire or to be satisfied, to
feare or to hope, to envy, to abhorre, to pittie, to rejoyce, to be ashamed, to
repent, and finally to be subject to the power of his speech whither soever it
tendeth. (p. 121)

In discussing pathopopoeia, the generic figure of *pathos*, Peacham emphasizes the same points as Wilson.

The Orator moveth the minds of his hearers to some vehemency of affection,
as of indignation feare, envy, hatred, hope, gladnesse, mirth, laughter, sadnesse
or sorrow: of this there be two kindes.
    The first is when the Orator being moved himselfe with anie affections (sor-
row excepted) doth bend & apply his speech to stir his hearers to the same . . .
to which diverse vehement figures do belong, as *Exclamatio, Obtestatio, Im-
precatio, Optatio, Exuscitatio, Interrogatio,* and such like. And to move mirth,
formes of speech serving to that purpose, as *Asteismus,* and others of that kinde.
. . . Examples hereof are common in Tragedies, but of mirth and laughter
in Comodies.
    The other kind of *Pathopeia,* is when the Orator by declaring some lamenta-
ble cause, moveth his hearers to pitie and compassion, to shew mercy, and to pardon offences. . . . A serious and deepe affection in the Orator is a mightie furtherance and helpe to this figure, as when he is zealous, and deeply touched
himselfe with any of those vehement affections, but specially if he be inwardly
moved with a pitifull affection, he moveth his hearers to the same compassion
and pitie, by his passionate pronuntiation. (*Ibid.*, pp. 143–45)

Exuscitatio is the stirring up of others to like or dislike, through the vehement affection of the speaker himself.

Doth it not abhor you to heare and understand of a rabble of so great and unaccustomed lewdnesse, a man every way so vile, to go thus freely unpunished? Surely I do thinke no honest mind but would bee of this opinion, that of all creatures living he were most worthy to be extirped. (Day, p. 389)

In a few figures of *pathos* the form of the language reveals the speaker's emotion. This is true of aposiopesis, by which

the Orator through some affection, as either of feare, anger, sorrow, bashfulnesse or such like, breaketh off his speech before it be all ended. *Virgil:* How doth the childe *Ascanius*, whom tymely *Troy* to thee: breaking off by the interruption of sorrow. (Peacham, p. 118)

Concerning ecphonesis, or exclamation, Hoskyns observes:

Exclamacion is not lawfull, but in extremity of mocion, as *Pirocles* seeing the milde *Philoclea* innocently beheaded, cryed out, oh Tyrant heaven. Traitor earth, blind providence, noe Justice, howe is this done? howe is this suffred? hath this world a government? (p. 147)

Fraunce and Fenner give examples of many species of the figure exclamation, which, they say, is an excellent means to the forcible stirring up of divers affections, such as wonder and admiration, despair, wishing, cursing, indignation, disdain, derision, scorn, mocking (often joined with irony), detestation, protestation, grief and misery, pity and commiseration. Thus the Ramists present under the one figure exclamation many species which the figurists treat as distinct figures, giving to each its own peculiar name. Thaumasmus is a figure by which one utters an exclamation of wonder.

O the deepenes of the riches, of the wisedome and knowledge of God &c. Rom. 11, . . .

By this figure the Orator sometime wondereth, at the boldnesse and impudency of wicked deedes . . . at the negligence of men, in not preventing danger, or at their brutish security when the battel axe of destruction hangeth over their heads . . . at impunitie, when he seeth great wickednes passe free without punishment or rebuke . . . at the accusation of some person, in whom he hath a good opinion. (Peacham, p. 72)

Erotema, or interrogatio, although expressed in the form of a question, does not ask for information but is rather a device whereby the Orator doth affirme or deny something strongly, Job 8.3.11: Doth God pervert the thing that is lawful, or doth the Almighty pervert justice? can a rush be green without moisture, or may the grasse grow without water? that is to say it cannot.

This figure giveth to speech not onely life and motion, but also great strength and a coragious countenance, which is much commended in the supporting of good causes. (*Ibid.*, p. 106)

Apostrophe often employs prosopopoeia, exclamation, or interrogation. Hoskyns thus explains it:

Apostrophe, is a turning of your speech to some newe person, as to the people, when your speech before was to the Judge. . . . Sometymes the occasion is to some quallitie, or thing, that your selfe gives shewe of life to as hope tell me, what hast thou to hope for? Love be ashamed to be called Love. (p. 162)

The figures of vehemence and affection sound the whole gamut of the emotions.

Three of them have as their purpose to recall and lament sorrow.

Anamnesis is a forme of speech by which the Speaker calling to remembrance matters past, doth make recitall of them. Sometime matters of sorrow, as did *Dido* a litle before her death . . .

An example . . . of the prodigall sonne: Then he came to himselfe and said, how many servants at my fathers house, have bread inough, and I die for hunger. Luke. 15.17. (Peacham, p. 76)

Threnos is a forme of speech by which the Orator lamenteth some person or people for the miserie they suffer, or the speaker his owne calamitie. . . . The greatest part of *Jeremies* lamentations, is framed by this forme of speech. . . . O that my head were full of water, and mine eyes a fountain of teares, that I might weepe day and night, for the slaine of the daughter of my people. Jeremy 9. (*Ibid.*, p. 66)

Apocarteresis is a forme of speech by which the speaker signifieth that he casteth away all hope concerning some thing, & turneth it another way. *Job* . . . signifieth that he hath no more hope of worldly prosperitie and comfort, and therefore he turneth the eye of his hope to heaven, saying: I know that my re-deemer liveth, &c. Whereby he comforteth himself the better to indure & suffer so great and heavy a burthen of misery. Job 19.25. (*Ibid.*, p. 83)

Three figures express desire or supplication.

Optatio is a forme of speech, by which the speaker expresseth his desire by wish-ing to God or Men. An example of *Cicero:* I would the immortall Gods had granted that wee might rather have given thankes to *Servius Sulpitius* being alive, then now to examine his honours being dead. (*Ibid.*, p. 72)

Deesis, when for God, or for mannes sake we vehemently desyre to have any thynge. As Cicero for Publius Sestius: O I praye you, & for the Gods sakes most herteli besech you, that as it was your wylles to save me, so you wyl vouchsaf to save them thorow whose helpe you received me agayne. (Sherry, Sig. D ii ʳ)

Mempsis is a forme of speech by which the Orator maketh a complaint, and craveth helpe. . . . King *David:* Why standest thou so farre O Lord, and hidest thy selfe in the needfull time of trouble? the ungodlie for his owne lust doth persecute the poore. . . . The poore committeth himselfe unto thee, for thou art the helper of the friendlesse, breake thou the power of the ungodlie and malicious. Psal. 10 (Peacham, p. 65)

Three figures are designed to console or to placate.

Paramythia is a forme of speech which the Orator useth to take away, or diminish a sorrow conceived in the minde of his hearer. An example of *Aeneas* in *Virgil,* and thus translated,

O mates (quoth he) that many a wo have bid, & borne ere this,
Worse have we seene, and these also shall end, when Gods will is.
(Ibid., p. 100)

Medela, when seeing the offences of our friends, or of them whom we defend, to be so great that we cannot honestly defend them, or so manifest that we cannot well deny them, we seeke to heale them with plastures of good words . . . The Apostle *Paul* giveth a verie good example of this figure in his Epistle to *Philemon,* where he useth sundry reasons & diverse meanes to salve and cure the fault of *Onesimus,* and to appease and pacifie the displeasure of *Philemon.* *(Ibid.,* p. 176)

Philophronesis . . . is a forme of speech by which the speaker perceiving the might of his adversary to be too great and too strong against him, useth gentle speech, faire promises, and humble submission, to mitigate the rygor and crueltie of his adversary: we have a notable example hereof in *Jacob:* who fearing the malice and might of his brother *Esau,* used this meanes to appease his rage and crueltie. . . . assoone as he saw *Esau,* he shewed a signe of dutiful submission, he bowed himselfe seven times most humbly before he came neare to him, calling him his Lord . . . his family also children came likewise in seemly and suppliant order, and humbled themselves at his presence . . . by meanes whereof the fiery and flaming wrath of *Esau* was turned into teares of compassion. *(Ibid.,* p. 96)

Mocks and taunts, not only in words but also in gesture, were treated in Renaissance rhetoric as figures. Puttenham calls mycterismus the fleering frumpe and defines it as a mock given with scornful countenance, as for example by drawing the lip awry. Sherry decribes it as

a skornyng by some jesture of the face, as by wrythinge the nose, putting out
the tonge, pointyng, or such lyke. (Sig. C vii ᵛ)

Peacham considers mycterismus to be a subtle mock with words and gives
this example:

To one that demanded of *Demonax* the philosopher, if Philosophers did use to
eate sweete cakes, *Demonax* made this answer, Doest thou thinke (quoth he)
that bees gather their hony for fooles onely? (p. 39)

Without naming it, Blundeville makes a logician's natural comment on
mycterismus in discussing what he calls confutation of person.

There be some that make two kinds of Confutation, the one belonging to person, the other to matter. Confutation of person is done either by taunting,
rayling, rendring checke for checke, or by scorning, and that either by wordes,
or else by countenance, gesture and action: which kinde of Confutation, because
it belongeth rather to scoffing then to true order of reasoning, I will leave to
speake thereof. (p. 183)

Sarcasmus, more open than mycterismus,

is a bitter sporting a mocke of our enemye, or a maner of jestying or scoffinge
bytynglye, a nyppyng tawnte, as: The Jewes sayde to Christ, he saved other,
but he could not save hym selfe. (Sherry, Sig. C vii ᵛ)

Chiding, reprehension, accusation, or abhorrence characterize five
figures. Epiplexis, or percontatio, is asking questions, not in order to
know, but to

chide, and set forth our griefe with more vehemencie . . . *Tullie* enveighing
against *Catiline* . . . beginneth his Oration chidingly . . . How long (*Catiline*) wilt thou abuse our sufferaunce? How long will this rage and madnesse
of thine goe aboute to deceive us? (Wilson, *AR*, p. 184)

Onedismus . . . is a form of speech by which the speaker upbraideth his adversary of ingratitude, and impietie. . . . *Dido* . . . upbraiding *Aeneas* with
the great and manifold benefites which he had received of her . . . exclaimeth
. . . No Goddesse never was thy Dam . . . Some Tigers thee did nurce
. . . it tendeth most specially to reprove and rebuke ingratitude. (Peacham,
p. 73)

Categoria . . . is a forme of speech by which the speaker openeth and detect-
eth some secret wickednesse of his adversary, and laieth it open before his face.
An example of Christ detecting *Judas:* He that dippeth his hand with me in the
dish, he shall betray me. Mat. 26.23. (*Ibid.*, p. 80)

Proclees . . . is a forme of speech by which the Orator provoketh his adversary to the conflict . . . either by a vehement accusation, or by a confident offer of justification. By accusation, this of *Eliphaz* provoking *Job* . . . Is not thy wickednesse great? and thine ungratious deeds abhominable? for thou hast taken the pledge from thy brother for nought, and spoyled the clothes of the naked. . . . By offer of justification, this example of Christ . . . Which of you can rebuke me of sinne? (*Ibid.*, p. 83)

Bdelygmia . . . is a forme of speech which the speaker useth to signifie how much he hateth and abhorreth some person, word, deed, or thing, and it is used commonly in a short forme, and in few words. Against a person thus: Out upon him wretch . . . Against an odious deed, thus: Fie upon it. (*Ibid.*, p. 82)

The vehement figures of threatening and cursing Peacham illustrates from the Bible.

Cataplexis is a forme of speech by which the Orator denounceth a threatening against some person, people, citie, common wealth or country . . . declaring the certaintie or likelihood of plagues, or punishments to fall upon them for their wickednesse, impietie, insolencie, and generall iniquitie. . . . Jonas 3. Yet fortie daies, and Ninivy shall be destroyed. (p. 79)

Ara is a forme of speech by which the Orator detesteth, and curseth some person or thing, for the evils which they bring with them, or for the wickednesse which is in them. Psalm 109. Let the ungodly have dominion over him, and let Sathan stand at his right hand. (p. 64)

In contrast, two figures express blessing and rejoicing.

Eulogia is a forme of speech by which the Orator pronounceth a blessing uppon some person for the goodnesse that is in him or her. . . . Psal. 41. Blessed is the man which considereth the poore and the needie. (*Ibid.*, p. 65)

Paeanismus is a forme of speech which the . . . speaker useth to expresse his joy, either for the cause of some good thing obtained, or some evil avoyded. . . . To this forme of speech perteineth this saying in the song of the virgine *Mary:* From henceforth all generations shal call me blessed. . . . He hath filled the hungry with good things, and the rich he hath sent emptie away. . . . This figure after a sort is lively represented in the Larkes song, which she singeth everie morning, in joy that the darknesse is gone and the light come. (*Ibid.*, p. 81)

2. *Ethos*

That mode of persuasion which Aristotle calls *ethos* is, in a sense, included in *pathos*, for the attitude of the audience toward the personal character of the speaker, their confidence in him and in his good will toward them, constitutes part of their feelings or frame of mind as they listen. And *logos,* the sum of the ideas in the speech, helps not only to inspire in the audience confidence and good will toward the speaker but also to affect their feelings favorably or unfavorably toward the persons or matters being discussed. Consequently, although each of these three modes of persuasion, *ethos, logos,* and *pathos,* has special reference either to the speaker, to the speech, or to those spoken to, they are, nevertheless, closely interrelated; all three are intrinsic to the speech, all are under the control of the speaker, and the measure of success of all three is the effect on the hearers, as Aristotle succinctly explains.

Since rhetoric exists to affect the giving of decisions . . . the orator must not only try to make the argument of his speech demonstrative and worthy of belief; he must also make his own character look right and put his hearers, who are to decide, into the right frame of mind. (*Rhetoric,* 2.1.1377 ^{b} 21)

In his *Rhetoric* Aristotle gives a clear and illuminating account of the mode of persuasion which he calls *ethos.*

Persuasion is achieved by the speaker's personal character when the speech is so spoken as to make us think him credible. We believe good men more fully and more readily than others . . . This kind of persuasion, like the others, should be achieved by what the speaker says, not by what people think of his character before he begins to speak. It is not true . . . that the personal goodness revealed by the speaker contributes nothing to his power of persuasion; on the contrary, his character may almost be called the most effective means of persuasion he possesses. (1.2.1356 ^{a} 4)

It adds much to an orator's influence that his own character should look right and that he should be thought to entertain the right feelings toward his hearers. (2.1.1377 ^{b} 25)

There are three things which inspire confidence in the orator's own character— the three, namely, that induce us to believe a thing apart from any proof of it: good sense, good moral character, and good will. False statements and bad advice are due to one or more of the following three causes. Men either form a false opinion through want of good sense; or they form a true opinion, but because of their moral badness do not say what they really think; or finally, they are both sensible and upright, but not well-disposed toward their hearers, and may fail in consequence to recommend what they know to be the best course. These are the only possible cases. It follows that anyone who is thought to have all three of these good qualities will inspire trust in his audience. (2.1.1378 ^{a} 6)

In the *Poetics* Aristotle treats character and thought as two of the six formative elements of drama, which has as its essential function to arouse pity and fear in order to purge the audience agreeably of an excess of those emotions.[2] Here again is the combination of *ethos, logos,* and *pathos.* Aristotle thus defines the two elements of character and thought.

Character in a play is that which reveals the moral purpose of the agents, i.e. the sort of thing they seek or avoid, where that is not obvious—hence there is no room for Character in a speech on a purely indifferent subject. Thought, on the other hand, is shown in all they say when proving or disproving some particular point, or enunciating some universal proposition. (*Poetics,* 6.1450 ^{b} 8)

Not only in their speeches but even in their actions the characters of drama employ *logos* and *pathos* to convey their thought.

The Thought of the personages is shown in everything to be effected by their language—in every effort to prove or disprove, to arouse emotion (pity, fear, anger, and the like), or to maximize or minimize things. It is clear, also, that their mental procedure must be on the same lines in their actions likewise, whenever they wish them to arouse pity or horror, or to have a look of importance or probability. The only difference is that with the act the impression has to be made without explanation; whereas with the spoken word it has to be produced by the speaker, and result from his language. What, indeed, would be the good of the speaker, if things appeared in the required light even apart from anything he says? (*Poetics,* 19.1456 ^{a} 36)

It is particularly at the beginning of a speech that a speaker endeavors to win for himself the confidence and favor of his audience. Consequently in treating of the exordium Wilson touches upon *ethos* as a means of persuasion.

We must advisedly marke the men, before whom we speake, and al the circumstances which belong unto the matter. If the matter be honest, godly, and such as of right ought to be well liked, we may use an open beginning . . . If the cause bee lothsome, or such as will not be well borne with all, but needeth much helpe and favour of the hearers: it shalbe the speakers part prively to get favour & by humble talk to win their good wils. First requiring them to give him the hearing, . . . Wee shall make the people attentive, and glad to heare us . . . if we promise to tell them things concerning either their owne profit, or the advancement of their countrie . . .

We shall get the good willes of our hearers fower maner of waies, either beginning to speake of our selves, or els of our adversaries, or els of the people and companie present, or, last of all, if we begin of the matter it selfe, . . .

[2] Lane Cooper, in *An Aristotelian Theory of Comedy,* shows reason to think that Aristotle, in a part of his work now lost, considered the function of comedy likewise to be a catharsis, one to be wrought through laughter. Aristotle remarks (*Rhetoric,* 3.18.1419 ^{b} 5): "Jests have been classified in the *Poetics.*" But they are not treated in the extant *Poetics.*

Wee shall get favour for our owne sakes, if we shal modestly set foorth . . .
our service done, without al suspition of vaunting . . . and lastly, if wee shewe
without all ostentation, aswell our good willes towards the Judges there, as also
pleasures done for them in tymes past. . . . in most humble wise to seeke favour . . .

We shall get favour by speaking of our adversaries, if wee shall make such
reporte of them, that the hearers shall either hate to heare them, or utterly envie
them, or els altogether despise them . . .

We shall get good will, by speaking of the Judges and hearers: if wee shall
commend their worthie doings, and prayse their just dealing . . . and tell
them in what estimation the whole countrey hath them . . .

We shall finde favour by speaking of the matter, if in handling our owne
cause, we commende it accordingly, and dispraise the attempt of our adversary. . . .

A privie beginning, or creeping in . . . must then, and not els be used,
when the Judge is greeved with us, and our cause hated of the hearers.

The cause selfe oftentimes is not liked for three divers causes, if either the
matter selfe be unhonest . . . or els if the Judge himself by a former tale be
perswaded to take parte against us, or last if at that time we are forced to speake,
when the Judge is weried with hearing of other. . . . evermore nothing
should be spoken at the first, but that which might please the Judge . . . when
the hearers are some what calmed, we may enter by little and little into the
matter, and say that those things, which our adversary doth mislike in the person accused, we also doe mislike the same. And when the hearers are thus
wonne . . . it were not amisse for the furtherance of our owne causes, closely
to speake our phantasie, and so, streight to aulter their hearts . . . But if the
adversarie have so tolde his tale, that the Judge is wholly bent to give sentence
with hym . . . we may take advantage, of some part of our adversaries tale,
and talke of that first, which he spake last: or els begin so, as though wee
doubted what were best first to speake . . . wondering . . . at the strange-
nesse of his reporte, and confirmation of his cause. For when the standers by,
perceive that the answerer (whome the adversaries thought . . . wholly
abashed) feareth so little the objections of his adversarie, and is readie to answere *Ad omnia quare* with a bolde countenance: They will thinke that they
themselves, rather gave rash credite, and were overlight in beleeving the first
tale. (*AR*, pp. 99–104)

It is evident that *ethos* is a pervasive quality running through a speech.
Yet there are four figures which seem designed to inspire confidence in
the speaker's goodness and in his good will toward the hearers and may
therefore be classified under *ethos*.

Comprobatio, when we see some good thyng eyther in the Judges or in our
hearers, or in any other. And therefore declare that we doo well allowe of it,

and also commende them for it. *Cicero.* I commende and prayse you, you Judges, for that most lovingly ye do advance the name of so famous a young man. (Peacham, 1577, Sig. L ii ᵛ)

Parrhesia, is a forme of speech by which the Orator speaking before those whom he feareth, or ought to reverence, & having somewhat to say that may either touch themselves, or those whom they favour, preventeth the displeasure and offence that might be taken, as by craving pardon afore hand, and by shewing the necessitie of free speech in that behalfe, or by some other like forme of humble submission and modest insinuation. An example of *Cicero* . . . I feare judges after what sort you may take my words, but for my continuall desire that I have to maintaine and augment your dignitie, I pray and beseech you, that if my speech be either bitter or incredible unto you . . . yet that you would accept it without offence . . . Neither that you will reject it before I have plainlie declared the whole unto you. . . .

This figure doth best beseeme a man of wisedome and gravitie, who is best able to moderate the forme of this speech . . . which is the onely forme that boldly delivereth to great dignities and most high degrees of men, the message of justice and equitie, sparing neither magistrates that pervert lawes, nor Princes that abuse their kingdomes. (Peacham, 1593, p. 113)

Eucharistia . . . is a forme of speech by which the speaker geveth thankes for benefites received . . . Sometime it is joyned with a confession of the unablenesse of the receiver to requite the giver . . . Psal. 16. What shal I give unto the Lord for all the benefites towards me? (*Ibid.,* p. 101)

Syngnome . . . is a form of speech by which the . . . speaker being a pacient of many and great injuries, or of some one great and greevous wrong, pronounceth pardon and forgivenesse to his adversary, who was the worker of all his miserie . . . An example of . . . *Steven* the Martyr at his death, who cryed with a loud voice, saying: Lord laie not this sinne to their charge. (*Ibid.,* p. 98)

In addition, a few figures which have been classified under other headings are likely to engender a favorable opinion of the speaker by revealing his courtesy or his goodness: anacoenosis, asking counsel of the adversary or of the judges; synchoresis, confidently asking one's adversary or judges to judge of one's cause; eustathia, promising constancy in purpose and affection; asphalia, becoming surety for another; philophronesis, gentle speech and humble submission; eulogia, pronouncing a blessing. Even prosopographia, as Aristotle shows, may contribute substantially to *ethos.*

With regard to the element of moral character: there are assertions which, if made about yourself, may excite dislike, appear tedious, or expose you to the risk of contradiction; and other things which you cannot say about your opponent without seeming abusive or ill bred. Put such remarks, therefore, into the mouth of some third person. . . . So . . . Sophocles makes Haemon appeal to his father on behalf of Antigone as if it were others who were speaking [*Antigone*, 688–700]. (*Rhetoric*, 3.17.1418 [b] 23)

3. Conclusion

Part III is a reconstruction, essentially complete, of the general theory of composition and of reading current in the Renaissance as it is embodied in extant sixteenth-century English texts on logic and rhetoric. Some passages from Aristotle have been included, because his work had an influence both direct and indirect on the Tudor logicians and rhetoricians, who frequently refer to him and sometimes use his very illustrations.

Careful study of the Tudor texts, which were based directly on Renaissance Latin texts used in the schools, discloses beneath obvious superficial differences the same fundamental doctrine among the traditionalists, the Ramists, and the figurists: all of them take account of the three modes of persuasion, *logos*, *pathos*, and *ethos*; all build on the topics of invention and recognize the same forms of reasoning and disputation. Logic was clearly regarded as the most important factor in composition not only by the Ramists and the traditionalists but also by the figurists. As has been shown in Chapters VII and VIII, one hundred and twenty-two of the two hundred figures of speech which the figurists distinguished are derived from the topics and forms of logic, a fact which they often explicitly pointed out. The figure diaeresis, for example, is equivalent to logical division, litotes to obversion, aetiologia to the enthymeme of the logicians, climax to sorites, epilogus to the hypothetical syllogism, apophasis to the disjunctive syllogism, dialysis to the dilemma.

The Renaissance theory, basically the same for all three groups, contains little that is altogether new to us, although the names of the figures and the sixteenth-century concept of figure, astonishing in its inclusiveness, present an initial obstacle. The precepts of all the arts are ultimately only codified good sense—rules derived by critics from the practice of creative artists whose native genius has produced results that have been admired, approved, and imitated throughout the ages.

The ancient classification of the figures, which the Renaissance rhetoricians retained, tends to obscure the simple and coherent functional pattern underlying their meticulous and comprehensive analysis of thought, emotion, and expression. It is hoped that the correlation of the works of the

logicians and rhetoricians here undertaken and the reclassification of the
figures according to their functions under the headings grammar, *logos*,
pathos, and *ethos* will both clarify the theory and contribute to a fuller
understanding of Renaissance literature.

BIBLIOGRAPHY

A. Primary

Aristotle. Works; tr. into English under the editorship of W. R. Ross. Oxford, 1928, 1924. "Organon," Vol. I; "Rhetoric" and "Poetics," Vol. XI.

Blundeville, Thomas. The Arte of Logick [1599]. London, 1617.

Butler, Charles. Rhetoricae libri duo [1598]. London, 1629.

—— Oratoriae libri duo. Oxford, 1629.

Cicero, Marcus Tullius. Brutus and Orator; tr. by George Lincoln Hendrickson and Harry Mortimer Hubbel. Loeb Classical Library. Cambridge, Mass., 1939.

—— De inventione rhetorica; texte revu et traduit avec introduction et notes par Henri Bornecque. Paris, 1932.

—— De oratore, De fato, Paradoxo stoicorum, De partitione oratoriae. 2 vols., tr. by E. W. Sutton and H. Rackham. Loeb Classical Library. Cambridge, Mass., 1942.

—— The Orator; tr. by E. Jones. London, 1808.

—— Rhetorica; recognovit brevique adnotione critica instruxit A. S. Wilkins. 2 vols. Oxford, 1901–1903.

—— Orations; tr. by C. D. Yonge, Vol. IV. Bohn's Classical Library. London, 1894–1903. "Rhetorical Invention" and "Topics."

Cox, Leonard. The Arte or Crafte of Rhethoryke [ca. 1530]; a reprint edited by Frederic Ives Carpenter. Chicago, 1899.

Day, Angel. The English Secretorie; with a Declaration of Tropes, Figures, and Schemes [1592]. London, 1635.

Fenner, Dudley. The Artes of Logike and Rhetorike. Middelburg, 1584.

Fraunce, Abraham. The Arcadian Rhetorike; or, The Praecepts of Rhetorike Made Plaine by Examples, Greeke, Latin, English, Italian, French, Spanish. London, 1588.

—— The Lawiers Logike; Exemplifying the Praecepts of Logike by the Practise of the Common Lawe. London, 1588.

Hoskyns, John. "Direccions for Speech and Style" [ca. 1599]; printed from MS Harley 4604, in The Life, Letters and Writings of John Hoskyns, 1566–1638, pp. 114–166, by Louise Brown Osborn. New Haven, 1937.

—— Directions for Speech and Style; ed. by Hoyt H. Hudson. Princeton, 1935.

Lever, Raphe. The Arte of Reason, Rightly Termed Witcraft; Teaching a Perfect Way to Argue and Dispute. London, 1573.

4

BIBLIOGRAPHY

Melanchthon, Philippus. Opera, Corpus Reformatorum, ed. by Bretschneider et
Bindseil. 28 vols. Brunswick und Halle, 1834–60. Vol. XIII, "Institu-
tiones rhetoricae" (Haganoa, 1521), "Elementa Rhetorices" (Witten-
berg, 1531), "Erotemata Dialectices" (Basel, 1521).
Peacham, Henry. The Garden of Eloquence. London, 1577.
—— The Garden of Eloquence; corrected and augmented by the first author.
London, 1593.
Puttenham, George. The Arte of English Poesie [1589]; ed. by Gladys
Doidge Willcock and Alice Walker. Cambridge, 1936.
Quintilian, M. Fabius. Institutio oratoria; with an English translation by H. E.
Butler. 4 vols. Loeb Classical Library. London and New York, 1922.
—— Institutes of Oratory; tr. by J. S. Watson. 2 vols. Bohn's Classical Li-
brary. London, 1891.
Rainolde, Richard. A Booke Called the Foundacion of Rhetorike. London,
1563.
Ramus, Petrus. Dialecticae institutiones. Paris, 1543.
—— Institutionum dialecticarum libri III. Paris, 1547.
—— Dialecticae libri duo, et his e regione comparati Philippi Melanth. Dialec-
ticae libri quatuor cum explicationum et collationum notis, ad utramque . . .
auctore Frederico Beurhusio, Meinertzhagense Scholae Tremoneanae Rec-
tore, 1586.
Ramus, Petrus. Dialecticae libri duo; cum commentariis Georgii Dounami
annexis. London, 1669.
Rhetorica ad C. Herennium; texte revu et traduit avec introduction et notes
par Henri Bornecque. Paris, 1932.
Shakespeare, William. Complete Works; ed. by George Lyman Kittredge.
Boston, 1936.
Sherry, Richard. A Treatise of Schemes & Tropes. London, 1550.
—— A Treatise of the Figures of Grammer and Rhetorike. London, 1555.
Susenbrotus, Joannes. Epitome troporum ac schematum et grammaticorum et
rhetoricorum [Zurich, 1540]. London, 1621.
Talaeus, Audomarus. Rhetorica e P. Rami praelectionibus observata [1544?];
per Claudium Minoem. Frankfort, 1579.
Wilson, Thomas. The Arte of Rhetorique; a reprint of the edition of 1585
[1553]; ed. by G. H. Mair. Oxford, 1909.
—— The Rule of Reason; Conteining the Art of Logike [1551]. London,
1567.

B. Secondary

Abbott, E. A. A Shakespearian Grammar. 3d ed. London, 1871.
Abelson, Paul. The Seven Liberal Arts; a Study in Medieval Culture. New
York, 1906.

Anders, H. R. D. Shakespeare's Books. Berlin, 1904.

Ascham, Roger. The Scholemaster. London, 1570.

—— The Whole Works of Roger Ascham; ed. by Giles. 3 vols. in 4. London, 1865.

Baldwin, Charles Sears. Ancient Rhetoric and Poetic. New York, 1924.

—— Medieval Rhetoric and Poetic. New York, 1928.

—— Renaissance Literary Theory and Practice. New York, 1939.

Baldwin, T. W. William Shakspere's Small Latine and Lesse Greeke. 2 vols. Urbana, 1944.

Berdan, John. Early Tudor Poetry 1485–1547. New York, 1931.

Boethius, Anicius Manlius. "De differentiis topicis," in Patrologiae cursus completus, series prima, ed. Jacques Paul Migne, Vol. LXIV.

Brinsley, John. Ludus literarius; or, The Grammar Schoole; ed. by E. T. Campagnac. Liverpool, 1917.

Cameron, Kenneth Walter. Authorship and Sources of "Gentleness and Nobility." Raleigh, 1941.

Campbell, Lily B. Shakespeare's Tragic Heroes, Slaves of Passion. Cambridge, 1930.

Campbell, Oscar James. Comicall Satyre and Shakespeare's 'Troilus and Cressida.' San Marino, 1938.

—— Satire in Shakespeare. New York, 1943.

Castiglione, Baldassare. The Book of the Courtier; tr. by Sir Thomas Hoby, 1561. New York, 1928.

Chambers, R. W. "Shakespeare and the Play of *More*," in Man's Unconquerable Mind (London, 1939), pp. 204–49.

Chapman, George. Works; ed. by R. H. Shepherd. London, 1874–75.

Clark, Donald Lemen. Rhetoric and Poetry in the Renaissance. New York, 1922.

Cooper, Lane. An Aristotelian Theory of Comedy; with an Adaptation of the Poetics and a Translation of the 'Tractatus Coislinianus.' New York, 1922.

Craig, Hardin. The Enchanted Glass. New York, 1936.

—— "Shakespeare and Formal Logic," in Studies in English Philology: a Miscellany in Honor of Frederick Klaeber (Minneapolis, 1929,) pp. 380–396.

—— "Shakespeare and Wilson's *Arte of Rhetorique;* an Inquiry into the Criteria for Determining Sources," *Studies in Philology*, XXVIII (October, 1931), 618–30.

Crane, William G. Wit and Rhetoric in the Renaissance. New York, 1937.

Curry, Walter Clyde. Shakespeare's Philosophical Patterns. Baton Rouge, 1937.

Dekker, Thomas. Dramatic Works; ed. by R. H. Shepherd. London, 1873.

—— Satiro-Mastix; ed. by Hans Scherer. Louvain, 1907.

Donnelly, Francis P., S.J. Literature, the Leading Educator. New York, 1938.

—— Persuasive Speech. New York, 1931.

Faral, Edmond. "Les Arts poetiques du XII⁰ et du XIII⁰ siècle," in Bibliothèque de l'École des Hautes Etudes, Paris, 1924.

Franz, Wilhelm. Die Sprache Shakespeares in Vers und Prosa. Halle, 1939.

Frasure, Louise D. "Shakespeare's Constables," *Anglia*, LVIII (1934), 384–392.

Gascoigne, George. Complete Works; ed. by John W. Cunliffe. 2 vols. Cambridge, 1907.

Gilbert, Allan H. "Logic in the Elizabethan Drama," *Studies in Philology*, XXXII (October, 1935), 527–45.

Gordon, George Stuart. "Shakespeare's English," in Society for Pure English, *Tract* 29 (Oxford), 1928, pp. 255–75.

Graves, Frank Pierrepont. Peter Ramus and the Educational Reformation of the Sixteenth Century. New York, 1912.

Greene, Robert. The Life and Complete Works in Prose and Verse of Robert Greene; ed. by A. B. Grosart (The Huth Library). 15 vols. London, 1881–1886.

Greenewald, Gerard M., O.M.Cap. Shakespeare's Attitude towards the Catholic Church in "King John." Washington, 1938.

Groom, Bernard. "The Formation and Use of Compound Epithets from 1579," in Society for Pure English, *Tract* 49 (Oxford), 1936, pp. 293–322.

Hart, Alfred. "Shakespeare and the Vocabulary of *The Two Noble Kinsmen*," in Shakespeare and the Homilies, (Melbourne, 1934), pp. 242–56.

—— "Vocabularies of Shakespeare's Plays," *Review of English Studies*, XIX (April, 1943), 128–40.

Hart, H. C., ed. Love's Labour's Lost. 3d ed., revised. The Arden Shakespeare. London, 1930.

Haskins, C. H. The Renaissance of the Twelfth Century. Cambridge, Mass., 1928.

Henderson, W. B. Drayton. "Montaigne's *Apologie of Raymond Sebond* and *King Lear*," *Shakespeare Association Bulletin*, XIV (October, 1939), 209–25.

Hermogenis. De ratione inveniendi oratoria, libri IIII; latinitate donati & scholis explicati atque illustrati a Jonane Sturmio, 2 vols., ed. by J. Cocin. [Argentorati], 1570.

Herrick, Marvin T. The Poetics of Aristotle in England. New Haven, 1930.

Hubbell, H. M. The Influence of Isocrates on Cicero, Dionysius, and Aristides. New Haven, 1913.

Hultzen, Lee S. Aristotle's "Rhetoric" in England before 1600. Unpublished dissertation presented to Cornell University, 1932.

Johnson, Francis R. "Two Renaissance Textbooks of Rhetoric: Aphtho-nius' *Progymnasmata* and Rainolde's *A Booke Called the Foundacion of Rhetorike*," *Huntington Library Quarterly*, VI (August, 1943), 427–444.

Jonson, Ben. Ben Jonson; ed. by C. H. Herford and Percy Simpson. 7 vols. Oxford, 1925–41.

—— Discoveries; a critical edition with an introduction and notes by Maurice Castelain. Paris, n.d.

—— The English Grammar [written *ca.* 1630–35]; ed. with introduction and notes by Alice Vinton Waite. New York, 1909.

Kellett, E. E. "Some Notes on a Feature of Shakespeare's Style," in Suggestions (Cambridge, 1923), pp. 57–78.

Kennedy, Milton Boone. The Oration in Shakespeare. Chapel Hill, 1942.

Kempe, William. The Education of Children. London, 1588.

Lever, Katherine. "Proverbs and *Sententiae* in the Plays of Shakspere," *Shakepeare Association Bulletin*, XIII (July and October, 1938), 173–83; 224–239.

Lewis, C. S. The Allegory of Love. Oxford, 1936.

Lodge, Thomas, and Robert Greene. A Looking Glasse, for London and Englande. London, 1598.

Lyly, John. The Complete Works of John Lyly; ed. by R. W. Bond. 3 vols. Oxford, 1902.

—— Euphues, the Anatomy of Wit, and Euphues and His England; ed. by Morris W. Croll and Harry Clemons. London, 1916.

Marlowe, Christopher. Works; ed. by C. F. Tucker Brooke. Oxford, 1929.

Massinger, Philip. Plays; ed. by William Gifford. 3d ed. London, 1845.

McBurney, James H. The Place of the Enthymeme in Rhetorical Theory. Reprinted from *Speech Monographs*, III (October, 1936), 49–74. An abstract of a dissertation presented to the University of Michigan.

McKeon, Richard. "Rhetoric in the Middle Ages," *Speculum*, XVII (January, 1942), 1–32.

Miller, Perry. The New England Mind. New York, 1939.

Milton, John. Artis logicae plenior institutio, ad Petri Rami methodum concinnata. London, 1672; in The Works of John Milton, Vol. XI, New York, 1935, ed. and tr. by Allan H. Gilbert.

Montaigne, Michel Eyquem de. Essayes; tr. by John Florio; ed. by Thomas Seccombe. 3 vols. London, 1908.

Moore-Smith, G. C. Gabriel Harvey's Marginalia. Stratford-upon-Avon, 1913.

Mulcaster, Richard. Elementarie [1582]; ed. by E. T. Campagnac. Oxford, 1925.

Nashe, Thomas. Works; ed. by R. B. McKerrow. 5 vols. London, 1904–10.

Osborn, Louise Brown. The Life, Letters, and Writings of John Hoskyns 1566–1638. New Haven, 1937.

Paetow, Louis John. The Arts Course at Medieval Universities; with Special Reference to Grammar and Rhetoric. Champaign, 1910.

The Pilgrimage to Parnassus with the Two Parts of the Return from Parnassus [three comedies performed in St. John's College, Cambridge, 1597]; ed. by W. D. Macray. Oxford, 1886.

Plato. Phaedrus, Ion, Gorgias, and Symposium; tr. into English with an introduction and prefatory notes by Lane Cooper. New York, 1938.

Rubel, Veré L. Poetic Diction in the English Renaissance from Skelton through Spenser. New York, 1941.

Rushton, William Lowes. Shakespeare and 'The Arte of English Poesie.' Liverpool, 1909.

Sidney, Sir Philip. Complete Works; ed. by Albert Feuillerat. 4 vols. Cambridge, 1912–26.

Skelton, John. The Poetical Works of John Skelton; ed. by Alexander Dyce. 2 vols. Edinburgh, 1843.

Smith, G. Gregory, ed. Elizabethan Critical Essays. 2 vols. Oxford, 1904.

Spencer, Theodore. Shakespeare and the Nature of Man. New York, 1942.

Spenser, Edmund. Poetical Works; ed. by J. C. Smith and E. De Selincourt. London, 1935.

Spingarn, Joel E. A History of Literary Criticism in the Renaissance. New York, 1899.

Spurgeon, Caroline F. E. "Imagery in the Sir Thomas More Fragment," Review of English Studies, VI (July, 1930), 257–70.

—— Shakespeare's Imagery and What It Tells Us. Cambridge, 1935.

—— "Shakespeare's Iterative Imagery," Proceedings of the British Academy (London), Vol. XVII (1931).

Taylor, Warren. A Dictionary of the Tudor Figures of Rhetoric. [Chicago], 1937. Distributed by the University of Chicago libraries.

—— The Tudor Figures of Rhetoric. Unpublished dissertation presented to the University of Chicago, 1937.

Tilley, Morris Palmer. Elizabethan Proverb Lore in Lyly's Euphues and in Pettie's Petite Pallace with Parallels from Shakespeare. New York, 1926.

Tuve, Rosemond. "Imagery and Logic: Ramus and Metaphysical Poetics," Journal of the History of Ideas, III (October, 1942), 365–400.

Van Hook, La Rue. "Greek Rhetorical Terminology in Puttenham's 'The Arte of English Poesie' " in Transactions of the American Philological Association, XLV (1914), 111–28.

Wagner, Russell H. Thomas Wilson's 'Arte of Rhetorique.' Unpublished dissertation presented to Cornell University, 1928.

Whiting, B. J. "The Nature of the Proverb," *Harvard Studies and Notes in Philology and Literature* (Cambridge, Mass.), Vol. XIV, 1932.

Willcock, Gladys Doidge. "Shakespeare and Rhetoric," *Essays and Studies by Members of the English Association* (Oxford), XXIX (1943), 50–61.

—— "Shakespeare as Critic of Language," *The Shakespeare Association Publications* (London), No. 18, 1934.

Wilson, Frank P. "Shakespeare and the Diction of Common Life," *Proceedings of the British Academy* (London), Vol. XXVII, 1941.

Wilson, Harold S. "Nature and Art in 'Winter's Tale,'" *Shakespeare Association Bulletin*, XVIII (1943), 114–19.

INDEX

ALL THE figures of speech and the vices of language are alphabetized under Figures of speech and vices of language. All the fallacies and the captious arguments are alphabetized under Fallacies and captious arguments.

Dilemma (dialysis), 185, 188-90, 216, 361, 363, 374, 398

Direccions for Speech and Style, see Hoskyns, John

Discoveries, see Jonson, Ben

Disjunctive proposition, 118, 186, 188, 314

Disjunctive syllogism, 185, 186 f., 362, 398

Disposition (judgment), or arrangement of a speech, 20, 21, 26-29, 354

Disputation, use by Shakespeare, 203, 208-41; by his predecessors and contemporaries, 203-8; his reference to, 212; the rhetorical figures which parallel logical disputation, 214-33, 380-85, outstanding instances of Shakespeare's dramatic use of, in serious matters, 224 ff.; rules of, 375-80

Dissimilarity, *see* Similarity and dissimilarity

Disticha moralia Catonis, 9

Division, genus and species, whole and parts, 111-19, 314-18; relation to definition, 111, 314; distinction between meanings a form of, 118, 164, 339; rules: the three kinds defined, 314

Donne, John, "Hymn to God the Father," 168

Donnelly, Francis P., 190*n*, 308*n*

Dreams, testimony of, 94

Education, *see* Grammar school

Education of Children, The, see Kempe, William

Effect, *see* Cause and effect

E. K., quoted, 50, 173

Elementa rhetorices, see Melanchthon, Philippus

Elizabeth, Queen, her methods of study described, 29, 324*n*

Elocution or style, 21, 31-40; *see also* Figures of speech

English Grammar, see Jonson, Ben

English Secretorie, The, see Day, Angel

English works on logic and rhetoric, 13-18

Enthymeme (or abridged syllogism), 39, 177, 358-61; identical with aetiologia, 178, 359, 398; sorites a series of, 180; counterpart of dialectical syllogism: form of: relation to the maxim, 358; refutative, 359

Epicheirema, 37, 39 f., 365

Epitaffe of the . . . Duke of Beddeforde, The, 172

Epithet, transferred, 56, 288, 295; compound, 124, 288

Epitome troporum . . . , see Susenbrotus, Joannes

Equals, comparison of, *see* Comparison

Erasmus, Desiderius, 10, 16, 204, 310*n*; *De duplici copia verborum ac rerum,* 9; *De ratione studii,* 8; *Modus conscribendi epistolas,* 9, 182*n*, 287

Erotemata dialectices, see Melanchthon, Philippus

Essence, implications of, 109, 110 f.

Ethos, Aristotle's discussion of, 37 f., 274, 393-95; figures of speech related to, 34 ff., 273 f., 396 f.; relationship of *logos, pathos,* and, 244, 272, 394 f.; defined, 272, 393 f.; Shakespeare's use of, 272-86, 288; in Antony's speech *logos, pathos,* and, combined, 283-86; treatment by rhetoricians and logicians, 395-97; affected by prosopographia, 397 f.

Etymology, 162, 339

Euphues . . . , see Lyly, John

Euripides, 340; excerpts: *Hecuba: Troades,* 358

Evasion through digression, 213, 221, 384; seeking "starting holes," 376, 378

Example, relation between induction, the syllogism, and, 363 f.

Faerie Queene, The, (Spenser), 130; excerpt, 299

Fallacies and captious arguments, accent, 194, 369; accident, 194, 229, 230, 369; amphibology, 193, 368; antistrephon, 199, 373; assistaton (or assistation), 201, 373, 374; begging the question (Cuckoes Song), 198, 207, 372; (a special failing of women, 162, 198, 199, 372; one form same as utis, 373); cacosistaton, 200, 373, 374; ceratin (or horned argument), 201, 373, 374; composition, 193, 369; consequent, 197, 238, 371; crocodilites (crocodile's argument), 202, 373, 374; division, 194, 369; equivocation, 191, 231, 341, 368; (used in broad sense, 195); false cause, 198, 371; form of speech, 194, 369;

nesis, 106, 312; paralipsis, 139, 285, 325; paramythia, 252, 391; parecbasis (or digression), 155, 332 f.; parelcon, 69, 294; parenthesis, 32, 57, 289, 294, 295; pareuresis, 222, 385; paroemia (adage or proverb), 98, 310; paromologia, 216, 382; paronomasia (or agnomination), 32, 165, 166, 170, 340, 341; parrhesia, 273, 276, 397; pathopopoeia, 388; periergia, 70, 302, 303; periphrasis, 32, 125, 303, 320; perissologia (or macrologia), 69, 302; peristasis, 121, 319; philophronesis, 253, 391, 397; pleonasmus, 69, 302; ploce, 84, 85, 306; polyptoton (paregmenon or tranlacer), 83, 306, 339; (relation to conjugates, 162, 339); polysyndeton, 32, 59, 297; pragmatographia, 128, 321; procatalepsis, 215, 382; proclees, 257, 393; proecthesis, 221, 384; prolepsis, 116, 316, 317; proparalepsis (or paragoge), 51 f., 293; propositio, 115, 316; prosapodosis, 188, 362; prosopographia, 126, 321, 397; prosopopoeia, 32, 126, 321, 390; prosthesis, 51, 293; protrope (or adhortatio), 223, 385; prozeugma, 296; pysma, 222, 385; reditus ad propositum, 155, 333; restrictio, 115, 316; sarcasmus, 255, 392; scesis onomaton, 296; schematismus, 171, 172, 341; simile, 32, 144, 327; solecismus, 64, 300; soraismus (or mingle-mangle), 65, 74, 115n, 300; syllepsis, 58, 165, 166, 168, 288, 296, 341; syllogismus (or intimation), 179, 360; symploce, 79, 305; synaloepha, 52, 294; synathroesmus, two meanings: congeries, recapitulation, 117, 317; synchoresis, 215, 381, 397; syncope, 52, 294; syncrisis, 137, 324; synecdoche, 32, 36n, 112, 315; syngnome, 274, 397; synoeciosis, 135, 323, 324; synonymia, 154, 332; systole, 53, 294; systrophe, 109, 313; tapinosis, 67, 301; tasis, 53, 294; tautologia, 68, 301, 302; taxis, 123, 319; thaumasmus, 245, 389; threnos, 248, 390; tmesis, 54, 55, 294, 295; topographia, 129, 321; topothesia, 130, 321; zeugma, 32, 58, 289, 296

Figurists, 21, 62, 330, 348, 388, 389; reason for name, 4; the authors and their

books, 14; subjects treated, 17, 37; theory and analysis of logicians and, essentially the same, 4, 34, 36, 308, 381n, 398

Floures of Terence, The, 353

Franz, Wilhelm, 61n

Frasure, Louise D., quoted, 77n

Fraunce, Abraham, 14 f., 17, 29, 35, 213n, 307, 330, 338, 389; writers and works from which illustrations drawn, 14 f.

—— *The Arcadian Rhetorike,* 14, 20n, 28n, 33, 35, 44; excerpts, 180, 305, 306, 317, 325, 382

—— *The Lawiers Logike,* 14, 28n, 30n, 34, 44; excerpts: 27, 30, 157; on topics of invention, 309, 312-39 *passim;* on genesis or composition, 342; examples of analysis or reading, 344-48; translation of Vergil's second eclogue into English hexameters, 345 f.; syllogistic reasoning, 354-63 *passim;* Socrates' love of disputation, 375; technique of disputation, 377-80

Freigius, analysis of Vergil's eclogue from, 347

Garcilasso de la Vega, 15

Garden of Eloquence, The, see Peacham, Henry

Gascoigne, George, 287; quoted, 303; *The Adventures of Master F. J.,* 204; *Supposes,* excerpt, 190

Genesis or composition, *see* Composition

Gentylnes and Nobylyte . . . (Heywood?), excerpt, 205

Genus and species, in definition, 108, 308, 312; *see also* Division

Gesture, 21, 37

Gilbert, Allan H., 30n, 208n; quoted, 190n

Golding, Arthur, tr., Ovid's *Metamorphoses,* 124n

Goodness and integrity, Shakespearean characters excelling in, 275 ff.

Gordon, George S., 50n; quoted, 44n, 49, 52, 134n

Gorgias, 16, 19, 20, 31

Gorgias (Plato), 19

Grammar, figures of speech related to, 34, 36, 37, 48-64, 293-99; Shakespeare's references to, 45, 47; *see also* Figures of speech; Schemes

1967